Research Methods for Reading Digital Data in the Digital Humanities

D1424039

RESEARCH METHODS FOR THE ARTS AND HUMANITIES

Research Methods for Reading Digital Data in the Digital Humanities

Edited by Gabriele Griffin and Matt Hayler

EDINBURGH
University Press

Edinburgh University Press is one of the leading university presses in the UK. We publish academic books and journals in our selected subject areas across the humanities and social sciences, combining cutting-edge scholarship with high editorial and production values to produce academic works of lasting importance. For more information visit our website: www.edinburghuniversitypress.com

Edinburgh University Press Ltd
The Tun – Holyrood Road
12(2f) Jackson's Entry
Edinburgh EH8 8PJ

Typeset in 11/13 Ehrhardt by
Servis Filmsetting Ltd, Stockport, Cheshire,
printed and bound in Great Britain by
CPI Group (UK) Ltd, Croydon CR0 4YY

A CIP record for this book is available from the British Library

ISBN 978 1 4744 0960 5 (hardback)
ISBN 978 1 4744 0962 9 (webready PDF)
ISBN 978 1 4744 0961 2 (paperback)
ISBN 978 1 4744 0963 6 (epub)

Contents

Acknowledgements

The editors would like to thank the University of Birmingham College of Arts and Law for generously providing a grant to make the colour-printing of the images in this volume possible.

Gabriele Griffin would like to thank the University of Umeå's Media and Communications Department, and in particular Professor Britta Lundgren and the Dean, Per-Olof Erixon, for the visiting professorship period in 2014 during which this project was begun. She would also like to thank the University of Uppsala for a brief visiting professorship in 2014–15 during which the project was further developed.

Finally, the editors would like to thank the commissioning and production team at Edinburgh University Press, especially Jackie Jones and Adela Rauchova, for their support for this project, always prompt and with good grace. It has been a pleasure!

CHAPTER I

Introduction

Gabriele Griffin and Matt Hayler

Digital Humanities has become one of the – albeit contested[1] – new domains of academe at the interface of technological development, epistemological change and methodological concerns (see Schreibman et al. 2008; Berry 2012; Gold 2012). At present there is a variety of research centres dedicated to Digital Humanities spread across the UK, to some extent Europe (e.g. Bergen) and, more prominently, the USA, with more recent centres such as HumLab at Umeå University in Sweden arising at reasonable speed. In many instances digital humanities are understood, as we do for the purposes of this volume, as distinct methodological practices developed in conjunction with and in response to new digital tools, with all that this implies for the related construction of knowledge. Two broad developments in the use of digital research methods in the Humanities might be discerned: one is the creation and curating of digital data to which we devote another volume (Hayler and Griffin 2016); the other is the development of new reading methods, often for new kinds of texts, including the 'farming' or analysis of existing digital data, a practice increasingly common among Humanities researchers exploring the new forms of textualisation and visual display that digital media afford. It is these new forms of reading in the Humanities with which we are concerned in this volume, not least because it is one of the most common forms of digital data research. The reading of 'born digital' fiction such as fan fiction, for example, or the analysis of online blogs, Twitter and other social media materials are all part of reading digital data as a comparatively new mode of conducting Humanities research.

An important feature of this rise in the use of digital research methods is the concomitant rise of interdisciplinary research collaboration. Indeed, as a number of the chapters in this volume attest, such collaborations are not only necessary between, for example, the visual and the textual arts, but also between academics and technicians due to the demands of the technical knowledge required to conduct, for example, online network analyses. These requirements are such that a conventionally trained literary scholar would be unable to conduct the technical work necessary to create the online structures required for the kinds of analyses s/he might want to do. Part of the role of this volume, then, is to demonstrate the potentials, viability and usefulness of such collaborations. And, as Bruno Latour and Steve Woolgar (1986), Karen Barad (2007) and others have discussed, such collaborations mean that technicians and the digital environments that they devise co-create the knowledge produced in the use of these digital environments. At this stage, these types of collaboration remain largely unarticulated, under-discussed and under-researched; work needs to be undertaken to examine quite what the effect of such collaborations is on the knowledge produced and that must start, in preliminary fashion, with raising awareness of the kinds of work being done.

Digitally based research methods that analyse textuo-visual online material are increasingly common across all humanities disciplines, and the range of specific research methods one might employ are vast, as an Arts and Humanities Research Council-funded project on digital research methods made clear.[2] There is, therefore, no way in which we might do justice to all relevant disciplines and/or viable methods within this volume. The new forms of aerially based visual data analyses now common in Archaeology, for example, are beyond the scope of our work here. What we have decided to do instead is to focus on digital research undertaken broadly within the frame of arts and literature, history and ethnography since these domains have had histories of mutual influence and engagement which digital humanities research has extended and expanded.

Such work has to be seen in a context where the number of academics engaged in digital humanities research is still relatively small but rapidly expanding, in which digital humanities has not yet developed – and possibly never will, at least in the traditional sense of the term – a canon of what constitutes the field, and where digital humanities is not systematically taught, particularly at undergraduate level. This is in part a function of the rapidly developing technologies involved: today – in 2015 – app construction is a big topic in the context of digitisation, but whether or not this will be the case in 2018, for example, is not clear. Moreover, since the field is in its infancy, most current practitioners of Digital Humanities research are autodidacts who have acquired detailed knowledge of maybe one or two specific methods that they then employ and develop. Robert Glenn Howard's chapter in this volume provides a good account of this. Such creation and refinement is very much in evidence in the chapters in this volume where contributors engage critically with reading digital data. This means that they – mostly academics rather than technicians – discuss both the pros and cons of the methods that they engage with, and the ideological underpinnings which structure and de/inform those methods. It is still the case that the vast majority of Humanities researchers encounter Digital Humanities research methods as postgraduates or later as academics, and usually in a haphazard fashion. But the need to think more systemically about the field is clearly evident, and in our view it is necessary to have volumes available that introduce researchers to Digital Humanities methods and practices beyond the small set that may be practised in their immediate environment.

Given the points made above, this volume is aimed broadly at Humanities scholars, especially from the arts, literature and history, who wish to engage with digital humanities research methods but do not necessarily know much about such methods or how they might be put into practice. We therefore hope that this collection will encourage colleagues, postgraduates and any interested researchers to begin to explore and use digital methods to research visual and textual digital material. In this volume we are particularly concerned with the ways in which digital data might be researched, how they might be interpreted and what such interpretations yield that other methods might not deliver.

Thinking about digital research methods and reading digital data has to be considered in the research methods training context which has gained prominence in higher education in the humanities over the past fifteen years or so. Unlike the Social Sciences where research methods training has had a sustained and articulated history, in many arts and humanities disciplines such training has only more recently come to the fore, not least as a function of the advance and advocacy of interdisciplinary work, the increasingly sustained calls for research collaboration and the calls for the impact and dissemination of academic research beyond the academy. Simultaneously we have seen the rise in digital technologies which facilitate all manner of conventional and new forms of Humanities research. Many of the chapters in this volume point to the, at times, seemingly easy ways in which one can access free software online in order to conduct digital data analyses. But, as several contributors also argue here, and as still needs to be better understood throughout academe, retrieving, storing and analysing digital data is neither easy nor quick – it involves a serious investment of time and effort, meaning that it is important to think through quite carefully what one wants to do and why. Several authors in this volume, for example, warn against the seductiveness of digital data. Those data seem a – possibly the only – 'sexy' thing to engage with, and appear to align with what might be described as the current scientisation and technologisation of the humanities, in which, *inter alia*, engagement with social media and with the diverse audiences that the Internet provides are called for, and where quantification – for a long time only practised in very particular avenues of humanities research – seems to create a scientific edge that other methods might seemingly lack.

However, as Gelfgren, Blanke and Prescott, and others in this volume show, the fetishizstion of quantity, the seeming plausibility, immutability and facticity of figures, can lead to a morass of data that, at the end of the day, may say nothing more than 'a lot', i.e. might only point to their own quantity as something of significance, but in fact be beyond the useful interpretive scope of the academic/s concerned. One function of sheer volume may well be its leading to a scenario where the generation of more and more data comes at the expense of analysis and meaningful engagement with those data. Quantity, in short, does not necessarily count or produce meaning per se.

Simultaneously it is important for Humanities academics to engage with the fact that more and more data of diverse kinds are available on the Internet and that humanities academics' interpretive, hermeneutic skills have much to offer by way of making sense of those data. Many of the chapters in this volume highlight the textual and other databases that now exist online and which enable academics to engage with texts and artefacts otherwise found in archives and other depositories that might previously not have been available to them. Such digital databases remain under-used (Hedstrom 1997; Borgman 1999; Eshet 2004; Bell et al. 2009; Ge 2010). Much of the current research in this area continues to revolve around the question of the use of (digital) libraries as these are among the key institutions for making digital data preservation decisions, weighing up the logics of material presence (the maintenance of books and journals in hard copy etc.) against the particular affordances of digitality. In the latter case, a recurrent issue that researchers also face is the acceleration of technological change where software and hardware become obsolescent within very short periods of time. This means that humanities researchers engaged in reading digital data – an act, or rather an iterative process, which requires access to both the data themselves, for example to fan fiction or particular blogs, and access to the software required to support the analyses to be undertaken – have to think of that engagement as a constant learning process where tools that they might be able to utilise one day are unsupported or withdrawn the next, and where digital skills have to be consistently and regularly updated, even as we live in an academic world in which it is assumed that technological literacy is osmotically acquired and demands no time to be set aside in order to systematically upgrade and train that literacy. Digital literacy, unlike the convention of print, is not for life, but instead only for the time span during which the knowledge of particular software, hardware and techniques that one has acquired remain *au courant*. That time span can be less than six months if one catches the end of a wave of a particular technological development. The point is that the skills- and training-related disposition that academics have conventionally displayed needs to be significantly reconstructed if one is to engage with digital methods effectively and sustainedly and academics, as much as their institutional bases, still need to integrate that recognition into their everyday practices.

When one engages with digital data, a distinction is commonly made between so-called 'born digital' data, i.e. data that exist only digitally, and those that have had (prior) lives in other media such as books, documents, artefacts, etc. Where once digitally born data were supported by arguments such as speed of communication and the green vision of the 'paperless office' (Sellen and Harper 2003), such rationales for digitally born data have long since given way to understandings of the range of affordances that digital technologies can provide and the dissemination and capture possibilities inherent in digital data manufacture and reading. These have, of course, been highly controversial, not least because of the associated issues of 'netiquette', ownership of digital content, the ethics of conducting research with data available online, questions of what constitutes the private and the public online, issues around surveillance, and so on. The debates around these issues are in full flow across a whole range of contexts, often associated with interpersonal behaviours ranging from cyberbullying to trolling (Sturges 2002; Helsper and Whitty 2010; Yarmohammadian et al. 2012; Park et al. 2014). All of this indicates that analysing digital data is a dynamic and changing field where participation requires significant input from the researcher at every level. The chapters in this volume discuss such requirements and the ways in which scholars have gone about addressing these issues in the field.

The chapter following this Introduction, 'Matter Matters: The Effects of Materiality and the Move from Page to Screen' by Matt Hayler, argues that the digital humanities are tasked with exploring new kinds of texts that require new ways of reading. With videogames, digital archives and code, this demand is immediately clear: traditional methods cannot do these forms full justice. But there are also texts which do not seem to ask for a change in methods or reading practices even as they might significantly require them. The digital version of a printed text, appearing to show no alteration beyond the move from page to screen, often falls into this under-theorised gap; what is an obvious demand for new practice when reading a videogame is a far more subtle requirement when asking what changes occur in the experience of reading a formerly printed novel on a Kindle. Hayler's chapter explores the ways in which digital texts can, however, speak beyond dramatic changes in the presentation of the script of a work; he suggests that a new default of close attention to phenomenological concerns in reading, from the subtle effects of pages and covers to hyperlinks and seemingly ethereal electronic texts, may be required in order to avoid assumptions about how a digital text 'should' be read. By exploring the ways in which readers encounter combinations of script and media we can better understand the act of meaning-making in all forms of reading and how this act might particularly be changed in a digital reading environment. Drawing on Katherine Hayles' notion of 'material metaphors' (Hayles 2002), this chapter demonstrates the importance of interrogating the ways in which materiality impacts upon meaning-making in both printed and digital texts, and brings this approach to bear on an artwork which straddles the boundary between the two.

As Nathalie Houston argues in her chapter on 'Reading the Visual Page in the Digital Archive' large-scale digitisation projects (by Google, research libraries and others) have already begun to transform the ways in which humanities research is conducted by providing access to a greater range of materials than most physical libraries can offer and by making them available to computational analysis. This access to historical cultural materials is provided through the digital surrogate, which typically consists of a photographic scan of the document's pages accompanied by text extracted via optical character recognition (OCR). Smaller scholarly textual editions and archives provide carefully corrected text transcriptions, frequently with additional metadata or interpretive information encoded in TEI-standard XML,[3] but they usually also include the scanned page images because Humanities scholars recognise that the visual and bibliographic aspects of historical texts conveyed in page images have research value. Yet most computational tools for large-scale analyses of digitised texts focus only on the linguistic element, the extracted plain text information. Drawing on examples from nineteenth-century books and periodicals, Houston first outlines a taxonomy of the kinds of information encoded in the spatial arrangement of text and white space on the page. This can signal the genre, function, theme and structure of the text. This visually encoded information can be valuable for researchers seeking to navigate large digital collections, but has only been available to the human eye scanning thumbnail images for recognisable patterns. She then presents some of her current research which utilises image analysis software to computationally access these visual features of digitised texts, including biomedical imaging tools and the VisualPage software which she and Neal Audenaert developed with a grant from the National Endowment for the Humanities. This proof of concept software adapts image recognition technology to identify and extract quantified measures for specific visual features in books of poetry. Using such tools can provide researchers with a computational 'bird's-eye' view of a large document collection and reveal clusters of related items and historical trends in physical layout and identify unique or visually representative items. 'Teaching' the computer to identify and report on the visual aspects of digitised page images extends our ability as Humanities researchers to navigate and use the deep resources of the digital archive now available to us.

Maria Lindgren Leavenworth's chapter on 'Paratextual Navigation as a Research Method: Fan fiction Archives and Reader Instructions', like Houston's, draws on her own research, in this instance fan fiction. She explores how such fiction might be interrogated utilising Gérard Genette's delineation of the paratext ([1987] 1997) in analyses of media specificity, of authoring functions and of altered reading habits following new modes of textual production. This chapter mobilises the notion of the paratext as a means of addressing how to research particular online texts. It provides an account of one way of conducting such research by focusing on websites that archive fan fiction: online-published, most often pseudonymously authored stories which take a pre-existing fiction as a starting point to develop new fictions based on these. Leavenworth's chapter speaks to how Genette's traditional, narratological delineation can be usefully expanded and modified to account for particular methodological challenges when researching virtual environments and approaching isolated works within them. In Genette's definition, the paratext constitutes 'a *threshold* . . . that offers the world at large the possibility of either stepping inside or turning back' (Genette [1987] 1997: 2). Despite the seeming concreteness of the threshold image he later goes on to specify that '"[t]he paratext," properly speaking, does not *exist*; rather, one chooses to *account in these terms* for a certain number of practices and effects, for reasons of method and effectiveness' (ibid.: 343). Online publishing entails particular forms of thresholds with websites, online archives, fanfic-specific genres, categorisations and tags representing specific aspects of the paratext. The choice of publication venue, filing options at the selected site and a host of more or less descriptive labels attached to the work thus signal what type of text form we are concerned with and what genre(s) it belongs to: preliminary indications for how that work is to be approached and giving visitors to the sites options to either pursue reading the fan fic or turn elsewhere. A sustained analysis of different paratextual functions, structuring the site as well as the presentation of the fiction, thus profitably accounts for the particularity of the fan fic text form as well as of the material mediation of the text.

Where Leavenworth is concerned with the analysis of a particular online genre, Dawn Archer in 'Data Mining and Word Frequency Analysis' adopts a more quantitative approach in her use of a number of studies – representative of different Humanities and Social Science disciplines – to demonstrate: (1) the techniques of data mining (frequency profiling, concordancing, collocations, n-gram clustering, etc.); and also (2) how these techniques are used to uncover not only the aboutness of a text or texts by researchers but also, for example, the similarities and differences between different types of genres, authorship attribution, the author's ideological stance, the construction of othering and the language characteristics of psychopaths. In these discussions she focuses in particular on studies which have exploited the keywords, key domains and/or key parts-of-speech methodology.

Stefan Gelfgren engages with a particular source of digital data that has been the object of a range of research projects, Twitter. In 'Reading Twitter: Combining Qualitative and Quantitative Methods in the Interpretation of Twitter Material' Gelfgren deals specifically with the use of Twitter material (i.e. tweets) in research. He does so in relation to two specific cases dealing with how authority is negotiated online in religious communities. The analysis of digital material and tools provides different possibilities to retrieve and interpret empirical research material relative to working on non-online data. Gelfgren explores how the combination of traditional and digital methods and tools offers new interpretive opportunities to the researcher. As he suggests, tweets are fairly easy to collect, organise and also to visualise, but there is still a need to contextualise them in order to 'read' them meaningfully. Gelfgren argues that the combination of quantitative and qualitative methods which researching Twitter-based material allows provides different ways to answer research questions than is the case for non-online-based material. Through a combination of close readings of tweets and computer-generated network visualisation, for example, other patterns and interpretations are made possible compared to the use of only one method.

Coppélie Cocq engages with the issue of using Twitter feeds in one's research from an ethics perspective. Her concern is with small data, meaning a relatively small amount of material coming, in this instance, from within a very well defined small community where Twitterers can be easily recognised by others. This has obvious implications around issues of privacy and the relation between online articulation and the reading of that articulation for research purposes. Exploring the preservation of native languages through the use of digital media, Cocq discusses what it means to deal with small data from communities with few individuals ethically and advocates for the close co-production of knowledge, with involvement from the community at every step.

Gabriel Wolfenstein's chapter has a rather different take in that it concerns itself with the attempt to harness other people online for doing various kinds of 'work'/research/data collection. Such mobilisation of people, also known as crowd-sourcing, has interesting potential for the Humanities. Crowdsourcing, or community-sourcing (different terms for what is broadly the same thing) is, at its most basic, a mode of research, knowledge-gathering and analysis, whereby a researcher engages a community to provide answers to questions or solutions to problems or analysis of material. In 'Knowing Your Crowd: An Essential Component to Crowdsourcing Research', Wolfenstein argues that there are many different forms of crowdsourcing, but they are all linked by the idea that a large group of people can offer solutions to research questions and data analysis that would be unavailable to the individual or small group. Because of the possibilities of wider engagement, crowdsourcing offers opportunities to advance humanities work with and beyond the walls of the academy. At Stanford's Center for Spatial and Textual Analysis, Wolfenstein and colleagues have been engaged in a Mellon supported project to study the question of whether crowdsourcing is useful for Humanities research. For this, they have conducted three simultaneous crowdsourcing projects: the Year of the Bay, Living with the Railroads and 500 Novels. Each project engaged with different kinds of crowds and asked different questions. And each, in different ways, explores the possibilities of partnering with non-academic media bodies. In the case of Year of the Bay and Living with the Railroads, the partner was Historypin, 'a global community collaborating around history', which offers users a web-based platform where memories (in the form of images and audio/visual materials) can be pinned to a map, locating the material in both time and space. Wolfenstein discusses what he sees as one of the major challenges of crowdsourcing: knowing your audience. He argues that this is one of the earliest questions one has to ask oneself if one wants to engage in crowdsourcing. He discusses the different crowds they engaged with in their three projects and the challenges associated with each. One of the key lessons learned was that in order to undertake successful crowdsourcing, one must be able to answer a certain, in his view fundamental, question, namely: what does your crowd want? Wolfenstein also makes very clear that creating or engaging with a community for crowdsourcing purposes requires more leg work than the idea of crowdsourcing suggests in the abstract. His chapter illuminates the levels of researcher commitment required to generate a successful crowdsourcing project.

Where the crowd is uppermost on Wolfenstein's mind, the closeness to data is what is at stake for Anna Johansson and Anna Sofia Lundgren in 'Fantasies of Scientificity: Ethnographic Identity and the Use of QDA Software'. They suggest that much debate on the use of qualitative data analysis software has revolved around the risks of losing 'closeness to the data' (cf. Agar 1983; Mangabeira 1996; Fielding and Lee 1998; Gilbert 2002) and the complexity and context of its creation. At the same time, the use of software is often seen as adding to the sense of scienticity of one's research. It is as if the use of software will somehow alone improve the quality of their work. Johansson and Lundgren analyse their initial responses to using ATLAS.ti and reflect on the different reasons for those reactions in order to think through the workings and effects of using qualitative software for analysing ethnographic materials. They draw on experiences from their research, including interviews and ethnographic observations as well as web and media materials, to discuss some possible consequences of the retrievability, opportunities for visualisations and quantifiability that QDA software offers. The chapter touches upon certain possible pitfalls of using QDA and discusses how the software can trigger a proclivity towards positivism, where the qualitative researcher may find herself subjected by, and attracted to, a positivist paradigm. They argue that QDA – when used critically and reflexively – may also assist the poststructuralist researcher in formulating context-sensitive strategies and methods for qualitative analysis.

The opportunities afforded a digital humanities researcher are also discussed by Robert Glenn Howard who, in 'Digital Network Analysis: Understanding Everyday Online Discourse Micro- and Macroscopically' suggests that using

computational methods offers communication researchers the distance necessary to see not just individual digital discursive performances but also the vast
webs of vernacular expression that are now accessible to us online. To fairly
consider these huge amounts of everyday expression, he suggests that we need
both close event analysis and distant computational analysis. Howard utilises
the concept of 'vernacular authority' to explore informal and everyday communication occurring online. He suggests that event- or performance-based
analytical methods are necessarily limited in their ability to discern the large-
scale processes of vernacular communication in the online environment. He
describes the computational method he has developed to address this limitation, and briefly analyses vernacular networks of belief on two very different
forums – a liberal parenting forum and a conservative gun forum – to outline
what network analysis can offer the Humanities researcher.

In 'Dealing with Big Data' Tobias Blanke and Andrew Prescott introduce
the concept of big data and its relevance for humanities research. They begin
by first contextualising Big Data and why it needs to be critically evaluated.
Here they focus on why size of data sets is not necessarily a good measure for
when something becomes Big Data. They then present some of the Big Data
research data sets that are available already as well as some that might appear in
the near future. Here, they elaborate the concept of long-tail data sets and their
complexity. Their chapter also covers big data analytics and explains some of
the foundations of the algorithms that drive research. They are interested in
'traditional activities' in humanities research and how these translate. They
finish with some epistemological questions that will position (future) Big Data
research in a particular understanding of the human condition.

Each of these chapters, then, provides compelling examples of methods in
action. The specificities of using particular software or hardware are not the
primary focus here, but rather a demonstration of what digital methods can do,
how they might be made appealing for those researchers not already engaged,
and a continuation of the defence for the legitimacy of digital research as a
multi-faceted practice.

The chapters also raise some interesting questions. One of these concerns
the prominence of relationality in connection with digital data. Almost all
chapters discuss the reading of digital data in relation to other sets of data
or texts, adopting, without necessarily explicitly reflecting upon this, a comparative stance to the data they discuss, be that with book-based or some other
material. The phrase 'social media', mostly not used in conjunction with
digital archives, for instance, itself already points to sociality and connectiv-
ity as a key structuring device in our understanding of digital data. This is
reinforced here where relationality is partly given through the rhyzomic con-
nectivity that digital data enable through hyperlinks and other such devices.
The quantity of that connective data often posits a dilemma for researchers

trying to set parameters for their work. We think that the frequent focus on the relationality of the data that appears in the various chapters has something to say, in itself, about the non-neutrality of digital methods and about the nature of relations in and of themselves. Researchers investigating digitisation from the point of view of organisation and quantification will always have an interest in making data dance in particular ways, and the question of whether Digital Humanities methods produce a particular kind of relation is certainly alive here. Tied to this, the continuing establishment of the dialogue between quantitative and qualitative approaches is clearly also still being worked out in this collection, both within and between the chapters. Some of the contributors such as Gelfgren, Howard, and Johansson and Lundgren make very explicit the seductiveness of the scienticity attributed to figures and notions of quantification, but are also very clear about the fact that numbers do not speak for themselves. Rather, they require a hermeneutic approach to make their meaning apparent. This recognition suggests the imbrication of diverse methods – quantitative and qualitative – in ways that move beyond the conventional 'two cultures' approach to the humanities and the sciences. And, indeed, many of the chapters here show how researchers employ a multi-method approach to deal with their digital data.

Another relational dimension of the work discussed is that between its online and its offline dimensions. While some chapters maintain, either explicitly or implicitly, an unquestioned division between online and offline data, Hayler's chapter, for example, goes far beyond the notion of digital data as emanating from the flat space of the screen. In describing a project, the *Theatre Book*, where a three-dimensional object incorporating pop-up pages and projections is constructed, he moves into the world of what Griffin would term 'digital plasticity' (*pace* Malabou 2008) where the digital is no longer confined to the flat screen but rather melds into and moulds the object world such that the material divisions between the page and the digital become uncertain, if not eroded. His project highlights the relational imbrication of the page and the digital in the production of technologised cultural artefacts, and thus challenges the division between the online and the offline which haunts conventional cultural readings of texts.

Hayler's project is an explicitly relational effort in that it involves artists, a theatre company and himself. Digital projects thus give rise to new forms of sociality. That sociality and its associated processes are as yet very much under-researched. We might ask, for instance, why we so rarely hear from the technicians involved in projects like those described here. The currently under-theorised role of technical and support staff in academic investigation is going to become an increasingly significant concern, with implications for our understanding of authorship and the ownership of knowledge, the expectations of technical proficiency for those who might want to reflect in some nuanced fashion on their practice and the biases built into assumptions about the neutrality of data and software.

It is important that such questions become manifest in reading through these chapters; they point to further work that needs to be undertaken. This volume offers a view of the kinds of reading of digital data that might be done, from the underlying code through to the phenomenological experience of reading a single text. We would like this work to encourage other scholars to become (more) involved in digital research and to do so, as these chapters do, with a critical and reflective eye.

NOTES

1. This contestation centres on whether or not Digital Humanities is an appropriate term to cover the wide range of practices it references and disciplinary arenas in which it is utilised.
2. See <http://www.arts-humanities.net/ictguides/methods> unfortunately currently not maintained; refers to <http://dhcommons.org/> (last accessed 25 August 2014).
3. TEI-standard XML refers to the standards set by the Text Encoding Initiative to represent text in digital form. See <http://www.tei-c.org/index.xml> (accessed 4 September 2015).

REFERENCES

Agar, M. (1983) 'Microcomputers as field tools', *Computers and the Humanities*, 17: 1, pp. 19–26.

Barad, K. (2007) *Meeting the Universe Halfway: Quantum Physics and the Entanglement of Matter and Meaning*. Durham, NC: Duke University Press.

Bell, G., Hey, T. and Szalay, A. (2009) 'Beyond the data deluge', *Science*, 323: 5919, pp. 1297–8.

Berry, D. M. (ed.) (2012) *Understanding Digital Humanities*. Basingstoke: Palgrave Macmillan.

Borgman, C. L. (1999) 'What are digital libraries? Competing visions', *Information Processing Management*, 35: 3, pp. 227–43.

Eshet, Y. (2004) 'Digital literacy: a conceptual framework for survival skills in the digital era', *Journal of Educational Multimedia and Hypermedia*, 13: 1, pp. 93–106.

Fielding, N. G. and Lee, R. M. (1998) *Computer Analysis and Qualitative Research*. London: Sage.

Ge, X. (2010) 'Information-seeking behavior in the digital age: a multidisciplinary study of academic researchers', *College and Research Libraries*, 71: 5, pp. 435–55.

Genette, G. ([1987] 1997) *Paratexts: Thresholds of Interpretation*, trans. J. E. Lewin. Cambridge: Cambridge University Press.

Gibbs, G. R. (2002) *Qualitative Data Analysis: Explorations with Nvivo*. Buckingham: Open University Press.

Gilbert, L. S. (2002) 'Going the distance: "closeness" in qualitative data analysis software', *International Journal of Social Research Methodology*, 5: 3, pp. 215–28.

Gold, M. K. (ed.) (2012) *Debates in the Digital Humanities*. Minneapolis: University of Minnesota Press.

Hayler, M. and Griffin, G. (eds) (2016) *Digitizing and Curating Digital Data*. Edinburgh: Edinburgh University Press.

Hayles, N. K. (2002) *Writing Machines*. Cambridge, MA: MIT Press.

Hedstrom, M. (1997) 'Digital preservation: a time bomb for digital libraries', *Computers and the Humanities*, 31: 3, pp. 189–202.

Helsper, E. J. and Whitty, M. T. (2010) 'Netiquette within married couples: agreement about acceptable online behavior and surveillance between partners', *Computers in Human Behavior*, 26: 5, pp. 916–26.

Latour, B. and Woolgar, S. ([1979] 1986) *Laboratory Life: The Construction of Scientific Facts*. Princeton: Princeton University Press.

Malabou, C. (2008) *What Should We Do With Our Brain?* New York: Fordham University Press.

Mangabeira, W. C. (1996) 'CAQDAS and its diffusion across four countries: national specificities and common themes', *Current Sociology*, 44: 3, pp. 191–205.

Park, S., Na, E. Y. and Kim, E. M. (2014) 'The relationship between online activities, netiquette and cyberbullying', *Children and Youth Services Review*, 42, pp. 74–81.

Pötzsch, H. and Hayles, N. K. (2014) 'FCJ-172 posthumanism, technogenesis, and digital technologies: a conversation with N. Katherine Hayles', *Fibreculture Journal*, 23: General Issue.

Schreibman, S., Siemens, R. and Unsworth, J. (eds) (2008) *A Companion to Digital Humanities*. Oxford: Blackwell.

Sellen, A. and Harper, R. H. R. (2003) *The Myth of the Paperless Office*. Cambridge, MA: MIT Press.

Sturges, P. (2002) 'Remember the human: the first rule of netiquette, librarians and the internet', *Online Information Review*, 26: 3, pp. 209–16.

Yarmohammadian, M. H., Iravani, H. and Abzari, M. (2012) 'Information and communications technology, culture, and medical universities; organizational culture and netiquette among academic staff', *Journal of Education and Health Promotion*, 1: 6.

CHAPTER 2

Matter Matters: The Effects of Materiality and the Move from Page to Screen

Matt Hayler

INTRODUCTION

In an interview about his striking book, *Tree of Codes* (2010a), Jonathan Safran Foer considered why his project felt particularly meaningful to him: 'I started thinking', he said, 'about what books look like, what they will look like, how the form of the book is changing very quickly. If we don't give it a lot of thought, it won't be for the better' (2010b). Foer was worried, maybe still is, about the expectant rush from page to screen, about what he saw as a delighted rejection of the body of the printed book. His response was to work with the British publishing company Visual Editions to produce a paperback where every page is individually die-cut, perforated with large holes, as if the black bars of a redacted document had been removed entirely to render each leaf like lacework.[1] Foer had gone through his favourite novel, Bruno Schulz's *The Street of Crocodiles* (1977), and erased words in order to construct a new story; the final form of *Tree of Codes* then re-performs and reinforces his productive subtraction. For Foer, his book acts as a reminder that there's something about the visceral materiality of paper that is worth preserving:

> I just love the physicality of books. I love breaking the spine, smelling the pages, taking it into the bath . . . I thought: What if you pushed it to the extreme, and created something not old-fashioned or nostalgic but just beautiful? It helps you remember that life can surprise you . . . I love the notion that 'this is a book that remembers it has a body.' When a book remembers, we remember. It reminds you that you have a body. So many of the things we may think of as burdensome are actually the things that make us more human. (2010b)[2]

In this quotation, Foer raises issues of materiality and embodiment and the complex of their relationship with heritage, aesthetics and phenomenal experience, the rich practice of reading. In this chapter I similarly want to think through some of the diversity of implications of the materiality of texts at a moment of continuing, if not transition, then increasing oscillation between print and digital reading experiences.

Digital Humanities, in its broadest sense, is tasked with exploring the new kinds of texts and new kinds of reading that emerge given increasingly ubiquitous computing; the other chapters in this volume focus on exploring new kinds of reading methods, and the companion volume (Hayler and Griffin 2016) on the creation and curation of digital data will investigate some of the new kinds of text that are being made available. Here, however, I want to explore how a sensitivity to the particularities of the transition that Foer alerts us to functions as a reading method. There are texts that seem to sit indistinctly between the old and the new, which do not appear to ask for a change in methods even as they might significantly require them: the digital version of a printed text, appearing to show no alteration beyond the move from page to screen, often falls into this under-theorised gap. What is an obvious demand for new practice when reading a videogame such as *Call of Duty* is a far more subtle call when asking what changes in the experience of reading the Kindle edition of a novel like *Thérèse Raquin* – the videogame is an evidently new experience with different requirements, but little, at first, seems to change in the presentation of a nineteenth-century fiction on a twenty-first-century screen. This chapter therefore focuses on the ways in which literary texts speak beyond the script of the work, beyond the ordering of the words; I'm interested in the often-ignored impacts of physical form – what do the objects do? How are they meaningful and how do they make meaning?

And, although it will not be my primary concern here, I also want to position this chapter within a new default of attention to phenomenological concerns in the digital humanities and in all kinds of literary reading, concerns which may be required in order to avoid assumptions about how a digital text 'should' be read. By exploring the ways in which readers encounter combinations of script and medium we can better understand the act of meaning-making in all forms of reading and how this act might particularly be changed in a digital reading environment. And by paying attention to the role that the reader's own embodiment plays we enrich our model further, showing why readers might read as they do or have the textual experiences that they might have. The affordances of the text will provide me with more than enough material for discussion here, but the embodied reader holding the paperback or Kindle in her hands necessarily haunts everything that I want to say.

I sit on the board for a European research network tasked with exploring the effects of e-reading, Evolution of REading in the Age of Digitisation

(EREAD), headed up by Anne Mangen, a reading researcher at the University of Stavanger. This COST-funded action aims to

> improve scientific understanding of the implications of digitization, hence helping individuals, disciplines, societies and sectors across Europe to cope optimally with the effects . . . [C]ombining paradigms from experimental sciences with perspectives . . . from the humanities, the Action will develop new research paradigms, and metrics for assessing the impact of digitization on reading. These metrics enable the development of evidence-based knowledge of paper and screen reading, and provide guidance for practitioners, policy makers, publishers and designers. (Mangen 2015)

The interdisciplinary scope of the project ('which unites researchers from thirty-three countries' and a huge diversity of scientific, social science and humanities backgrounds) is captured in its central commitment to a 'multidimensional, integrative model of reading'. Such a model is what the researchers involved feel must be considered as a minimum for understanding the effects of digital reading on readers, and I suspect that some version of it must become the norm for future work on reading in the Digital Humanities whether it is interested in the readers' cognitive health, their affect or a text's literary potential. Many aspects of this integrative approach are not new, they have been part of textual studies for a long time, but their combination is likely unique and certainly richer than the current default tends to be. In this regard, the action is committed to exploring reading as an embodied and multi-sensory experience, and as a human–technology interaction that demands that we consider the entanglement of the rich physicality and related cognition of the user and the particular affordances of the device being used.

As Foer suggested in the quotation above, the investigation of such concerns must include ergonomics and haptics, attention and cognition, phenomenological experience, and sociological and cultural forces. So I want to unpack some of these ideas across experiences of print, digital texts and a case study of the form of an art book that limns between the two in order to try and demonstrate some of this richness and what it might offer to our understanding of reading, particularly at this moment.

THE EMBODIED TEXT

When we consider the ways in which a book might be meaningful, we are trained from our school days to interpret the language captured on the page, to work our way through the symbols, metaphors and echoes of social context trapped within a series of marks that, more or less, approximate speech. While more advanced English studies troubles or enriches these methods, it is only a small subset of work that focuses on the role of the printed form that holds the words. Part of my claim here, however, is that a work's embodiment always plays a structuring role in our reception of the text, particularly as we gain an affinity and expertise with the medium, and it also provokes ways of thinking that can carry over long after we leave the text behind; in short, textual embodiment is something.

Printed books' most significant material features are their covers, their pages, their typography and the formal arrangement of words on the page, and the interactions that the comingling of each of these aspects afford the reader. As I am predominantly interested in physicality, I will focus on pages and covers, but in Foer's *Tree of Codes* and a work that I will look at in the next section, Mark Z. Danielewski's *House of Leaves* (2000a), formal arrangement and typographical choices are also clearly important, clearly meaningful. So what kind of response might come from the seemingly simple physicality of a printed book? I must be careful when dealing with the suggestion that certain kinds of thinking may inhere in a codex. A book does not determine any kind of thinking in its users, but it can be seen as provoking certain kinds of thought from within the cultural context in which it operates (or, perhaps more often, to restrict certain kinds of thinking).

The cognitive linguists and philosophers George Lakoff and Mark Johnson (1999) give us a way of thinking about these structuring capacities of reading equipment in their discussion of the role of metaphor. One of their most provocative explorations describes how we give 'faces' to things based on the ways in which we interact with them: the 'front' of a television is the side we want to view, the 'front' of a car faces the direction that we tend to want it to go. This seems a fairly logical way of bounding and orienting the world, of producing an enabling model for otherwise faceless things: making the bodies of objects akin to our own bodies which tend to act in the direction that our eyes face. But we also ascribe faces or fronts to objects with which we do not have a particular plane of interaction; if we place a ball between ourselves and a rock or a tree we tend to think of the ball as being 'in front' of the rock or tree despite their being no actual or really actionable 'face' for any of these objects. 'In other languages (e.g. Hausa), speakers project fronts onto such objects in the opposite direction, facing away from the speaker' (Lakoff and Johnson 1999: 34), but in English-speaking cultures the whole world looks toward us. This convention, whether in Hausa or in English, is always an embodied phenomenon:

> The concepts front and back are body-based . . . If all beings on this
> planet were uniform stationary spheres . . . perceiving equally in all

directions, they would have no concept of front or back . . . Our bodies define a set of fundamental spatial orientations that we use not only in orienting ourselves, but in perceiving the relationship of one object to another. (34)

Metaphorical use here reveals the impacts of our bodies on our cognition – we do not think neutrally or from nowhere, but always in concert with the physics of ourselves, of our environments and of the objects that we find there.[3]

In the same way that our bodies condition the ways in which we think about the world, by exporting conventions of our own form out onto other objects with which we interact or locate ourselves in reference to, in some smaller fashion so to do the embodied objects that we encounter project elements of their form back into our way of thinking. To think this through in terms of print I would like to appropriate a term from the work of digital literature theorist N. Katherine Hayles (2002): 'material metaphor'. For Hayles, a material metaphor 'foregrounds the traffic between words and physical artefacts' (2002: 22), interrogating the connection between a book's script content and the tangible medium:

We are not generally accustomed to think of a book as a material metaphor, but in fact it is an artifact whose physical properties and historical usages structure our interactions with it in ways obvious and subtle. In addition to defining the page as a unit of reading, and binding pages sequentially to indicate an order of reading, are less obvious conventions such the [sic] opacity of paper, a physical property that defines the pages as having two sides whose relationship is linear and sequential rather than interpenetrating and simultaneous. (22–3)

Hayles here recognises the ways in which the form of a printed book can promote or suggest things to the reader. The privileging of linear thinking that goes hand in hand with the relentless forward process of turning pages is something that I have spoken about elsewhere (Hayler 2015: ch. 1) and that Foer plays with in his rupturing of the pages of *Tree of Codes* – what was once 'sequential rather than interpenetrating and simultaneous' becomes, in Foer's book, penetrable and synchronous, a set of iterations where you see the same words in different company, windowed through the ever-changing leaves of the novel. We might also think of Jane Austen's aside to the reader at the end of the playful *Northanger Abbey* where she notes that her characters' 'anxiety . . . can hardly extend, I fear, to the bosom of my readers, who will see in the tell-tale compression of the pages before them that we are all hastening together to perfect felicity' (2003: 185). The amount of pages resting in our right hands constantly updates us as to the time we have left to spend with the story world, and this might raise or lower the tension that the author has set up so far: as it thins we know that there is not long to go.

The material form of the codex, then, can structure the reception of at least the content within it. I would further argue that it has the potential to structure the kinds of thinking that follow on after its use. Walter Ong, an early and influential theorist of digital writing, gives us a way into this by grounding his discussion of new media in the radically freeing effect of the introduction of the written word:

> Since in a primary oral culture conceptualized knowledge that is not repeated aloud soon vanishes, oral societies must invest great energy in saying over and over again what has been learned arduously over the ages. This need establishes a highly traditionalist or conservative set of mind that with good reason inhibits intellectual experimentation. Knowledge is hard to come by and precious. (1982: 41)

Societies which have adopted writing hugely expand their capacity for novel thinking,[4] not only through the elimination of repetition for the sake of memory, but also of repetition between people working on the same problem. Writing, particularly that which is presented in a form which is easily copied, preserved, stored and/or distributed, transcends space and time, and reaches audiences beyond those immediately bodily present. In this way, the uses of the codex and codex-like forms have been radically democratising with implications for, for example, religion[5] and the transmission and availability of ideas.[6]

But the history of the use of writing stored within the codex does not uniformly match the message of its physicality; particularly in the age of the Internet and its swiftly produced, amateur-led and often brief and fleeting texts, it becomes clear that the codex does not inherently afford caprice or rapid response, instead promoting the positives and negatives of the glacial flow of received wisdom. The forces of history, culture and society interacting with the equipment have undoubtedly shaped each user's phenomenological experience of the form, but they are not the enduring aspects of its brute embodiment. The defining positive features of the codex are not its provision of freedoms and novelty, but its order, its stability and its sense of authority, products of its boundedness. The covers of a printed text enact this clearly: the object is finished all around with a hard shell; it is discrete.

Sven Birkerts, an early critic of reading on screen, invokes the codex's biblical origins when describing those features indelibly connected to the experience of the object itself: 'What [codex] reading does, ultimately, is keep alive the dangerous and exhilarating idea that a life is not a sequence of lived moments, but a destiny. That God or no God, life has a unitary pattern inscribed within it' (2006: 85). The belief displayed here is in '[t]he stable hierarchies of the printed page' (3), where the linear order marks a steady teleological progression towards the enlightenment of the conclusion. The form wins out over the history of its deployment in the repeated phenomenological experience. A history of new freedoms and the democratisation of information is supplanted by the particular forces of preservation and continuity that are tied to the arrangement of the pages themselves.

The above gives some sense of the ways in which the form of the printed codex might impact upon the reader. It itself has become meaningful across a timeline of long and intensive usages, at times supporting and at others contradicting the messages of the words that it might contain and their ready dissemination. I will now turn to the much younger technology of electronic text in order to consider the kinds of metaphorical impact its own strange embodiment might already have begun to accrue, particularly in light of its troubled relationship with print.

THE DISEMBODIED TEXT?

The way in which we receive digital texts' more complex materiality is conditioned by their divided relationship with both print and computing. Set against a history of print we can understand at least some of the concerns of commentators such as Birkerts: digital texts appear to be intangible (even if e-reading devices such as the Kindle and iPad clearly are not) and this can lead to a sense of a problematic change. Birkerts' argument in *The Gutenberg Elegies* (2006), for instance, revolves around the ways in which the physicality of print enables us to build up sense memories that are denied us by the resilient and depthless plastic and glass of electronic screens. I have written extensively elsewhere about digital materiality with regard to these fears of moving from page to screen (Hayler 2015), so I will focus, instead, on reading two aspects of digital and digital-inspired texts that are intimately connected with materiality: the phenomenological experience of intangibility and the meaningfulness of hyperlinking. My aim is to demonstrate that the physicality and reception of digital texts are becoming just as subtly meaningful as those of print.

In *Writing Space* (1991), *Hypertext* (1992) and *Hyper/Text/Theory*[7] (1994) Jay David Bolter and George Landow set out theories and theoretical implications for the new digital literature, databases and environments that were starting to impact upon English studies. These texts were enthusiastic about the new forms and largely sought to see how the American academy's poststructural strategies of the time could be mapped onto digital products; little interest was shown in the potential downsides of a shift in media from print to pixels, nor in what was occurring during programming, what effects code and coding might have upon the reader's reception of a text, etc. These works largely treated digital media as evanescent, setting the tone for approaches to digital texts throughout the 1990s that work in the Digital Humanities since the turn of the millennium has sought to rehabilitate.

Moving on from Bolter and Landow's theoretical position, Hayles, first with *Writing Machines* (2002) and then with *Electronic Literature* (2008), brought the close reading of classical English studies to bear on digital works, and also explored the effects that those works had started to have on more conventional printed material. Hayles' increasing sensitivity to the particularities of every aspect of digitisation has been hugely influential on the theoretical aspects of contemporary Digital Humanities study and has made it both accessible to traditional media scholars and pushed it forward for a new generation of researchers.

Hayles' influence can be felt in Matthew Kirschenbaum's *Mechanisms* (2008), a work which has been similarly important for theoretical discussions regarding the importance of materiality for the Digital Humanities, meticulously picking apart the physical particularities of the computer and refuting the illusion of the digital as an ethereal realm. As mentioned above, phenomenologically, digital texts do not appear to be there, they seem to be insubstantial ghosts on the screen that disappear when they are to be replaced by other content. As Mangen describes them,

> [u]nlike print texts, digital texts are ontologically intangible and detached from the physical and mechanical dimension of their material support, namely, the computer or [e-reader] . . . When reading digital texts, our haptic interaction with the text is experienced as taking place at an indeterminate distance from the actual text, whereas when reading print text we are physically and phenomenologically (and literally) in touch with the material substrate of the text itself. (2008: 405)

In terms of the specificity of the script instantiation's substrate this is largely correct, but the physicality of the script does remain in other ways, although hidden to all but the minority of users involved with the guts of the machine and with access to the reality of the forensic realm that Kirschenbaum describes in *Mechanisms*.[8] As Kirschenbaum notes, '[e]lectronic textuality is . . . locatable, even though we are not accustomed to thinking of it in physical terms. Bits can be measured in microns when recorded on a magnetic hard disk. They can be visualised with technologies such as magnetic force microscopy (MFM)' (2008: 3). Studies such as Kirschenbaum's alert us to the meaningful potential inherent in electronic ways of presenting texts by reminding us of a rich and intricate physicality and layering of readable strata that we often neglect when contemplating the digital projection of words on a screen.[9]

As well as discussing a typically invisible forensic materiality, Kirschenbaum also asserts that all software has an extensive entailment of material elements that should not be forgotten as evidence of its very real place in the world:

> Software is the product of whitepapers, engineering specs, marketing reports, conversations and collaborations, intuitive insights, professionalised expertise, venture capital . . . late nights (. . . labour), caffeine, and other artificial stimulants. These are material circumstances that leave material (read: forensic) traces – in corporate archives, on whiteboards and legal pads, in countless iterations of alpha versions and beta versions and patches and upgrades, in focus groups and user communities, in expense accounts, in licensing agreements, in stock options and IPOs, in carpal tunnel braces, in the Bay Area and New Delhi real-estate markets, in PowerPoint vaporware and proofs of concept binaries locked in time-stamped limbo on a server where all the user accounts but one have been disabled and the domain name is eighteen months expired. (2008: 14–15)

Most significant for us here is that this litany demonstrates that to suppose intangibility at any level of the digital text is simply a misreading: the software has a physical forensic materiality at the level of the hard disk image and in the materiality that it entails from production to distribution to use, and it is instantiated on a device which is equally physical and entailed.[10] That the phenomenological experience is of a potentially discomforting immateriality is born of naivety and the limitations of our senses rather than a valid ontological claim. What can seem alienating, however, is that not only has our reading experience changed, but what and how that experience can mean.

Talking about electronic writing on a PC screen, Hayles' detailing of this seemingly spectral materiality is equally applicable to the e-reader:

> In the computer, the signifier exists not as a durably inscribed flat mark but as a screenic image produced by layers of code precisely correlated through correspondence rules, from the electronic polarities that correlate with the bit stream to the bits that correlate with binary numbers, to the numbers that correlate with higher-level statements, such as commands, and so on. Even when electronic [texts] simulate the appearance of durably inscribed marks, they are transitory images that need to be constantly refreshed . . . to give the illusion of stable endurance through time. (2004: 74)

This leads Hayles to argue that 'electronic text is a process rather than an arte-fact one can hold in one's hand' (2004: 79). When a book becomes a process to be run on a machine, rather than a coherence of inked writing and paper substrate to be held, this must have implications for how we conceive of it. The digital document, instantiated as a block of script, drives us to our history of print and to writing more generally. But its appearance on an electronic device also sends us to our experience of various other screens:

> Readers come to digital work with expectations formed by print, including extensive and deep tacit knowledge of letter forms, print conventions, and print literary modes . . . At the same time, because electronic literature is normally created and performed within a context of networked and programmable media, it is also informed by the powerhouses of contemporary culture, particularly computer games, films, animations, digital arts, graphic design, and electronic visual culture. (Hayles 2008: 4)

Here, Hayles identifies the struggle in producing a new model for what a text can be, a shape that does not settle easily and that can only come through repeated interaction: our first uses, if they are to have any chance of success, must rely heavily on our prior experience. We have a default gestalt for bound-book reading that has emerged out of a long history of experience. We are initially forced to apply that paradigm to electronic reading, but such reading is capable of and promotes interactions – such as clicking, scrolling, swift changes and communication between content, etc. – which do not fit our printed-book experience and we must therefore find a suitable model from elsewhere in order to get us through the experience. The new gestalt expands to include the diversity of prior contexts that Hayles identifies which we might draw upon in order to attempt action and understanding; all of these things are suddenly part of both what 'book' and 'digital/electronic text' can mean.

As the Digital Humanities continues to work out its theorisation of reading the multiple layers of digital texts, from source code to human-readable layers and on to the final presentation of the text and the materiality of the medium on which the script is called into being, readers too are developing a new series of learnt expectations that structure our reception of texts. As with print, we are developing a new history, a new set of models that condition all of our future uses, and these models, as with Foer's interrogation of the printed page, can be drawn on by authors in order to produce meaningful responses. To think through one example of this, I want to consider electronic hyperlinks, a method of navigating documents that, from the earliest digital theorists onwards, have come to represent the potential for new ways of reading, thinking about reading and reflecting on what reading has always been.

A hyperlink, most typically represented as an underlined blue word, when clicked takes the reader from the page that they are on to somewhere else, known or unknown. The author of the document sets the hyperlink marker – which word or image is clickable – and they set the destination; the reader chooses whether or not they are going to click the link. But even an unclicked link has come to possess meaning.[11] Steven Johnson describes hyperlinks as an entirely new linguistic element, 'the first significant form of punctuation to emerge in centuries' (2005: 111), and this is an apt description; like a comma, question or exclamation mark, hyperlinked words do not change the words themselves at the level of their letters, but instead augment and alter their meaning and capacity to mean. In early writing systems pictographic script largely attempted to represent spoken words: the spoken 'bird', in the simplest pictogram, would have a representational or symbolic parallel with the image of a bird. A text was accurate if the interpretations of each image matched some value of what the author intended. A chirographic or typographic written word is different: it is more precise, capable of far greater nuance, and part of its ability to better capture both more specific and more abstract meanings stems from its representing, or coming to represent, a spoken word that has been inscribed many times, iterated with its own growing history and malleable context. As the cognitive neuroscientist Maryanne Wolf notes in her exploration of the reading brain:

> [l]inguists classify English as a morphophonemic writing system because it represents both morphemes (units of meaning) and phonemes (units of sound) in its spelling . . . [T]he linguists Noam Chomsky and Carol Chomsky use words like 'muscle' to teach the way our words carry an entire history within them[12] . . . For example, the silent 'c' in 'muscle' may seem unnecessary, but in fact it visibly connects the word to its origin, the Latin root musculus, from which we have such kindred words as 'muscular' and 'musculature.' In the latter words the 'c' is pronounced and represents the phonemic aspect of our alphabet. The silent 'c' of 'muscle,' therefore, visually conveys the morpheme aspect of English. (2008: 42–3)

A pictogram of a muscle always means the concept of 'muscle'; whatever the culture dictated that concept to be, the image would always suggest to the reader their current interpretation of that conventional concept. But if we look at the word 'muscle', with its silent 'c', then we also get the full morphopho-neticism of English coming to the fore: the Latin root, with its pronounced 'c', hides within a conceptual trace, a history more or less known and more or less affective to the reader. But now paint that word blue and underline it, put it on a screen and it becomes imbued with *possibility*. This contraption now means the interpreted cultural concept of the spoken or inscribed 'muscle', like the pictogram; it alludes to 'musculus' and to a history of use, like the inscribed word; but it also reminds us of everywhere that it might take us: anatomical diagrams, bodybuilding, bodyguards, seafood even, or somewhere we have yet to learn. Even if the link is not clicked and followed, hyperlinks still have implications for interpretation. Hyperlinks, and their apparent manifestations, represent a personal aspect to every underlined word, of choices made to access or not, a unique link or combination. They are hypermorphophonemic: conceptual, historical, possible.

This becomes significant in a time of ever-increasing electronic reading. Hyperlinking has been an important part of the promise of digital documents since Ted Nelson's coining of the term in the 1960s,[13] but the rise of Internet-based reading has normalised the mechanism – it is as much part of reading on screen as pagination is to codex reading. Reading books on Kindles and iPads has only served to further the default of words as hypermorphophonemic, with every e-reading space now offering the potentials of hyperlink-inflected reading and ensuring that every word on screen explicitly carries this weight, reminding us of the potential inherent in every word, its myriad connotations and relations. Amazon's Kindle, for instance, allows you to search for any word within a document, and this parallels and extends one of the first hyperlinking systems created: the printed index. But any word, or word string, can also be searched for in your entire Kindle corpus, binding all of your texts together, drawing links and associations, or it can be searched for in the Kindle store, linking together the millions of available documents there. The dictionary search function, highlighting any word on the page you're reading and looking up a definition in the built-in database, similarly parallels a pre-existing linking mechanism. But that same highlight and search function, with one more button push, can search for the term in Wikipedia or on Google. Every single word in a Kindle text is always already effectively a hyperlink to somewhere beyond the text that you're working with. As Nancy Kaplan asserted, eight years before e-reading really took hold,

> [t]urning a book's pages . . . adds nothing to signification: the end of
> a page is an arbitrary boundary imposed by an intransigent material
> world. Taking a link from here to somewhere is not the same thing at
> all, for in the aggregate the set of chosen links and each link's place in
> the set play off against all the sets passed over. That doubleness – the
> links taken and those passed by – brings a particular reading into being.
> (2000: 227)

And this kind of reading cannot help but mean differently.

Mark Z. Danielewski spent much of the 1990s writing his debut novel *House of Leaves* (2000a) against the backdrop of the growing Internet. For all of its relations to the new digital era, *House of Leaves* was written in a time

largely before Google changed search (1998), before the iPod changed the
music industry (2001) and well before YouTube changed the distribution of
moving images (2005). But the Internet, ubiquitous home computing and the
beginnings of the 'threat' to the codex that digitisation was meant to pose are
written deeply into the pages of Danielewski's book.

It would be both irrelevant and impossible to accurately detail the complexities of *House of Leaves*' plot, but it can loosely be thought of as a haunted
house novel about a house bigger on the inside than the outside, a reworking
of the minotaur in the labyrinth myth, a critical theory-heavy film studies
monograph, a meditation on the power of the codex and at least two family
dramas – all combined into arguably the first great English language novel
of the millennium.[14] The script appears as a beautiful mess of footnotes,
nested images, index and appendices. Throughout, *House of Leaves*' layout
and typography is visually intense in one form or another. Most famously,
in its colour edition every instance of the word 'house' is coloured blue and
offset slightly, a constant reminder of the space that is haunted and that
haunts the story, and arguably a reference to the infinitely inscribable space
of blue screen projections for cinematic special effects (see McCormick 2011).
There is, however, another explanation for the motif, also associated with an
infinite blue: the hyperlink. In his essay on *House of Leaves*, the new media
theorist Mark B. N. Hansen (2004) is more focused on the filmic aspects of
the text and somewhat dismissive of this connection: 'Making pseudoseri-
ous reference to the blue highlighting of hyperlinks on Web pages, the blue
ink of the word "house" in the work's title transforms this keyword into
something like a portal to information located elsewhere, both within and
beyond the novel's frame' (598). But I think that, though he is playful with
it, Danielewski is deadly serious about the importance of this interpretation,
particularly in light of, as Sonya Hagler notes, '[p]urple, the color of visited
links, mak[ing an] appearance, in chapter twenty-one: "I'm sorry, I have
nothing left. Except this story, what I'm remembering now, too long from
the surface of any dawn" . . . Fittingly, this purple text deals with memory'
(2007: n.p.).

House of Leaves draws extensively on the digitisation of the written word
as it was already established at the end of the 1990s during the book's gesta-
tion. From the sizeable index's functioning as a search engine (long a skill of
the codex, but given greater weight in the novel with its more trivial entries
(including 'all', 'and', 'back', 'can', 'for', 'here', 'in', 'into', 'just', 'more', 'my',
'not', 'nothing', 'only', 'out', 'so', 'something', and the significant single use of
the word 'Yggdrasil') giving the impression that every word is searchable,[15] to
the myriad footnotes acting as hyperlinks that actually form entire parallel narratives, *House of Leaves* interrogates the new specificities of the digitisation of
texts and the ways in which their remediation can be put to work in subverting

the printed page. Like Foer, Danielewski regards his book as a challenge to the abandoning of one medium for another:

> Older generations . . . will find *House of Leaves* difficult because they're prejudiced. They've been taught what a book should look like and how it should be read . . . But books don't have to be so limited. They can intensify informational content and experience . . . Passages may be found, studied, revisited, or even skimmed. And that's just the beginning. Words can also be colored and those colors can have meaning . . . Hell pages can be tilted, turned upside down, even read backwards . . . But here's the joke. Books have had this capability all along . . . Look at early 16th century manuscripts. Hell, go open up the Talmud . . . [S]omehow the analogue powers of these wonderful bundles of paper have been forgotten. (Danielewski 2000b: n.p.)

House of Leaves never allows us to forget this agenda, enriching both print and the digital in its demonstrations of possible meanings. The novel shows the explosion of potential for *all* texts once readers become experienced in reading the possibilities written into form and mechanism, not just the illusion of translated speech that words on the page are often reduced to. Ink is rejuvenated in the text as meaningful, acting as a material metaphor for the equipmental structures surrounding the novel. 'Why do we deprive ourselves', Danielewski seems to ask, 'of any opportunity to layer meaning?' Every instance of 'house' in blue is a sore thumb, sticking out to remind us that a book is always more than evanescent content: these are words in thick, black ichor, hammered into place by a metal reflection or corralled into shape with lasers. But, simultaneously, that same materiality points to the potential of phenomenologically intangible links and their implications for print; Danielewski drags the materials and means of production into the text. Knowing well the traces that would intentionally or unavoidably permeate his work, Danielewski brings the Internet and the threat of digitisation into meaning, makes them indispensable to the text and simultaneously mounts a defence of the codex as a form. This defence seems to be an act of pedagogy on Danielewski's part, an attempt to strengthen and broaden our sense of what a codex is, not simply as a response to a perceived threat, but also as a response to the provocations and excitements of the new electronic forms.

Danielewski's remediation of hyperlinks comes as part of his broader revivification of paper. As reading new digital scripts initially relies upon drawing on the history of print before expanding outwards, Danielewski's text shows the meaningful impact of the digital as it goes the other way, as new metaphors born of repeated use become available for authorial manipulation. I will conclude this chapter with a brief look at an artwork which, even further than

Danielewski's *House*, straddles and interrogates this division between print and the digital and pulls each form's various aspects into meaning-making.

A BRAND NEW BODY

In early 2014 I acted as lead academic in developing a project with the Royal Shakespeare Company and an art team, Kristin and Davey McGuire. We received funding from the AHRC REACT research hub, a prototyping grant for what would become described as a 'Theatre Book'. Kristin and Davey had been working with digital and projection technologies for a number of years, most significantly with *The Icebook*.[16] *The Icebook* straddles print and digital literature; it is a pop-up book that receives digital projection from a large external device. A helper turns the pages as the story unfolds at a fixed pace, bringing up new scenes for the projection to meet. The effect is that of being read a story by a parent, having the images come to life, but remaining, yourself, a passive if excited recipient. *The Theatre Book* project extends and enriches, in my view at least, the effectiveness of *The Icebook*'s impact by bringing all of the technology within the bounds of a single object and enabling the reader, alone, to trigger the story at his or her own pace. I shall describe the appearance of the *Theatre Book* below, but would also recommend visiting the McGuires' website[17] to watch a short video of the project in action in order to better appreciate some of what I am about to discuss.

The reader is first faced with a large wooden-covered book, almost a box, laser engraved on its front with 'Macbeth' informing us that this is a retelling of Shakespeare's play. Best viewed in a darkened space, upon opening the book a paper pop-up scene is brought out of the flat folded page and there is a slight whir and click as a mirror, unseen behind the proscenium arch of the pop-up, raises into position. The paper itself bears key lines from the play, and if you move slightly to one side you can see a little of the hidden mechanism. Tiny paper lighting riggers, directors and grips act as a good-natured reminder that you are looking where you should not, trying to spoil the secret behind the scenes of the 'theatre' – the visual gag becomes a little extra magic while simultaneously extending the theatrical metaphor and revealing it as an illusion; that is not quite how this story will be made.

A pico projector built into the book's spine automatically comes to life as the covers are opened; it shines on the mirror and is reflected back onto the paper, brightly illuminating it, filling in its shapes with images of a wood. Music from internal speakers begins to play, composed for the project, ethereal and beautiful. As the projected image comes to life with small characters walking into a clearing in the trees, not animated but real human figures that begin to silently act out key scenes from the play, the illusion is complete. The physical form of the book is wholly bounded – no wires and nothing to plug in; the story has come to life.

As the first element of the tale draws to a close, the music winds down and the scene fades away to re-reveal the blank cream of the paper and its skeletal pop-up forms. There is no prompt, but the reader knows what to do: she reaches out and turns the page, returning one set of paper models to the flat and bringing another up and out into being. New music begins, a newly projected scene fades up into animating this new paper set, and the next part of the story starts to be enacted. The reader can go back or skip on just by turning the pages, interrupting the flow of the story at his or her leisure.

So how do we go about reading a text like this, one that dances across the line between an electronic projected screen and a paper page? What do we need to be sensitive to? What aspects might play into its particular meaningfulness? I want to focus on three things in line with my discussion in the previous sections: how *The Theatre Book* draws on print, how it draws on the digital and how it brings these concerns together in a cultural moment that lends them particular weight.

With regard to print, the *Theatre Book*, like *Tree of Codes*, offers constant reminders of its commitment to the power of materiality. The magic of unfurling layered paper landscapes, the beautifully etched wooden covers that speak back to the trees the paper came from, the small figures that seem to be hard at work making the projection function in the background – each of these elements keeps the power of books at hand. With each turn of the leaves our hands are put to work in bringing the text, as a combination of material, materiality and human experience in context, into being. We act as directors, as we always have – never wholly responsible, but the driving force behind the combination of aspects which produce the final thing that we encounter. For the McGuires, the most important relationship between the *Theatre Book* and traditional print is its evocation of reading a book under the covers with a torch as a child, a secretive world-building.

Its relationship with the digital is more assiduously hidden, but no less meaningful. There is little magic to a projector anymore, hence the joke of the little paper figures around the mirror – the mirror is not enough. In order to more thoroughly understand the digital elements of the work we could maybe look back beyond the contemporary publishing industry to the pre-cinematic moving images captured by magic lantern shows and shadow plays of all kinds. The *Theatre Book* seems to riff on these forms more than cinema in its combination of static sets and lively moving elements within the bounds of the paper surfaces. The reader is sent out to consider all kinds of moving images, all manner of references. But we, of course, still know that this is a peculiarly twenty-first-century product – these images, captured in their portable form, could have been produced at no other point in human history. The paper, the pop-up, the mirror, the light, the recorded sound, the engraved wooden box: these elements each have an extensive tradition of at least a century. But the paper is connected to a micro-switch system that changes the scenes; the pop-ups and the mirror and the light form an unfathomably tiny and accurate cinema (not the smallest screen, but among the smallest gestalt of light thrown and received); the recorded sound is an mp3 played through a tiny amp and speakers; the box is laser etched. This is not a traditional item at any level; from the binary code of its underlying computer platform to the reassuring wood and print materiality that rests upon the table it has been mediated by digital processes.

The *Theatre Book* derives much of the intensity of its meaningfulness from its subversions of our expectations regarding prior art in print; as with *House of Leaves*, part of its effect is in closing a reciprocal loop between print and the digital. Printed pages are meant to be fixed, but here they are brought to life. The digital is meant to be ghostly, ephemeral, independent of the structures that mobilise it, but here it is fixed, bound up with the surfaces that it animates, triggered by their movements. It is in its weaving together of both forms, and at this time, that the meaning of each is heightened – the *Theatre Book*, again similarly to *House of Leaves*, offers an antidote to fear in the face of the new and a commitment to showing the already-present meaning-making potentials of existing forms. Above all else, this project implicates the reader in bringing the story to life, in conjuring up its world and making it matter (in at least a couple of senses of that word).

We might always question where a text *is* – in music it is perhaps more readily problematic: is the piece in the notation, the performance, the recording or the act of listening? Does the text necessarily always subtly spread across each of these aspects as the reader, performer or producer at each level is at least partly informed about and inflected by the other aspects? In a printed book is the text in the story's script, in the reader's head or in some communion between the instantiation of the work, the reader, their cultural contexts and the current milieu in which they find themselves? In the *Theatre Book*, the active role that the reader plays in writing her specific text is brought to the fore in her participation in actually creating each setting that the work will manifest upon, causing the space to emerge from the leaves of the book – this materiality causes us to perform what we have always done. As Hayles noted, digitisation renders electronic script as a process rather than a thing – it is not waiting for us to discover it on the page, but is instead called into being just for us at the moment of contact. This is much the same concern, but from another angle. And so we find in the *Theatre Book* a private textual theatre moment: the magic of both modes' entanglement helps the reader remember the activity of reading, rendering the simple act of turning pages and interpreting images and words and music as anything but passive.

As the possibilities for meaning-making in literary texts change with the continuing development and adoption of digital technology, the Digital Humanities will continue to develop productive reading strategies. The remaining chapters in this volume all read new texts in new ways, but here I have wanted to defend a kind of sensitivity in reading that is often far simpler. We are, in our encounters with electronic pages, and with print in the light of digitisation, developing new meaningful grammars, i.e. structures for comprehension, which might also underpin authorial and other artistic strategies. By uniting theorisations of the experience of new reading practices with artistic work committed to troubling and exploring the kinds of reading that can occur, there is a mutual enriching of all kinds of literary work and of the viable strategies for comprehending its impact. As it is increasingly built into our lives, digital technology is becoming humanised: made subtle, not jarring, truly deep, not ghostly or shallow, and meaning-rich, like every page which has held the words that move us.

ACKNOWLEDGEMENTS

I would like to thank the REACT hub for their support and the Royal Shakespeare Company and Davey and Kristin McGuire for their collaboration on the 'Theatre Book' project described in this chapter.

NOTES

1. Images of Foer's book are available at the Visual Editions website: <http://www.visual-editions.com/our-books/tree-of-codes> (last accessed 19 June 2015).
2. I have written about this quotation before in 'The extent of text' (2012), an essay that considers some of the metaphorical significance of Foer's work. Foer's conception of his project, and his reflection on it in this quotation, is something that I keep returning to – the weight of embodied experience and the materiality of devices has come to underpin my understanding of twenty-first-century e-reading, and also of the young millennium's feelings toward technology more broadly.
3. The field of embodied cognition in cognitive science explores a whole host of ways in which this is the case. For more on this see, for example, Shapiro (2010), Varela et al. (1993) and Chemero (2011). For a thorough discussion of the importance of the embodiment of the reader in understanding the resistance to e-reading and technological interactions more broadly see also Hayler (2015).

4. For more on the power of the adoption of writing see Martin (1995) and Olson et al. (1985).

5. Christians were the foremost early users of the codex, adopting it in order to disseminate and work with their Bible:

> By the first century, Christians were tying loose-leaf sheets of papyrus or parchment together in tablets that opened down the middle. These codices were compact enough to be carried around in a satchel and produced at prayer meetings. The codex had two other advantages over the roll: with writing on both sides of the surface, it was more capacious; and whereas rolls had to be read sequentially, codices enabled readers to turn to individual pages at separate points in the book. (McNeely and Wolverton 2008: 45–6)

> See also Roberts and Skeat (1983).

6. The most influential book regarding the history and effects of printing is surely Eisenstein (1979). See also Febvre and Martin (1997) and Man (2002).

7. A collection edited by George Landow.

8. Kirschenbaum identifies two kinds of materiality: 'forensic' – 'no two things in the physical world are ever exactly alike' (2008: 10) – and 'formal' – the arbitrary material particularity, independent of forensic differentiation, of a particular interpretation of a data set, e.g. one set of image data producing a .jpeg, .tiff, .gif, metadata, histograms, watermarks, etc. depending on what program interprets that set.

9. *Tree of Code*'s layers of pages, for instance, seem to take on an extra resonance in light of the layers of machine- and human-readable code that underpin every electronic text. See also Hayles' 'Print is flat, code is deep' (2004).

10. For more on the discussion of the alleged ephemerality and infinite malleability of digital text see (Kirschenbaum 2008: 50–8).

11. I also briefly touch on this idea in 'Translating to digital' (2010) where I explore the move from page to screen as an act of translation.

12. Wolf cites Halle and Chomsky (1968) and Chomsky (1972) in this regard.

13. See Nelson (1980) for discussion of his work on hypertext and the Xanadu hypertext project over two decades.

14. The January release of Zadie Smith's *White Teeth* (2000) is really the beginning and end of the argument.

15. The index of *House of Leaves* allows

> readers to trace the different contexts in which the words appear and even the frequency of that appearance. So if you come across the listing for 'for', you don't have to look up all the passages where 'for' appears to be able to say, Wow, there's a prevalence of this word and here is a

certain stylistic habit statistically represented with page numbers. The index allows you to suddenly start asking questions about books you normally wouldn't think about in these terms. Wouldn't it be nice to have an easy way to find out how many and's [*sic*] appear in a Faulkner book or the King James? Or how many for's [*sic*] appear in a Virginia Woolf novel? Do they vary? What do these signs of reoccurrence reveal? Maybe nothing at all, but it brings that question to mind. And to me any feature of a book that invites readers to ask different sorts of questions is valuable. (Danielewski 2003: 118–19)

Danielewski's interest in his work being in some way pedagogical, or otherwise elucidating to the reader, is clear here.

16. See <http://www.theicebook.com> (last accessed 19 June 2015). This site hosts video of *The Icebook* in action with discussion from the artists.

17. Available at <http://www.davyandkristinmcguire.com/macbeth.html> (last accessed 19 June 2015).

REFERENCES

Austen, J. ([1817] 2003) *Northanger Abbey*. Oxford: Oxford University Press.

Birkerts, S. (2006) *The Gutenberg Elegies: The Fate of Reading in an Electronic Age*. New York: Faber & Faber.

Bolter, J. D. (1991) *Writing Space: The Computer, Hypertext, and the History of Writing*. Hillsdale, NJ: Lawrence Erlbaum Associates.

Chemero, A. (2011) *Radical Embodied Cognitive Science*. Cambridge, MA: MIT Press.

Chomsky, C. (1972) 'Stages in language development and reading exposure', *Harvard Educational Review*, 42, pp. 1–33.

Danielewski, M. Z. (2000a) *House of Leaves*. London: Anchor.

Danielewski, M. Z. (2000b) 'A conversation with Mark Danielewski', interview by Sophie Cottrell, *boldtype*, April, at <http://www.randomhouse.com/boldtype/0400/danielewski/interview.html> (last accessed 18 June 2010).

Danielewski, M. Z. (2003) Interview by Larry MacCaffery and Sinda Gregory, 'Haunted house – an interview with Mark Z. Danielewski', *Critique*, 44: 2, pp. 99–135, at <http://markzdanielewski.info/mzd/critique.pdf> (last accessed 19 June 2015).

Eisenstein, E. L. (1979) *The Printing Press as an Agent of Change Vols 1 and 2*. Cambridge: Cambridge University Press.

Febvre, L. and Martin, H.-J. (1997) *The Coming of the Book: The Impact of Printing 1450–1800*. London: Verso.

Foer, J. Safran (2010a) *Tree of Codes*. London: Visual Editions.

Foer, J. Safran (2010b) 'Jonathan Safran Foer talks *Tree of Codes* and conceptual art', *Vanity Fair*, 10 November, at <http://www.vanityfair.com/online/daily/2010/11/jonathan-safran-foer-talks-tree-of-codes-and-paper-art.html> (last accessed 26 January 2011).

Hagler, S. (2007) 'Mediating print and hypertext in Mark Danielewski's *House of Leaves*', *Cornell University*, 12 April, at <http://www.arts.cornell.edu/English/mode/documents/hagler.doc> (last accessed 14 July 2007).

Halle, M. and Chomsky, N. (1968) *The Sound Pattern of English*. New York: Harper & Row.

Hansen, M. B. N. (2004) 'The digital topography of Mark Z. Danielewski's *House of Leaves*', *Contemporary Literature*, 45: 4, pp. 597–636, at <http://www.jstor.org/stable/3593543> (last accessed 19 June 2015).

Hayler, M. (2010) 'Translating to digital', *PEER English: Journal of New Critical Thinking*, 5, at <http://www2.le.ac.uk/offices/english-association/publications/peer-english/5/12%20Hayler%20-%20Translating%20to%20Digital.pdf> (last accessed 19 June 2015).

Hayler, M. (2012) 'The extent of text: producing meaning beyond intuition', *Writing Technologies*, 4, pp. 20–42, at <http://www.ntu.ac.uk/writing_technologies/back_issues/vol_4/124935.pdf> (last accessed 19 June 2015).

Hayler, M. (2015) *Challenging the Phenomena of Technology*. Basingstoke: Palgrave.

Hayler, M. and Griffin, G. (eds) (2016) *Research Methods for Digital Humanities 2: Digitising and Curating*. Edinburgh: Edinburgh University Press.

Hayles, N. K. (2002) *Writing Machines*. Cambridge, MA: MIT Press.

Hayles, N. K. (2004) 'Print is flat, code is deep: the importance of media-specific analysis', *Poetics Today*, 25: 1, pp. 67–90.

Hayles, N. K. (2008) *Electronic Literature: New Horizons for the Literary*. Notre Dame, IN: University of Notre Dame Press.

Hayles, N. K. (2012) *How We Think: Digital Media and Contemporary Technogenesis*. Chicago: University of Chicago Press.

Johnson, S. A. (2005) *Everything Bad Is Good for You: Why Popular Culture Is Making Us Smarter*. London: Penguin.

Kaplan, N. (2000) 'Literacy beyond books', in A. Herman and T. Swiss (eds), *The World Wide Web and Contemporary Cultural Theory*. London: Routledge, pp. 207–16.

Kirschenbaum, M. G. (2008) *Mechanisms: New Media and the Forensic Imagination*. Cambridge, MA: MIT Press.

Lakoff, G. and Johnson, M. (1999) *Philosophy in the Flesh*. New York: Basic.

Landow, G. (1992) *Hypertext: The Convergence of Contemporary Critical Theory and Technology*. Baltimore: Johns Hopkins University Press.

Landow. G. (ed.) (1994) *Hyper/Text/Theory*. Baltimore: Johns Hopkins University Press.

McCormick, P. (2011) '*Houses of Leaves*, cinema and the new affordances of old media', in *Mark Z. Danielewski*, Manchester: Manchester University Press, pp. 52–67.

McGuire, D. and McGuire, K. (2011) 'The icebook', *The Icebook*, at <http://www.theicebook.com> (last accessed 19 June 2015).

McGuire, D. and McGuire, K. (2015) 'Theatre book', *davyandkristinmcguire* <http://www.davyandkristinmcguire.com/macbeth.html> (last accessed 19 June 2015).

McNeely, I. F. with L. Wolverton (2008) *Reinventing Knowledge: From Alexandria to the Internet*. New York: W. W. Norton.

Man, J. (2002) *The Gutenberg Revolution: The Story of a Genius and an Invention that Changed the World*. London: Headline Review.

Mangen, A. (2008) 'Hypertext fiction reading: haptics and immersion', *Journal of Research in Reading*, 31: 4, pp. 404–19.

Mangen, A. (2015) 'Evolution of reading in the age of digitisation (EREAD)', *COST*, at <http://www.cost.eu/COST_Actions/isch/Actions/IS1404> (last accessed 19 June 2015).

Martin, H.-J. (1995) *The History and Power of Writing*, trans. Lydia G. Cochrane. Chicago: University of Chicago Press.

Nelson, T. (1980) *Literary Machines*. Sausalito, CA: Mindful Press.

Olson, D. R., Torrance, N. and Hildyard, A. (eds) (1985) *Literacy, Language, and Learning: The Nature and Consequences of Reading and Writing*. Cambridge: Cambridge University Press.

Ong, W. J. (1982) *Orality and Literacy: The Technologizing of the Word*. London: Routledge.

Roberts, C. H. and Skeat, T. C. (1983) *The Birth of the Codex*. London: Oxford University Press.

Schulz, B. (1977) *The Street of Crocodiles*. London: Penguin.

Shapiro, L. (2010) *Embodied Cognition*. Abingdon: Routledge.

Smith, Z. (2000) *White Teeth*. London: Penguin.

Varela, F. J., Thompson, E. and Rosch, E. (1993) *The Embodied Mind: Cognitive Science and Human Experience*. Cambridge, MA: MIT Press.

Visual Editions (2010) 'Tree of Codes', *Visual Editions*, at <http://www.visual-editions.com/our-books/tree-of-codes> (last accessed 19 June 2015).

Wolf, M. (2008) *Proust and the Squid*. Cambridge: Icon.

CHAPTER 3

Reading the Visual Page in the Digital Archive

Natalie M. Houston

INTRODUCTION

Photography radically changes the meaning and impact of cultural objects, as Walter Benjamin ([1936] 2008) pointed out long ago in 'The work of art in the age of its technological reproducibility'. The possibility of reproducing identical photographic copies of an artefact transforms the contexts in which that artefact is encountered and alters the kinds of significance it produces. Benjamin's account of nineteenth-century reproductive technologies and the ascent of exchange value rather than ritual value for the artwork has significance for understanding the digital archive today (Benjamin 2008: 20–7). Although many twentieth-century technologies for preservation, dissemination and storage, such as microfilm and the photocopy, involved the photographic reproduction of texts, digital photographic technologies have transformed the methods by which researchers encounter and analyse printed artefacts. This chapter examines the effects of these technologies on the definition, constraints and possibilities of the digital archive today. It argues for the significance of the visual page in interpreting digitised textual artefacts, and describes methods for conducting exploratory data analysis with visual information in the digital environment.

THE DIGITAL ARCHIVE

In the mid-1990s, most digitisation efforts for historical printed materials were concentrated in particular scholarly editions or collections, such as the William Blake Archive, the Dante Rossetti Archive and the Walt Whitman

Archive. These projects adopted the term 'archive' to describe the digital reproduction of diverse materials by a single author, which were collected and made available from one website. By bringing together in virtual space texts whose physical manifestations only exist in geographically distant libraries, these scholarly projects demonstrated the possibilities for new kinds of knowledge production made possible in such archives. At the same time, the Rossetti and Blake archives in particular demonstrated the value of digital reproduction in analysing multi-modal historical works that consist of both text and image.

In 2004 the Google Books Library project ushered in a new kind of digital archive. This archive (currently standing at 13 million scanned volumes) is unselectively produced from the shelves of research libraries, in that the full contents of every shelf in a partner library are scanned for the project. But this unselective archive is of course predicated on generations of selective decisions by librarians, book collectors and others involved in the acquisition and retention of library items. By making the public domain segment of the project available on the open web, albeit with limited metadata and search functionality, Google opened the virtual doors to this archive to a mass audience. This truly large-scale archive demonstrates the possibilities newly available for digital humanities research. As Gregory Crane pointedly asked, 'What do you do with a million books?' (Crane 2006). Today, that question is still pressing as the numbers of digitised volumes continue to mount.

Most humanities researchers today conduct a significant amount of research using digital materials, whether or not they consider the focus of their research to include aspects of technology, digitisation or computation. Access to scholarly journals is frequently obtained through library databases, research libraries may offer materials in print or ebook formats, and a tremendous quantity of digitised cultural material is available on the open web through large-scale digitisation projects (such as those conducted by Google and major research libraries) as well as smaller scholarly editions, collections and archives.

The materials amassed by an individual scholar during the research process themselves also often constitute a sizeable digital archive, including downloaded copies of critical articles, public domain digitised objects and photographs of manuscript or printed materials taken for individual research purposes. In those libraries and archives that allow digital photography, many researchers spend their time in the traditional physical archive collecting digital photographs of documents rather than taking notes or transcribing documents in longhand or via computer keyboard. This change in the technologies of access and recording means that the kinds of effort and method that are applied in the physical archive are extended beyond the place and time of the researcher's visit to a specific physical location to additional time (at other location/s) for the archival tasks of reviewing, classifying and sorting digital photographs before the processes of reading, interpretation and analysis can begin. Additionally, the research process generates layers of metadata and annotation that should also be considered part of the researcher's digital archive, such as bibliographic tags or entries in a citation management system, digital annotations in the form of highlights, digital pen marks or textual notes attached to those digital objects, and the human- and machine-readable metadata contained in file names, date stamps and file formats. Photographic technologies have radically increased the quantity, variety and modes of access to digital research materials in today's new scholarly archives.

THE DIGITAL SURROGATE

Although large quantities of digitised page images are now available to researchers both in large digital libraries such as the Google Books project or the HathiTrust Digital Library, as well as in smaller editions and projects, most large-scale computational research with digitised cultural artefacts has focused on text analysis using the extracted linguistic text. Plain text is one of the simplest digital formats, readable on most hardware and software configurations. Transforming digitised cultural objects into plain text makes their linguistic content available for dissemination and analysis at new scales and by new methods. Large-scale text analysis methods like topic modelling, which computationally discovers semantic meaning within sets of documents without prior human interpretation, are only possible with large quantities of reasonably accurate plain texts. But as Joseph Viscomi (2002) suggests, 'Typographic transcriptions . . . abstract texts from the artefacts in which they are versioned and embodied' (29). There are layers of encoded historical meaning available from the visual layout of the page that are lost in plain text transcription. As Jacobs and Jacobs (2013) argue, 'Books and other printed information packages (e.g., journals, newspapers) don't just store and transport information; they also encode and present information. They *are* the user-interface: the layout of text on the page imparts meaning' (n.p.). This visual meaning is encoded at three distinct levels: the visual relation of ink to page, the spatial information hierarchy and historically specific conventions of page design. Today, most scholarly digital editions and archives include photographic images of the pages of textual artefacts as well as text versions of the linguistic content of those pages, produced either through optical character recognition (OCR) technology or through human transcription. Scholars recognise, at least implicitly, that there is value in being able to view document pages as they originally appeared. This chapter outlines some approaches to analysing the visual codes of digitised pages that could be implemented at a larger scale to explore historical meanings that would otherwise be available only to individual readers of specific texts.

Because of the scale of the new digital archive and the expanded access to the digital surrogates of historical artefacts it offers, today many research inquiries are conducted entirely with digital surrogates rather than physical print artefacts. For some kinds of research questions, access to the digital surrogate suffices; for others, access to the physical book is still required. Unless very detailed metadata is provided (which is not usually the case with large-scale projects), the digital surrogate cannot convey many of the physical or somatic dimensions of a textual artefact: the weight and feel of the book as an object, the texture of the binding, the thickness of the paper, or the depth of the impression of the letters on the page. In addition to these material aspects which contribute to the social, economic and aesthetic history of the book, other kinds of information are contained in multiple copies of physical books that are at risk today of being lost as libraries de-accession items because a digital surrogate exists online. Some of these include traces of the history of reading practices, such as script annotations, drawings, pressed flowers, and other evidence of how books were used (Stauffer 2014).

Although digital surrogates are frequently offered by libraries as expedient measures, it is nonetheless important to recognise that no matter how detailed the photographic reproduction is, a surrogate is a new digital object. Certainly, it bears a relation to a physical object, but they exist in separate ontological realms, and can be more or less closely tied together through bibliographic metadata or display technologies. User interfaces for digital libraries, collections and scholarly editions that offer users multiple ways to browse page images help address those aspects of the material book lost in the digital surrogate. As the eye skims over a screen filled with tiled thumbnail images, the human viewer can easily locate items that are visually distinctive, such as pages with illustrations or charts. Providing a facing-page layout that displays the verso and recto pages of a given opening of the codex book conveys important aspects of the book's design that may be lost in single page views or in text transcription. Facing pages may contain a poem and an accompanying illustration, or texts that are designed to be read together, as in multi-lingual editions. Such views are not merely nostalgic replications of the codex book reading experience. If the digital object is designed to function as a digital surrogate for the print object, then multiple views offer the best chance for users to apprehend the size, variety and arrangement of its contents.

DEFINING THE VISUAL PAGE

The inked page

The visual relation of ink to page is constituted by perceptual contrast: only if the page is light enough and the ink dark enough can the text be seen. Before the words of the text can be decoded, the human eye has already taken in the visual contrasts and spatial organisation of dark ink and lighter page. As Laura Mandell suggests, 'looking at a set of graphic marks set off by the frame of white space involves the same cognitive processes as would looking at any image' (Mandell 2007: 762). At the simplest level, page images appear predominantly dark if they are text-heavy and lighter if they are not. The proportions and shapes of text blocks and white margins reflect print conventions of indentation, word spacing and line length that distinguish poetry from prose, text from included quotations and paragraphs from one another. Such visual codes function at a pre-semantic level as the reader's eye skims over a printed page.

Because the linguistic content of printed documents is frequently the focus of interpretive acts, the uninked areas of the page are frequently termed 'white space' because the act of immersive reading typically transforms the textured, coloured, odorous, tactile leaf of paper into blankness, air, a screen on or in front of which we perceive the text's semantic meaning. The term 'white space' subsumes a wide variety of both actual paper tones and their digitised representation, which will vary in their hue and intensity depending on the conditions under which the item was photographed, the hardware and software settings for the photography, the processing, storage and transmission methods used with the digital files and the display settings used by viewers. White space is rarely simply white. And it is not necessarily what the word 'space' can seem to imply, a field or emptiness that surrounds more substantial objects or entities. To focus your attention on white space is to arrive at a figure/ground perceptual problem. As Edgar Rubin's famous optical illusion of the vase surrounded by a pair of faces illustrates, the mind has great difficulty in perceiving both figure and ground at the same time (Rubin 2000). We can see one or the other, or perhaps oscillate between them fairly rapidly. Because of our focus on reading the printed text, the white, or blank, sections of the printed page usually only enter our awareness through functional means (as when we seek space for annotations) or when the graphical nature of the page is called to our attention.

Instead of focusing on either figure or ground, text or white space, we can better see these aspects of the visual page as mutually constitutive. Johanna Drucker (2009) has suggested that the graphical nature of all printed pages should best be understood as a 'quantum system' in which the page's graphical elements are dynamically related to one another and activated in the moment of the reader's perception. Thus, she says, we can only perceive space as it surrounds, touches or exposes the inked area of a page: '"White" space is thus visually inflected, given a tonal value through relations rather than according to some intrinsic property' (Drucker 2009: 162). The page is only white as it stands in relation to the ink's black. In the digital environment, however, we can more easily perceive the uninked parts of the page, as the entire page image may be framed by the design of a website, a PDF software interface or a user's display screen. Additionally, we can manipulate digital page images in ways that would be impossible to do with the printed pages of a codex book, enhancing our ability to perceive them as constituted by graphical juxtaposition, contrast and spatial design.

The information hierarchy

Elements in page design present structured information in printed documents, allowing readers familiar with these visual codes to quickly distinguish a title page from a content page or to locate the start of a chapter. Titles in printed documents typically occur within a hierarchy ranging from book-level title and subtitle to section or chapter titles and subtitles that further divide the content. Titles are visually encoded through choices in typeface, size and weight, through horizontal and vertical placement on the page and by their separation by white space from other text blocks.

Other kinds of information, such as page numbers, running heads, footnotes and captions are also visually distinguished by white space and by their placement within the visual field of the page. Many of these elements become recognisable through repetition in a series of pages within a document. The placement of page numbers, for instance, may vary among printed materials from the same time period. Some books in the mid-nineteenth century place page numbers in the outer upper corners of each opening (that is, the upper-left corner of a verso page and the upper-right corner of a recto page); others place page numbers in the centre of the header line or in the centre of a footer line at the bottom margin. Still others vary the page number placement depending on whether the page contains the opening of a chapter or poem. Although there are several possibilities for page numbering, historical printing conventions limit those possibilities: one rarely sees page numbers in the side margin of the main text block, or surrounded by the text. My point here is that these informational structures are quickly perceived by experienced readers because they are visually coded. We can see if there is a page number on the page even in a much reduced thumbnail image without being able to read what the digits are.

Cultural conventions

The third level of visual encoding in historical printed documents encompasses those visual features that are applied to the text in historically specific and sometimes intentional ways. These include the indentation of selected lines of text (such as the first line of a paragraph, quoted material or lines of poetry), the spacing between paragraphs or stanzas, the use of dropped initial capital letters and/or ornamented capital letters at the beginning of chapters, sections, poems or works and the use of bullet points or other list markers. The choice of a particular typeface can, in some instances, indicate the publisher or author's intention to frame a printed book in particular ideological or aesthetic terms (Bristow 2005: 19). Whether the intentions behind design choices are known or not, such choices inevitably impact on the reading experience (Genette 1997: 34). Identifying how these visual features change over time, how they align with the economic, aesthetic and political aspects of historical text artefacts and what they might have signified to their original audiences is of interest to scholars in a wide range of humanities disciplines.

THE VISUAL PAGE OF VICTORIAN POETRY

In the sections that follow, I describe several methods for analysing the visual codes of digitised printed materials, with specific reference to research I have conducted as part of an ongoing project entitled 'The Visual Page as Interface'. Starting from Jerome McGann's observation that 'A page of printed or scripted text should thus be understood as a certain kind of graphic interface,' this research seeks to discover the graphic or visual codes that are at work in books of poetry published in the nineteenth century (McGann 2001: 199). Although, as I have suggested above, all printed texts communicate through visual codes, poetry offers an especially interesting field for investigation. One of the primary ways poetry is distinguished from prose in printed books since the early modern period is by printing each poetic line as a separate line of text. Because lines of poetry are frequently shorter than the full page width typically filled by paragraphs of prose, the white space around the printed poem is a key visual signal for the presence of poetry.

In addition to the visual codes of the inked page and informational hierarchy outlined above, which are present in books of poetry as in other texts, there are specific visual codes that structure the printing of poetry in the nineteenth century, including the use of white space between stanzas and between poems, the use of ornaments or numbering between stanzas and the use of ornaments, numbering, white space and/or titles between poems or groups of poems. An important feature of nineteenth-century printing conventions is the indenting of lines of verse to indicate the rhyme scheme of the poem. This printing convention translates the audible feature of poetic rhyme into a visual code that makes poetic form apprehensible prior to semantic interpretation. Typographic choices, such as the use of large, dropped initial capital letters or ornamented letters for the first word of a poem, also function in both the linguistic and the visual realms. Although I have been using the analytic methods I describe here with sets of digitised books of poetry from the 1860s, many of these approaches would work equally well on cultural artefacts from other periods and in other forms of writing.

READING THE VISUAL PAGE

To analyse the visual page, we must first perceive the page as containing visual or graphic data (Gitelman and Jackson 2013: 3). As data, rather than seemingly transparent windows onto the physical artefact, digital page images become available for exploratory analysis. Jerome McGann and Lisa Samuels (2001) offer a critical account of textual deformance as a kind of experimental analysis: 'in our deformative manoeuvers, interpretive lines of thought spin out of some initial non-discursive "experiment" with the primary materials' (McGann and Samuels 2001: 129). Although McGann also describes some experiments conducted by manipulating images of paintings in photo-editing software, most of the deformations McGann and Samuels discuss are at the linguistic level of the text (McGann 2001: 84–7). The transformations I describe here involve experimenting with the visual aspects of the printed page in order to reveal patterns of similarity, difference, order, disorder, consistency and variation. Rather than examining the linguistic authored text (the object of traditional literary interpretation and aesthetic value) my experiments in transformation engage with the material object as it is mediated through the digital surrogate. The transformations and deformations available in the digital environment make possible new experiments and explorations of historical artefacts. Such transformations strategically defamiliarise the printed book in order to expose the limits of accepted knowledge and suggest new paths for exploration.

The strategies I present in the remaining sections of this chapter constitute a method for exploratory data analysis of the visual page. The tradition of exploratory data analysis begun by John Tukey examines data 'to see what it seems to say' (Tukey 1977: 2). Tukey outlined methods for the visual exploration of quantitative data, including plotting the measures now enshrined in statistical software as the five-number summary, as well as stem-and-leaf plots and boxplots. Such visual methods for perceiving the distribution of data points in a large data set are today made widely available through software tools ranging from basic office spreadsheet software to advanced statistical programs. Here I describe several methods for visually and mathematically exploring data sets consisting of digitised page images.

Reduction

As discussed above, thumbnail, or reduced size, images are frequently used in web design to offer a preview of hyperlinked materials. Because there is so much information available from the visual page of digitised documents, thumbnail browsing can allow viewers to explore multi-page contexts in the digital object. But when the viewing size of the thumbnails is reduced past the point of legibility for the text, such displays transform the digitised text object into a purely graphical one. At reduced size, graphical patterns in the individual page images can be easily perceived by the human eye: sequences of pages with similar layouts, pages with distinctive elements such as ornaments or illustrations and items that are set off by white space such as poems, epigraphs and section breaks.

The digital environment enables the comparison of page images from different books in ways that would be difficult or impossible to achieve with printed volumes. By setting the pages of multiple books next to each other, one can perceive the graphical relationships among them more easily than one could by looking at each one individually. Tiling highly reduced thumbnail images, especially with a large display screen, also enables the perception of patterns across hundreds of pages that would be impossible due to the physical size constraints with print volumes.

Overlay

Another experiment in transforming digitised page images in order to understand them differently was inspired by the work of digital information artist Jason Salavon, whose *Amalgamation* series of paintings layer multiple examples of a photographic genre to explore their conventions. The painting *Newlyweds*, for instance, part of the 2004 series *100 Special Moments*, overlays 100 photographs and calculates the mathematical average of them to create a ghostly composite image that reflects tendencies in popular culture. (Other paintings in the series transform pictures of high-school graduates and children with Santa Claus.)

Adjusting the transparency of the digital page images from Victorian books of poetry and overlaying them on top of each other visually reveals which areas of the page are consistently filled with text and which are not. The result of such experiments is deliberately not meant to be legible, with lines of text faded through transparency and overlaid directly on top of other lines (Figure 3.1).

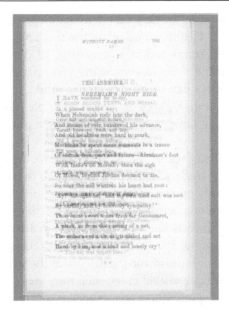

Figure 3.1 Overlay experiment with pages
from six books of poetry published 1860–9
(Source: The author)

Instead this experiment transforms the lines of text, which human readers inevitably want to read for semantic meaning, into purely graphical shapes. The darker areas in the stacked images represent spaces of coherence where lines of text exist in multiple pages. Lighter text areas in the composite image reveal traces of text from pages that differ from others in the stack. To be sure, these differences are fairly small: the central text block used in nineteenth-century printing is fairly consistent. But variations in the placement of headers, titles and page numbers are visible as well as those graphical variations introduced by poems of different forms with lines of different length. Such composite images reveal the coherence of the visual conventions used in the printing of poetry in the mid-Victorian period: even though the original books are of different sizes, the size of the printed area varies little, and the spatial relationships between page numbers, titles and text blocks remain remarkably consistent across sampled volumes.

Text density

The manipulations described above depend upon the human eye to examine and interpret the transformed digital object. Digital image analysis software can offer more precise tools for comparison through quantitative analytics.

For example, I have used ImageJ, an open-source program developed by the National Institute of Health, to calculate the text area of a page image, both as a numerical pixel count and as a percentage of the total page area. This provides more specific ways of comparing text-sparse and text-dense page design. Such measures can be used to understand the range and average of text density within a given book or across multiple volumes from different publishers during the same year or from the same publisher over a number of years.

Calculating the text area of the page provides a measure of text density, which is integral to readers' perceptions of page design and its impact on reading. The eye easily perceives a crowded or full page of text and contrasts a page with more generous margins. Victorian collections of sonnets frequently printed these small poems one to a page, with generous margin space surrounding them, which was seen as advantageous for focusing the mind to study the poem's meaning (Houston 1999: 249). Since the perceptions of historical readers are not directly available to us, such measures offer an approximation that can be used to explore questions about how different printed documents might have been perceived or used by readers.

Even the simple measure of text area calculated in ImageJ for individual pages can also be used as a filtering mechanism to locate particular kinds of visually distinctive material. Within multi-genre collections, for example, pages with poetry will frequently have lower text density than pages filled with prose. Within collections of verse, pages with greater text density will typically include poetic forms with longer lines, such as narrative poems in blank verse. Such approximations are very rough and are best developed and used when exploring a well-defined data set of digitised objects. But even as a rough approximation, the measure of text density, which is quickly calculated with ImageJ, offers researchers ways to computationally browse, explore and navigate among large data sets of digitised pages.

Text density measurements and other data extracted from the digital surrogate object, can be understood to bear some relation to the original print artefact but should not substitute for accurate empirical measurements taken of the print pages. In particular, different hardware and object manipulation methods used during the digitisation process can result in different inner margins in the photographed page. (Since most items currently being digitised are drawn from library collections, it is also important to note that the practices of library book binding can affect the viewable margin space in a codex book.) However, to take such measurements of a large number of pages would be impractical and almost certainly impossible at the very large scale of materials now available to researchers through large digital libraries. The methods described here are not intended to substitute for the analysis of print artefacts except in those cases when access is only available through digital means, when the scale of the research being conducted is greater than would allow for human observations, or when a research question can be answered through relative comparisons between the digital surrogates without reference to the original artefact.

Finally, it is important to note that human observations are prone to bias and subjective change over time. As a human reader recording observations of graphic design in printed books or their digital surrogates, the patterns and relationships I notice after examining 200 books are very likely to be different from those I observed in the first twenty books examined. Of course, there are data coding and validation best practices, such as collecting independent observations from multiple researchers, designed to minimise subjective variance. But the computational measure of text density as the ratio between dark and light pixels is an objective measure that will not change no matter how many observations are recorded.

VisualPage

In order to access the informational hierarchy and historically specific visual conventions in printed materials through computational analysis, Neal Audenaert and I have recently developed a prototype software application called *VisualPage* that demonstrates the possibilities for exploratory analysis of the visual codes of digitised printed materials. In the initial prototype, we repurposed algorithms for page layout analysis from Tesseract, an open-source OCR application. The first step in optical character recognition involves identifying blocks or areas of text on a page. By combining that page layout analysis with a domain-specific model of visual features, we are able to extract quantitative measures for text density, line length, margin size, line spacing and line indentation. Such features are among the visually distinctive elements in the books of nineteenth-century poetry that make up our initial data set for this prototype development. Because the cultural conventions of page design vary over time as well as by genre, function and purpose of the documents, input from domain experts is required in order to tune the software to provide useful analytic information. For example, line length is an important feature of poetry but might not be a useful analytic dimension in assessing prose texts.

Because the appearance of poems on the page in the nineteenth century corresponds to aspects of their poetic form, such as the length and number of lines, these quantitative measures can be used to identify pages with a high probability of containing certain forms, such as the sonnet or blank verse. Line length can also be used to distinguish front matter (title pages, prefaces, tables of contents, etc.) and end matter (afterword, index, etc.) from the body of the book.

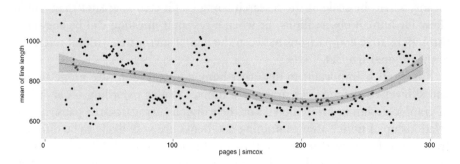

Figure 3.2 Mean line length per page in George Augustus Simcox, *Poems and Romances*. London: Strahan, 1869
(Source: The author)

Because *VisualPage* produces a set of quantitative measures for each line and each page in a book, it enables the production of summary snapshots of the visual data of that historical object as mediated through its digital surrogate. This is similar to Tukey's five-number summary, but for visual information. For example, a measure of mean line length per page can be used to compare the formal variety within a particular volume of poetry or across multiple volumes. The graph of mean line length in Figure 3.2 offers a way of perceiving the range and distribution of line length in George Augustus Simcox's 1869 *Poems and Romances*. The visible clusters of consecutive pages with mean lines of similar length correspond to groups of poems written in similar verse forms. This graph provides one summary view of how the pages in this book of poetry would appear if you were to thumb through them. This summary representation of the visual data of the book enables high-level exploration of a data set and comparison of items within it without the potential distraction of actually looking at the pages' visual codes themselves. Such data summaries offer important methods for exploring large data sets precisely because they are abstracted from the object. But, unlike the abstraction of plain text transcription, which drops the visual codes of the printed artefact, these snapshot statistics can be combined with text analysis to explore the interrelation of visual and linguistic codes.

The large-scale collections available in the digital archive today require data analysis methods that can be scaled beyond the human capacity to perceive and remember limited quantities of data. Exploring the visual codes of digitised print artefacts opens up new ways of thinking about the material objects that now circulate in digital simulacra. Transforming digitised page images through the exploratory methods described here can open up new questions for research befitting our age of technological reproduction.

NOTE

1. This work was supported by a Level II Start Up Grant (HD-51560-12) from the National Endowment for the Humanities Office of Digital Humanities. Any views, findings, conclusions or recommendations expressed in this publication do not necessarily reflect those of the National Endowment for the Humanities.

REFERENCES

Benjamin, W. (2008) 'The work of art in the age of its technological reproducibility: second version', in M. Jennings, B. Doherty and T. Y. Levin (eds), *The Work of Art in the Age of Its Technological Reproducibility, and Other Writings on Media*, trans E. Jephcott, R. Livingstone et al. Cambridge, MA: Harvard University Press, pp. 19–54.

Bristow, J. (2005) 'Introduction', in J. Bristow (ed.), *The Fin-de-Siècle Poem: English Literary Culture and the 1890s*. Athens: Ohio University Press, pp. 1–46.

Crane, G. (2006) 'What do you do with a million books?', *D-Lib Magazine*, 12: 3, n.p.

Drucker, J. (2009) *SpecLab: Digital Aesthetics and Projects in Speculative Computing*. Chicago: University of Chicago Press.

Genette, G. (1997) *Paratexts: Thresholds of Interpretation*, trans. J. E. Lewin. Cambridge: Cambridge University Press.

Gitelman, L. and Jackson, V. (2013) 'Introduction', in L. Gitelman (ed.), *'Raw Data' is an Oxymoron*. Cambridge, MA: MIT Press, pp. 1–14.

Houston, N. M. (1999) 'Valuable by design: material features and cultural value in nineteenth-century sonnet anthologies', *Victorian Poetry*, 37: 2, pp. 243–72.

Jacobs, J. A. and Jacobs, J. R. (2013) 'The digital-surrogate seal of approval: a consumer-oriented standard', *D-Lib Magazine*, 19: 3/4.

McGann, J. J. (2001) *Radiant Textuality: Literature after the World Wide Web*. New York: Palgrave.

McGann, J. J. and Samuels, L. (2001) 'Deformance and interpretation', in J. J. McGann, *Radiant Textuality: Literature after the World Wide Web*. New York: Palgrave, pp. 105–36.

Mandell, L. (2007) 'What is the matter? What literary theory neither hears nor sees', *New Literary History*, 38: 4, pp. 755–76.

Ramsay, S. (2011) *Reading Machines: Toward an Algorithmic Criticism*. Urbana: University of Illinois Press.

Rubin, E. (2000) 'Figure and ground', in S. Yantis (ed.), *Visual Perception: Key Readings*. Philadelphia: Psychology Press, pp. 225–30.

Salavon, J. (2004) 'Newlyweds', *in Jason Salavon: Brainstem Still Life*. Bloomington: SoFA Gallery & Earl Lu Gallery; also online at <http://salavon.com/work>.

Stauffer, A. (2014) *Book Traces*, online at <www.booktraces.org>.

Tukey, J. W. (1977) *Exploratory Data Analysis*. Reading, MA: Addison-Wesley.

Viscomi, J. (2002) 'Digital facsimiles: reading the William Blake archive', *Computers and the Humanities*, 36: 1, pp. 27–48.

CHAPTER 4

Paratextual Navigation as a Research Method: Fan Fiction Archives and Reader Instructions

Maria Lindgren Leavenworth

As with many other activities, the consumption of fiction has increasingly moved online, and works by professional and amateur authors migrate to digital environments or are born in them. Fan fictions (or fanfics) are today almost exclusively digitally born, stored on individual authors' home pages, in archives of various sizes and scopes, or disseminated through social media or designated web applications.[1] In different ways, a fanfic author engages with an already existing text, referred to as the *canon*, be this a single work or an extensive, often transmedial, storyworld. By expanding the narrative arc in prequels and sequels, altering romantic pairings or narrative perspective, fanfics evince particular engagements with the canon, presenting, in most cases, stories that take a considerably different turn. Archived and easily accessible, fan fiction constitutes an underused resource in literature studies, due in part to unfamiliarity with the text form, but also to the seemingly unmanageable vastness of the output.

Emerging methods for data scraping and distant reading hold potential for large-scale mapping of fanfic archives,[2] but the present chapter works from the premise that knowledge of particular paratextual functions (explained below) facilitates the literary research process and leads to more manageable text samples. As 'a *threshold*' of interpretation, the paratext in Gérard Genette's definition is 'a zone not only of transition but also of *transaction*' (2).[3] A reader is invited into the text (or pushed away) by an array of paratexts, ranging from a work's title and preface to author statements made in interviews, and negotiates the meanings transmitted by these paratextual functions. Migrating online, literary texts such as fan fiction retain many similarities with traditionally printed works (Genette's object of study) and some paratextual functions remain relatively unaltered; their recognition may facilitate various transitions and transactions. However, specificities of digital publishing, where the mere choice of archive may serve as a paratextual marker, and user-generated elements that frame and tag fanfics demand a modification of how we identify paratexts as well as their function.

In dialogue with Genette and with subsequent critics who have shifted attention to paratextual functions in other media, this chapter examines how digital venues for archiving fan fiction can be navigated, highlights systems for categorising the texts and analyses the use of paratexts in the author's communication with her readers. It speaks to how Genette's delineation of the paratext can be usefully expanded and modified to account for particular challenges when researching selected virtual environments and when approaching isolated works within them. A sustained analysis of different paratextual functions, structuring sites as well as the presentation of and communication around fiction, thus profitably accounts for the particularity of the fanfic text form as well as of the digital mediation of the text.

THE PARATEXT AND FAN FICTION IN 'NEW' MEDIA

Since the publication of *Seuils* 1987, and the English translation *Paratexts: Thresholds of Interpretation* a decade later, Genette's extensive narratological mapping has been debated, applied and modified, testifying to the continued use-value of considerations of the borderlands of texts: the 'invitat[ion] to understand how we unwittingly are manipulated by [the book's] paratextual elements' (Macksey 1997: xxi). A work's title sets up expectations, a foreword or an epigraph may address a certain readership and exclude another, a new edition may include notes and annotations with slight or profound impact on the reader. The function of these elements may in turn be affected by whether their sender is (perceived to be) the author, the publisher or a third party. Genette had no reason to move away from the printed book in his examinations, but suggests a development that necessitates continuous modifications. 'The ways and means of the paratext change continually,' he writes, 'depending on period, culture, genre, author, work, and edition [and even] the sole fact of transcription . . . brings to the ideality of the text some degree of materialization [that] may induce paratextual effects' (Genette [1987] 1997: 3). The appearance of texts in 'new' media consequently brings with it new forms of materiality that directly or indirectly impact on the function and effects of the paratext, and the culture producing and consuming texts similarly affects how the paratext manipulates the reader.

Genette's gesture towards discursive particularities, as well as the continued relevance of seeing new media texts in relation to previous paradigms, have led several critics to recently investigate paratextual functions in other text forms and in other media than the printed; discussions that contribute to our understanding of the altered approaches to both production and consumption of texts. Jonathan Gray suggests that both promotional and audience-generated materials can no longer be seen as peripheral to meaning-making in large text worlds. '[P]aratexts', he argues, 'fill the media landscape and can be as responsible for popular culture's encounters with countless storyworlds and texts as are film and television' (2010: 221). Mia Consalvo similarly shifts attention from what has previously been regarded as peripheral materials to supplemental information and activities engaged with when playing, and cheating in, videogames. These paratexts, she maintains, 'may alter the meanings of texts, further enhance meanings, or provide challenges to sedimented meanings' (Consalvo 2007: 182). Rather broad definitions are here usefully employed to decentralise the notion of the text itself.

A more problematic assessment emerges in Gavin Stewart's analysis of paratexts surrounding and embedded in the multi-modal hypertext *Inanimate Alice*. He argues that its less than 'clear-cut [. . .] separation between the author function and the publisher function' necessitates caution when applying Genette's taxonomy since 'it is not always possible to establish a line between the paratexts and the wider context' (Stewart 2010: 59). Stewart's hesitation is echoed in the concluding section of Dorothee Birke and Birte Christ's recent introduction to a cluster of articles in *Narrative*, in which they note the risk of loss of 'analytic value [when] paratextual elements that negotiate the space between text and context, become increasingly difficult to isolate' (80). The risk, highlighted here, is that everything comes to be perceived as paratext and, tellingly, the articles Birke and Christ introduce focus on paratexts in connection with DVDs and e-readers (by Paul Benzon and Ellen McCracken, respectively). These 'digital phenomena [. . .] do not revolutionize reading and viewing habits in an instant but are part of a long process of development that is in close dialogue with the printed book as the long-term cultural paradigm' (Birke and Christ 2013: 66). DVDs and devices like Kindles and iPads can therefore be considered as 'transitional texts [that] engage in much more moderate adaptations of traditional printed literature' (McCracken 2013: 105) than an online text like *Inanimate Alice* and that can relatively comfortably be aligned with Genette's taxonomy.

My own article 'The Paratext of Fan Fiction', which provides a starting point for my more methodologically oriented elaborations here, similarly focuses on the strong links between fan fictions and the paradigm of print literature because, although digitally born, fan fiction is predominantly text-based, seldom using the affordances of hyperlinks, lexias or audio-visual materials in the story proper. I accordingly argue that fan fiction can be seen 'as an intermediary form between print literature and narratives which to a greater extent make use of the multimodal hypertext format' and that paratextual functions, in addition to illuminating text-specific aspects, draw attention to vulner-abilities associated with the paratext in print culture (Lindgren Leavenworth 2015: 57). I continue these discussions below, emphasising how an increased awareness of the organisation of fanfic archives, of the text form and of para-textual functions specific to both the presentation and reception of fan fiction helps to navigate the vast landscape of that fiction.

I am persuaded by Birke and Christ's elaboration of three paratextual functions, briefly explained below, salient in the contemporary context: *'navi-gational'*, *'commercial'* and *'interpretive'* (2013: 67–8). Although the majority of paratexts direct the reader to important aspects of the work, Genette's omission of a comprehensive delineation of the *navigational* function is due to his inability to 'perceive the book as a technology requiring user instructions' (ibid.: 68). The story presented in a fan fiction is similarly not dependent on user instructions – even a reader unfamiliar with a fanfic's overt intertextual-ity will recognise it as a work of fiction and its form (as a short story or novel) can likewise be easily determined. However, the path to access an individual story entails a number of navigational choices that are intimately connected to the text form and also to the interfaces of different archives and websites. The first section below, expanding the concept of the navigational paratext, thus demonstrates how the space in which fanfic is stored and accessed presents a tangible threshold.

The *commercial* function is increasingly important in the contemporary media climate, but in the case of non-remunerative fan fiction is rather tied to how a text can be aligned with and differentiated from others much like it. Fanfics are in the main produced and consumed within a specific fan group (or fandom). The use of text-specific categorisations and tags may appeal to readers who subscribe to a similar line of interpretation as the author, and who therefore want to peruse stories detailing their favourite alternative plot devel-opment or character pairing. An author's summary, however, presents options of indicating how the fanfic contributes something new: potential selling points in a competitive market. The *promotional* function is closely tied to the interpretative function, following from Genette's delineation and signifying how paratexts are utilised to produce 'a more pertinent reading of [the text]' ([1987] 1997: 2). The same paratexts that promote a fanfic – categorisations, tags and summaries – attempt to guide the text's reception; they indicate how the text and its author are positioned vis-à-vis readers and how the latter are (ideally) to respond.

Fanfic authors' use of Author Notes, especially when repeatedly inserted in chapters in the serial publication of a novel-length story, 'is one of the strongest indications of how the function of the paratext has changed with new publication forms and in a cultural climate where texts are produced in close temporal proximity to their readers' (Lindgren Leavenworth 2015: 50). In the last section of this chapter, I examine communication from author to reader, focusing on the various functions Author Notes fulfil. Whether attempting to guide the reception of the text, guard against what is perceived as faulty readings or initiate a more personal dialogue with readers, Author Notes highlight a productive tension between individual text production and collaborative meaning-making.

NAVIGATION AND SELECTION: THE SPATIAL THRESHOLD

Particularities of sites constitute specific thresholds that importantly carry paratextual meaning; as Genette claims, 'every context serves as a paratext' ([1987] 1997: 8). An active fandom may be dispersed, with individual participants engaging in discussions in various social media and publishing fanfic in a plethora of digital venues. A first step in the navigation of the vast landscape of fan fiction generally, is consequently an awareness of differences and similarities between different sites and of rules regarding story content and user interactions. Adult material, for example, may be permissible on one site but disallowed on another, and whereas some fanfic archives and communities are freely accessible, others are restricted to registered users, which introduces specific ethical research concerns. Below I focus on the two currently largest collective sites, *FanFiction.net* and *Archive of Our Own* (AO3), that require registration to publish stories but not to access texts and reader feedback.[4]

Genette's division into peritexts and epitexts, that together make up the paratext, is spatial and to an extent contingent on who can be identified as 'the sender' ([1987] 1997: 8). Various forms of peritexts are found in direct proximity to the text itself: 'the title or the preface and sometimes elements inserted into the interstices of the text, such as chapter titles or certain notes', whereas '[t]he epitext is any paratextual element not materially appended to the text within the same volume but circulating, as it were, freely, in a virtually limitless physical and social space' (ibid.: 5, 343). The sender behind peritexts is commonly the author, but a preface, foreword, notes and annotations may also come from the publisher or a third party and vary between editions. The epitext is intimately connected with the author when found in interviews, diaries and letters but may come from a third party, for example in reviews. To qualify as an epitext, however, an element has to carry meaning for the work, and in the following discussion I maintain that systems for filing and categorising, although pre-dating the actual work stored, can be seen as instances of the contemporary publisher's epitext. This is a departure from Genette's taxonomy[5] and a radical expansion of the notion of epitext, but whereas Genette was solely interested in the book and saw no reason for examining the bookstore, in the contemporary publishing context we need to pay attention to both.

FanFiction.net and AO3 store fanfics connected to a vast number of fandoms, arranged in the first instance according to media format: literature, film, anime, computer games and so on. To exemplify, there were, in November 2014, over 2,000 canon novels in the book section alone on *FanFiction.net* ('Books'), and 16,619 fandoms on AO3 ('Welcome'). Authors therefore need to upload their stories in the correct section and sub-section, to ensure that they are found. Media format and fandom in this way work as overarching epitexts and facilitate the visitor's initial navigation. As elsewhere in this article, I use the production by the *Sherlock* fandom as a case study, that is fan fictions working from Mark Gatiss and Steven Moffat's ongoing BBC series (2010–). Selecting 'TV-shows' in the first step and *Sherlock* in the second results in unwieldy lists: in November 2014 almost 50,000 fanfics working from this canon were archived on *FanFiction.net* and close to 65,000 at AO3. Further navigation is called for, and both sites offer the visitor the useful option of filtering stories.

On *FanFiction.net*, a button labelled 'Filter' appears above the extensive list and on AO3 a filter box appears on the right-hand side of the computer screen. The sites have three major filtering options in common, and these furthermore work the same across all the gathered fandoms. Firstly, the visitor may choose to view only completed stories. Although works in progress can be valuable if the aim is to investigate the writing process, many incomplete stories are only just begun, and may be abandoned after the first instalment. Secondly, one may specify language, a filtering option that drastically limits the sample in the *Sherlock* fandom only if the chosen language is not English.[6] Finally, it is possible to indicate what rating the stories should have, ranging from appropriate for a general or teen audience (K to T on *FanFiction.net*) to mature or explicit. Numbers resulting from this latter filtering process demonstrate that the majority of *Sherlock* fanfics at both sites is rated for a general and teen and up audience.

Fanfic authors generally exhibit a strong interest in characters and in specific forms of relationships, and Catherine Driscoll argues that character pairings grouped under the overarching categories 'het, slash and gen' – stories featuring heterosexual, homosexual or no romance at all – overshadow other categories by which to store and search (2006: 84). On *FanFiction.net*, filter options can be set either to indicate what characters the stories should feature, which does not signal a specific relationship, or what pairing is of interest, which does. Using a slightly different terminology, the same options are available on AO3. The 'Character' filter determines, precisely, what characters the story revolves around, whereas the filter labelled 'Categories' is used to signal what type of romantic or sexual relationship is featured. In the *Sherlock* archive, the majority of fanfics depict a male–male relationship (M/M), but there is also a sizeable amount of stories in the gen category. Driscoll maintains that gen is exceedingly rare, to the point that it is usable only to label stories that cannot be seen to fit into any category (ibid.: 85–6), but the nature of the canon is arguably influential in the choice of categorisation. Although interpersonal relationships are important in *Sherlock*, the series' foregrounding of mystery-solving and deduction may also resonate with fans, giving rise to a production less invested in examining romance and sex.

Traditional and fanfic-specific genres present additional useful navigational options. On *FanFiction.net* authors in all fandoms choose between twenty-one pre-set genres or genre elements. Some are easily recognisable, such as horror and sci-fi, whereas others are specific to the fanfic text form, among them 'angst', featuring dark and potentially depressing themes, and its subgenre 'hurt/comfort', in which one character suffers and another consoles. On AO3, genre-filtering of this type is instead to be made under 'Additional Tags', which testify to fandom specificity and the user-generated nature of materials (see Figure 4.1).

The tags appended to the most fanfics in the *Sherlock* section are the general 'Angst' and 'Fluff' (indicating either themes or styles that are light-hearted) but they are followed by the fandom-specific tag 'Post-Reichenbach'. The final episode of the TV series' second season, 'The Reichenbach Fall' (Haynes 2012), ends with Sherlock Holmes' apparent suicide, a plot development that left fans distraught and suspended in the two-year-long hiatus that followed. Almost five thousand stories are set in the aftermath of this moment, testifying to the creativity it and the absence of canon production inspired.

What is indicated above is that lines at times blur between navigational epitexts built into the archival systems and the interpretations emerging in fandoms. As Louisa Stein and Kristina Busse argue, subgroups within a fandom entail 'established presuppositions [that] are vital to the community's sense of cohesiveness, clearly demarcating the intended readers as those that share a common reading' (2009: 198). Categories and tags demonstrate the formation of such subgroups, but so does AO3's 'Fandom' filter by indicating how plot strands and characterisations are linked to other fictional worlds, resulting in stories that are commonly labelled as 'crossovers'. Nine fictional worlds have attracted enough authors to appear as crossover options in AO3's initial filtering process. Among these are worlds featuring time travel (such as *Dr Who*) or other speculative elements (such as *Supernatural*), narrative aspects that may facilitate the crossing of fictional universes, but also the Bond-film *Skyfall*. Although close readings are needed to elucidate precisely why this film has resulted in nearly three hundred crossover fanfics, one may speculate that its plot focused on national turmoil and its 2012 premiere being

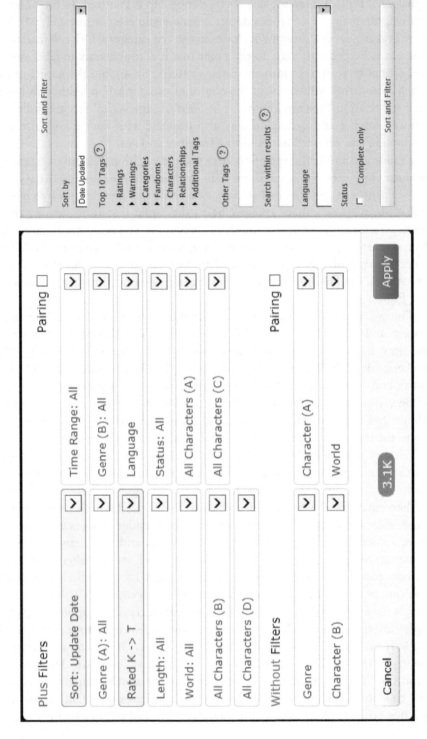

Figure 4.1a Detail from screen shot of FanFiction.net (Source: <www.FanFiction.net>; screengrab by the author)

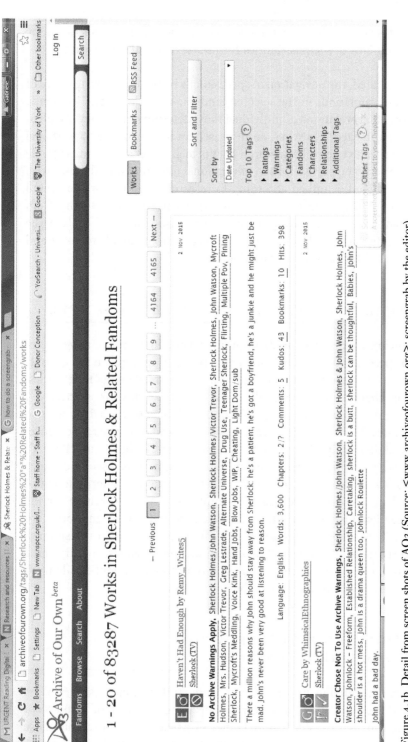

Figure 4.1b Detail from screen shots of AO3 (Source: <www.archiveofourown.org>; screengrab by the editor)

temporally close to the above-mentioned second season finale of *Sherlock* may have prompted fans to see possibilities for intertextual links between the two worlds.[7]

As demonstrated, the navigation of space entails being or becoming aware of prominent interpretations in the selected fandom, since the stories' contents, reflecting the interpretations of individual fans, determine how they are filed, categorised and tagged. However, an increased awareness of the navigational aspect of the paratext helps limit search results to arrive at a more manageable sample of stories to be perused. Each navigational filter provides the user with limiting options to be applied according to research questions or the overall design of individual projects. But the navigational epitexts, ranging from media formats to specific pairings or crossovers also concretely present the specificities of fan fiction: they enable the transition from outside to inside and constitute sites of transactions of meaning.

EPITEXTUAL NAVIGATION: THE *SHERLOCK* SAMPLE

In the following sections I examine promotional and interpretive materials in the form of peritextual elements and summaries, and investigate the centrality of paratexts in authors' communication with their readers. As long stories, published in chapter instalments, illustrate the latter aspect most clearly, I have limited my search to *Sherlock* works on *FanFiction.net* exceeding 100,000 words and rated K to T to get a sense of works aimed at a general audience. On 17 November 2014, these settings (made under 'Length' and 'Rating') resulted in sixty completed works in English. One story was discounted since it is an RPF (Real People Fiction) rather than depicting an interpretation of the canon. I have cross-referenced the sample with AO3, searching for the authors' pseudonyms and the titles of the fanfics and seventeen stories are published at both sites, sometimes rated differently.[8] Although the summaries, categorisations and Author Notes of all fifty-nine fanfics, by fifty-three authors, have been perused (on both sites), I refer to sixteen fanfics, identifying and discussing salient features in the production.

PROMOTION AND INTERPRETATION: THE TEXT-SPECIFIC THRESHOLD

The intertextual relationship between a fanfic and its canon is part of its paratext and the reader and/or researcher needs to be aware of it to accept the invitation to step in. Very short fanfics in particular, for example those that depict one character's intense emotional response to an isolated event, are completely reliant on the reader's understanding of the relationship between canon and fanfic. No background is given in stories of this kind; rather, the reader is thrust immediately into the situation, and is expected to either understand the character's reaction or negotiate an interpretation that is widely different from her own. Accepting this invitation and using the pre-set and fandom-specific epitexts discussed above to navigate, the reader can arrive at a story she expects will conform quite closely to her own proclivities regarding pairings and genre/category. The fanfic author's filing and tagging, her use of categorisations and her summary prepare the reader and create certain expectations. These paratexts conform closely to Genette's taxonomy: they are epitexts and peritexts that frame individual works and negotiate their transfer to the public.

On both *FanFiction.net* and AO3, story headers include the fanfic's title and author's pseudonym as hyperlinks, categorisations and tags appended to the work, as well as a short summary. Clicking on the hyperlinked title brings the reader to the text, and on the pseudonym onto the author's profile page. The latter corresponds to what McCracken defines as navigation along the 'centrifugal vector': without leaving the medium through which the summary is accessed, 'exterior' material is reached (2013: 107, 106). The centrifugal move consequently leads to epitexts that give additional information about the author's production and interpretive proclivities. The author Writingwife83, for example, indicates that her preferred pairing is Sherlock/Molly Hooper and assures visitors that they 'will never find graphic love scenes in [the] stories' ('Profile page'). These epitextual comments, if accessed, frame the reception of her fanfic *I Told You So* by stressing the author's individual selling points.

Other readers can also assist in promotion as statistics appear below the story's summary in the form of numbers of 'reviews', 'favs' and 'follows' on *FanFiction.net* and 'comments' and 'kudos' on AO3. At the former site, a reader simply clicks a button in the top right-hand corner of the screen after accessing the story itself, and then indicates whether she wants to mark the story or the author as a favourite, and whether she wants to follow the story's progression or the author's production. The agency behind this kind of promotion rests with the audience and it is common for authors to request their readers to take action. 'Read and review!' is an often inserted exhortation in summaries as the mere number of reviews signals that the fanfic is worthy of attention (whether they are all positive can only be substantiated by a close reading).

On AO3 tags appear below the title and pseudonym. Appended to texts by the author herself, there is in some cases seemingly no limit to how many are deemed necessary to correctly frame the story and demonstrate the author's interpretation. Howlynn appends eighty tags to her story *A Statue in the*

Temple of Mendacity that indicate what characters and pairings are featured, text-specific genre elements such as hurt/comfort, and elements that in other, often overlapping, ways describe the story's contents, among them 'Psychological Trauma'. The tags are hyperlinked and the link mentioned takes you to a page listing close to two thousand unfolding and completed fanfics featuring, then, depictions of psychological trauma in a variety of fandoms. Despite challenges produced by this type of cross-referencing, the detailed lists framing individual stories are clear indications of the authors' interpretations and, again, the selling points of their fanfics.

The summary inserted after the title and pseudonym (and after tags on AO3) can be aligned with Genette's discussions about the 'please insert' ([1987] 1997: 104). Initially, the 'please insert' was directed at critics and appeared as a separate document in the text to be reviewed, 'describing . . . in a value-enhancing manner, the work to which it refers' (ibid.: 104–5). Today, the closest analogy would be the blurb on the back of a book that gives the reader an idea of the text's contents. Fanfic summaries, however, are often reliant on text-specific descriptions that enhance the value predominantly for the initiated reader. To exemplify, 16magnolias' *Lessons in Love* is described as containing 'sweet, slow Sherlolly' and 'minor OCs' whereas SailorChibi's *Walking Together* is labelled an 'AU' featuring 'Johnlock & mentions of Mystrade'. An OC is an Original Character of the author's own invention and AU signifies an Alternate Universe, a what-if scenario in which elements of the canon are played with. Both abbreviations may fulfil a promotional function, although the OC can also be perceived as a mild warning for readers not interested in non-canon characters. AUs are less controversial since all fanfics are expected to offer a twist on the canon narrative, SailorChibi's being that 'everyone has one soul mate that they usually meet early in life.' The selling point of her story is its exaggeration of the canon friendship between Holmes and Watson and her inclusion of the, in the fandom frequently occurring, portmanteau 'Johnlock' (John/Sherlock) suggests that it is also transformed into a romantic and/or sexual relation. 16magnolia's combination of Sherlock and Molly (Sherlolly) is also relatively common in the fandom's heterosexual pairings, and denotes stories in which Molly's canon infatuation with Sherlock is reciprocated. Mystrade (Mycroft Holmes/Greg Lestrade) is less frequent in the sample and is the pairing most difficult to align with the canon, since the characters (Sherlock's brother and Scotland Yard boss, respectively) never share scenes in which a possible subtext can be transformed into fanfic text. An unlikely pairing may nevertheless resound profoundly with subgroups in the fandom, and by including the portmanteaus in their summaries, the authors cater for readers with similar interpretive proclivities.

In addition to alerting the reader to what type of story it is and what pairing it features, three main aims of summaries appear in the sample, two of which work in various ways to situate the fanfic. The most common formulations specify the point in the canon at which the fanfic is inserted and what major issues it therefore engages with. As noted, 'Post-Reichenbach' fanfics are numerous enough to have occasioned their own tag on AO3, and it appears in several of the sample stories' summaries. This descriptor is nuanced, however, in ways that specify the author's contribution. Formulations such as 'John jumps in Sherlock's stead' (nmqttps, *4,916*) prepare the reader for an AU treatment, whereas 'Sherlock returns' signals the author's wishes for or expectations of a particular development when the canon narrative continues (solojones' *The Sign of the Four*). Despite positioning themselves in relation to an ongoing narrative, the authors in the sample do not supply the reader with a level of specificity greater than in these examples. I have elsewhere examined fans' engagement with a transmedial storyworld in which written and visual instantiations tell partially different stories, and in which weekly TV episodes quickly alter conditions (Lindgren Leavenworth 2014). In that context, an author's exact starting point becomes crucial to framing her story and creating the appropriate circumstances for its reception, whereas in the case of *Sherlock* fanfic, the need is not as pressing.

A second aim is to situate the story within an author's own production. Several of the fanfics in the sample are part of the author's own series or in other ways contingent on previous works. librarianmum's *After the Storm* '[f]ollows on immediately from Lighting Fires', a previous fanfic by this author, and *The Mouse and the Spider* and *The Moon and the Stars* are cross-referenced by author I'm Over There in her summaries, the latter being an independent sequel to the former. Implied by this type of information is in the first case that the previous work should be consulted for a complete enjoyment of *After the Storm*, and in the second that another story is available if the first has met the reader's expectations. Both authors thus use the paratextual space of the summary to promote their own, extensive fanfic production and to guide readers to the relevant chronology in it.

The summary can finally also be used to issue warnings for elements that may be perceived as difficult or disturbing.[9] Author fantasybean signals that her fanfic *Hugs* contains 'SLASH [and if you] don't like it, don't read it' while kate221b issues '[w]arnings for references to mental illness and abuse' in her *The Box*. Warnings are surrounded by some controversy as they indicate normativity and some (such as for slash) have rather come to be perceived as promotion. To signal other types of potentially disturbing contents, as kate221b does, has on the other hand become increasingly common and the warnings seem more seriously intended. Readers to whom depictions of abuse act as triggers or reminders of a personally experienced trauma are hence overtly informed that they may want to give the story a miss.

Summary formulations precede a more direct communication expressed in Author Notes (discussed below) but similarly, and like authorial prefaces in printed literature, work to ensure 'a more pertinent reading' if heeded (Genette [1987] 1997: 2). So do the specific tags and categorisations found in story headers, but they are simultaneously designed to keep an undesired audience away, and in this way avoid potentially inappropriate readings of the text not yet perused. Summaries and user-generated descriptions are therefore a clear instance of authorial authority when seeking to determine a readership.

PARATEXTUAL COMMUNICATION

As spaces of transition and transaction, paratexts generally delineate the positions of author and reader. As Genette argues, their purpose is 'to ensure for the text, a destiny consistent with the author's purpose' and this is made especially clear in what he labels the *'original authorial preface'* ([1987] 1997: 407, 196). In fan fiction, prefaces correspond to Author Notes (A/Ns) inserted before the story proper, or at the end of individual chapters or the complete text, and as is the case with the written preface, it is no longer a matter of attracting the reader: he or she has already made the choice of perusing the text. The preface's 'location', Genette writes, 'is introductory and therefore monitory (this is *why* and this is *how* you should read this book)' (ibid.: 197).[10] The why and the how are foregrounded also in A/Ns, but a distinct difference between traditional and contemporary communicative situations emerges. Instead of reaching a 'definitely assumed' reader (ibid.: 209), A/Ns allow the author to address those she already knows have a predisposed interest in her type of fiction and who constitute a concrete presence: available for instant communication.

The monitory function of A/Ns, however, is underscored in long, serially published fanfics, as each chapter brings with it a new opportunity to signal how to read or how not to read. This aspect of the author's communication divorces it from the paradigm of print literature but also illustrates a difference from paratexts in other digital media. Genette notes that 'the reader [is] not required to read a preface (even if such freedom is not always opportune for the author)', that is even if the author strongly opposes it, a preface may easily be bypassed in a printed work (ibid.: 4). Any desire to re-read a preface, or any preliminary paratext, is thwarted on Kindles and iPads that open to the page where the reader has left off. As McCracken notes, 'the conventions of viewing important paratexts that some writers count on readers engaging with before reading the main text' disappear in this form of digital programming (2013: 113). Although readers can naturally opt to bypass fanfic A/Ns as well, their integration into the text, often in the same type and formatting as the narrative portions, arguably makes this choice more difficult to make. And when inserted repeatedly, there is no need to back click to reach the information; it is rather attached to each chapter, underscoring the presence of the author and enforcing her intentions.

As fan fiction inherently builds on a destabilisation of traditional authorial power, the author function is surrounded with some ambivalence. On the one hand, fanfic authors' own renditions contest messages and depictions in the canon, on the other hand they 'attempt to actively direct the story's audience into a certain, premeditated reader position' (Herzog 2012: § 2.7). Using the peritextual space of A/Ns, fans enforce their own interpretation that is not to be gainsaid through the same process that has precipitated their own engagement with the canon. This author function, communicating a 'statement of intent' (Genette [1987] 1997: 222) further competes with what is at times a highly participatory process. If gaps are detected in an unfolding story, they can be filled in the next chapter or addressed in subsequent A/Ns, but the author may also steer the story in a new direction based on feedback from the community. The authoritative and collaborative author may further coexist as A/Ns oscillate between enforcing the signalled interpretation and being sensitive to the fandom's reactions.

MorbidbyDefault's humorous *Sherlock Holmes and the Case of the Ginger Midgets* exemplifies a process which is exceedingly reliant on collaboration. Initially intended as a one-chapter fanfic, the author encourages her readers to send her prompts, that is specific ideas for new stories that can follow upon the first. Three months later the completed fanfic spans sixty-three chapters. Throughout, but particularly in the A/Ns for the last chapter, MorbidbyDefault addresses her readers and offers personalised thanks that illustrate the communal effort and the way feedback spawns creativity. The acknowledgements' placement divorce them from Genette's 'at the head of the book' and the known readership represents a slight difference from his identification of the function of the dedication as 'offer[ing] the work as a token of esteem to a person, a real or ideal group, or some other type of entity' (117). The esteem Genette speaks of is not always correlated with the addressee's actual involvement in the production of the work (it can even be directed towards a symbolic idea), but the long lists of thanks amassed at the end of many of the sample fanfics usually denote concrete contributions to the creative process.

An oscillation between fandom expectation and creative freedom is noticeable in LizzeXX's *Welcome Holmes*. One of the central characters in the story is an OC who has 'a very long and very established relationship' with Sherlock depicted in stories published before *Welcome Holmes*, and this leads LizzeXX to present her readers with the 'caveat [that] you are a different person around your friends' (Ch. 1). The OC's long-time relationship with Sherlock may therefore result in the latter's non-canon behaviour in the story, but the background explanation attempts to deflect criticism of this aspect. LizzeXX in this way sets the rules for how her fanfic is to be perceived and serial publication enables her to re-inform her readers of the initial caveat and give additional instructions as to how the text is to be read. That is, although she does not bend to any hesitancy among her audience, she uses the peritextual space to develop the reasons for her creative choices. These forms of insurances against 'faulty' readings can be complemented with references to writing styles and experimentations with something new that similarly work to deflect criticism: it is difficult to chastise an author for potential issues she has already admitted to. Regardless of what detail is brought up to ensure a more appropriate reading of the work at hand, a notable difference emerges between fanfic authors and the author of a printed work. The latter has one opportunity to issue direct orders whereas the former can repeatedly supply information perceived to be missing and put her readers back on the intended track.

Repeated explanations and continuous commentary are also found in relation to titles and epigraphs. When directly referring to another work the title may, Genette argues, 'provide the text with the indirect support of another text, plus the prestige of a cultural filiation' whereas epigraphs commonly have a commentary function 'indirectly specif[ying] or emphasiz[ing]' the text which they preface ([1987] 1997: 91, 157). But, again, the author of a printed work seldom has the opportunity to enforce how these peritexts are interpreted by readers, whereas fanfic authors can use the space of the A/N to do precisely that. Zoffoli, one of the few authors in the sample who also includes visual images on AO3 where this option exists, intersperses song lyrics that set the mood for sections of each chapter of *NUTRISCO ET EXTINGUO*, and she translates as well as explains the deeper meaning of the Latin used. Storystuff goes further by detailing not only from where she has lifted her title: *Never the Twain Shall Meet*, but explicates her interpretation of Rudyard Kipling's poem and in what ways its theme suits her fanfic (Ch. 27). The prestige lent by intertextual links is thus made explicit and readers are concretely given the additional layers of meaning generated by their use.

Finally, A/Ns may be used for a commentary of a kind that becomes exceedingly intimate with the progression of a multi-chapter fanfic. The last chapter of Benfan's fanfic *Shot in the Dark* consists of one long A/N (removed on AO3) and illustrates the private nature of communication and the way the author, in hindsight, looks back on the writing process. The personal information centres on the one hand on a delineation of her personal situation – married, with a child and a full-time teaching job – and on the other on the difficulties of being 'a secret writer', a consequence of seeing herself as 'the only nerd in the world [and] more than twice the age of the average fangirl' (Ch. 48). Benfan refers specifically to *FanFiction.net* when detailing her re-evaluation of her nerd-status, finding 'that there are actually a LOT of people like [her].' Evidence of other authors' creative engagement with the canon and the communication with like-minded individuals through reviews provide the grounds for this reassessment and the A/N illustrates the process by which Benfan and fans like her 'cease to see themselves as the stereotypical lone Other and reconceptualize themselves as part of a vast, multivoiced, and powerful community' (Herzog 2012: § 4.11). The affinity space constituted by an active and supportive fandom thus exists simultaneously as the insistence on the relevance of being an author with important interpretations to contribute.

The continuous and multifarious use of A/Ns signals a very particular communicative situation as well as altered author roles in the contemporary production of fiction. On the one hand, as demonstrated, the author's intent is manifestly expressed and the interpretive path clearly and repeatedly marked. On the other hand, as participants are engaged in very similar creative processes (readers often writing their own fanfics), texts and ideas cross-fertilise each other, and the progression of a story may be perceived as a highly communal effort. The person behind the fanfic matters therefore, whether she foregrounds her authorial intent and power or whether she highlights her fictional production as one among many meaning-making activities.

CONCLUSION

Although modifications of the paratext's function and effects need to be made when leaving the paradigm of print behind, and although new functions appear in the digital space, Genette's detailed taxonomy continues to be useful when investigating how fictions are transmitted to the reading public. At the end of his seminal text, Genette adds to the image of the threshold that of the 'airlock that helps the reader pass without too much respiratory difficulty from one world to the other, a sometimes delicate operation, especially when the second world is a fictional one. Being immutable, the text in itself is incapable of adapting to changes in its public in space and over time. The paratext – more flexible, more versatile, always transitory because transitive – is, as it were, an instrument of adaptation' ([1987] 1997: 408).

To research the passing via the figurative airlock into the world of fiction is, as I have argued, no more difficult than other engagements with texts, provided that the overtly intertextual relationship between fanfic and canon is understood. The way the fanfic is framed by the archives' epitexts and the text-specific categorisations and labels, however, may result in more significant respiratory difficulties. To trace contingencies between printed and digital texts may therefore help the visitor's figurative breathing, may help lower the threshold constituted by the appearance of texts in a new medium. Conversely, to take note of the necessary adaptations alerts us to how new modes of production and consumption manipulate us in different ways.

I have therefore argued that an increased awareness of how fan fictions are archived and made searchable, how categorisations, labelling and descriptions frame individual texts, and how the paratextual communication operates, illuminates new forms of authorship and allows different ways of conducting digital research around this. Increased knowledge of the paratext's navigational function results in more manageable samples and text-specific awareness provides researchers with opportunities to make use of a dynamic and important material. When engaging with contemporary forms of consumption of fiction, the activities of fans need to be taken into account, and their production deserves serious attention as literary artefacts in their own right and as expressions of a highly active participatory culture.

NOTES

1. Archives may contain stories starting from a variety of source texts, such as *FanFiction.net* or *Archive of Our Own*, or have a narrower focus: *The Republic of Pemberley*, for example, stores fanfics based on Jane Austen's novels. Communities on social networks, for instance Tumblr and LiveJournal, circulate fanfics among their participants; the app Wattpad is designed for users accessing fanfic on tablets or smartphones.
2. The Fan Data project at UC Berkeley is particularly interesting from a quantitative standpoint. Statistical results from data scrapes come in the form of numbers of fanfics produced and authors involved, and specification of the times fan production spikes or wanes. These statistics allow for the employment of an 'engagement-production paradigm' when examining 'the many interrelated factors that cause media consumers to be engaged with media texts and to produce fan works in response' (De Kosnik, El Ghaoui, Cuntz-Leng et al. 2015: 148, 161).
3. All formatting in quotations as in original.
4. There are differences between the two sites concerning the cultural capital they are perceived as holding in the contemporary context that fall outside the scope of the present discussion. I address these in more detail in 'The Paratext of Fan Fiction' concluding that '[c]ontextual knowledge of . . . the differences between the sites prepare visitors in particular ways and may forcefully determine an author's choice when publishing a story' (Lindgren Leavenworth 2015: 46).
5. Genette's brief definition of the publisher's epitext hinges on materials

such as 'posters, advertisements, press releases and other prospectuses' whereas the *'publisher's peritext'* denotes a 'spatial and material [. . .] zone that exists merely by the fact that a book is published and possibly republished and offered to the public in one or several more or less varied presentations' ([1987] 1997: 347, 16). He is in the latter case concerned with aspects such as the individual work's cover, its typeface, the type of paper it is printed on and so forth (ibid.: 16–36). I prefer to term filing and categorisation systems as epitextual elements because, although influencing all fanfics stored, they are not specific to isolated works in the archives.

6. Choosing to view only completed stories in English results in around 20,000 stories being removed from the search list on *FanFiction.net* and 13,000 from AO3.

7. *FanFiction.net* has a separate section for crossovers, and *Sherlock* is there most commonly crossed with *Dr Who*. James Bond, although not necessarily *Skyfall*, comes in fifth place.

8. If authors use a different synonym and have changed the title of their fanfic when publishing on AO3, my method will not pick them up.

9. On AO3, the author may also choose to append warnings via an epitextual filter.

10. The spatial location of A/Ns is not always introductory, especially not when, as I have done here, conflating notes at the beginning of chapters with authors' End Notes, finishing a chapter or the entire fanfic.

REFERENCES

16magnolias (2014) *Lessons in Love, FanFiction.net,* 15 June. Web (accessed 25 November 2014), n.p.

Benfan (2014) *Shot in the Dark, Archive of Our Own,* 21 November. Web (accessed 25 November 2014), n.p.

Benfan (2014) *Shot in the Dark, FanFiction.net,* 7 November. Web (accessed 25 November 2014), n.p.

Birke, D. and Christ, B. (2013) 'Paratext and digitalized narrative: mapping the field', *Narrative,* 21: 1, pp. 65–87.

'Books' (n.d.), *FanFiction.net.* Web (accessed 19 November 2014), n.p.

Consalvo, M. (2007), *Cheating: Gaining Advantage in Videogames.* Cambridge, MA: MIT Press.

De Kosnik, A., El Ghaoui, L., Cuntz-Leng, V. et al. (2015) 'Watching, creating, and archiving: observations on the quantity and temporality of fannish productivity in online fan fiction archives', *Convergence: The International Journal of Research into New Media Technologies,* 21: 1, pp. 145–64.

Driscoll, C. (2006) 'One true pairing: the romance of pornography and the pornography of romance', in K. Hellekson and K. Busse (eds), *Fan Fiction and Fan Communities in the Age of the Internet*. Jefferson, NC: McFarland, pp. 79–96.

fantasybean (2012) *Hugs*, *FanFiction.net*, 27 September. Web (accessed 25 November 2014).

Genette, G. ([1987] 1997) *Paratexts: Thresholds of Interpretation*, trans. J. E. Lewin. Cambridge: Cambridge University Press.

Gray, J. (2010) *Show Sold Separately: Promos, Spoilers, and Other Media Paratexts*. New York: New York University Press.

Haynes, T. (dir.) (2012) 'The Reichenbach Fall', *Sherlock*. BBC 1, UK, 15 January.

Herzog, A. (2012) '"But this is my story and this is how I wanted to write it": author's notes as a fannish claim to power in fan fiction writing', *Transformative Works and Cultures*, 11.

Howlynn (2012) *A Statue in the Temple of Mendacity*, *Archive of Our Own*, 26 December. Web (accessed 25 November 2014), n.p.

I'm Over There (2012) *The Moon and the Sun*, *FanFiction.net*, 17 June. Web (accessed 25 November 2014), n.p.

I'm Over There (2012) *The Mouse and the Spider*, *FanFiction.net*, 12 June. Web (accessed 25 November 2014), n.p.

kate221b (2012) *The Box*, *FanFiction.net*, 8 October. Web (accessed 25 November 2014).

librarianmum (2014) *After the Storm*, *FanFiction.net*, 12 March. Web (accessed 25 November 2014), n.p.

Lindgren Leavenworth, M. (2014) 'Transmedial narration and fan fiction: the storyworld of *The Vampire Diaries*', in M.-L. Ryan and J.-N. Thon (eds), *Storyworlds Across Media: Toward a Media-Conscious Narratology*. Lincoln, NE: University of Nebraska Press, pp. 315–31.

Lindgren Leavenworth, M. (2015) 'The paratext of fan fiction', *Narrative*, 23: 1, pp. 40–60.

LizzeXX (2014) *Welcome Holmes*, *FanFiction.net*, 25 January. Web (accessed 25 November 2014), n.p.

McCracken, E. (2013) 'Expanding Genette's epitext/peritext model for transitional electronic literature: centrifugal and centripetal vectors on Kindles and iPads', *Narrative*, 21: 1, pp. 105–24.

Macksey, R. (1997) 'Foreword', *Paratexts: Thresholds of Interpretation*, trans. J. E. Lewin. Cambridge: Cambridge University Press, pp. xi–xxii.

MorbidByDefault (2012) *Sherlock Holmes and the Case of the Ginger Midgets*, *FanFiction.net*, 12 October. Web (accessed 25 November 2014), n.p.

nmqttps (2014) *4,916*, *FanFiction.net*, 13 March. Web (accessed 25 November 2014), n.p.

SailorChibi (2014) *Walking Together*, *FanFiction.net*, 15 March. Web (accessed 25 November 2014), n.p.

solojones (2012) *The Sign of the Four*, *FanFiction.net*, 17 June. Web (accessed 25 November 2014), n.p.

Stein, L. and Busse, K. (2009) 'Limit play: fan authorship between source text, intertext, and context', *Popular Communication*, 7, pp. 192–207.

Stewart, G. (2010) 'The paratexts of *Inanimate Alice*: thresholds, genre expectations and status', *Convergence: The International Journal of Research into New Media Technologies*, 16: 1, pp. 57–74.

Storystuff (2011) *Never the twain shall meet*, *FanFiction.net*, 19 July. Web (accessed 25 November 2014), n.p.

'Welcome' (n.d.) *Archive of Our Own*. Web (accessed 19 November 2014), n.p.

Writingwife83 (2014) 'Profile page', *FanFiction.net*, 31 October. Web (accessed 25 November 2014), n.p.

Writingwife83 (2014) *I Told You So*, *FanFiction.net*, 18 September. Web (accessed 25 November 2014), n.p.

Zoffoli (2013) *NUTRISCO ET EXTINGUO*, *Archive of Our Own*, 4 September. Web (accessed 25 November 2014), n.p.

CHAPTER 5

Data Mining and Word Frequency Analysis

Dawn Archer

In this chapter, the author uses a number of studies – representative of different Humanities and Social Science disciplines (and also the legal profession) – to demonstrate the techniques of data mining (lexical/statistical frequency profiling, concordancing, collocations, n-grams, etc.) and how these techniques are being used to uncover not only the aboutness of a text or texts by researchers but also, for example, to distinguish phenomena as diverse as (1) the similarities and differences between different types of genres, (2) relevant materials for the purposes of litigation (as part of ediscovery), (3) authorship attribution indicators, (4) the author's ideological stance, (5) the construction of *othering* and (6) the language characteristics of psychopaths. Particular attention is given to studies which have exploited the keywords, key domains and/or key parts-of-speech methodology.

1. INTRODUCTION

The term *corpus linguistics* (henceforth CL) can be used to define a cluster of computer-enabled methodological techniques or a theoretical approach (Tognini-Bonelli 2001: 1–2). In this chapter, I will assume the first perspective. My specific aim is to demonstrate the efficacy of some of the most widely used techniques of data mining (see section 2) by discussing how such techniques have enabled researchers to draw attention to:

- the linguistic similarities/differences which delineate genres (section 3);
- a more efficient means of engaging in ediscovery (section 4);
- authorship attribution indicators (section 5);
- the author's ideological stance (section 6);

- the (linguistic) construction of *othering* (section 7);
- the language of psychopaths (section 8).

For some readers, my mention of *data mining* may particularly bring to mind 'big data' analysis methods, for example predictive coding (aka machine learning), inductive statistics, Boolean searches, etc. This is not the focus of my chapter. Rather, I focus on those techniques (associated with the CL methodology) which have been found to be profitable to researchers regardless of the size or their data set(s).

2. OUTLINE OF POPULAR CORPUS-LINGUISTIC TECHNIQUES

The prototypical techniques associated with the types of data mining I have in mind are (lexical and statistical) frequency profiling,[1] concordancing,[2] collocations,[3] n-grams,[4] etc. This said, according to Wulff et al. (2010: 4), the days of corpus linguists solely relying on the first two in the list – lexical frequency lists and their related concordances – are 'long gone', by and large. This is because lexical frequency lists and their concordances (i.e. citations of the target 'word in context') provide an indication of the frequency with which/how the different words in a given text – or across a given corpus of texts – are being used. In English at least, this tends to mean that function words such as *the*, *of*, *and*, *a*, *in*, *to*, etc., are at the top of such lists when we are exploring written texts, and that *I*, *you*, *it*, *the*, *'s*, *and*, etc., are at the top of such lists when we are exploring spoken texts.[5] Yet, this is not always the case – as I am finding in respect to a current project which is exploring people's perception(s) of cancer awareness advertisements – specifically, the 'Be Clear on Cancer' campaigns produced on behalf of Cancer Research UK. The most frequent lexical item in respect to one participant (interviewed by a team at the University of Central Lancashire[6]), for example, is *err* – and a quick check of the concordance results suggests that this particular participant was somewhat indecisive when it came to expressing their opinion. There are at least two lessons to take from this. First, we should not ignore something as simple as lexical frequency lists, as they may well throw up results that suggest the need for further investigation/ (in)validation using other CL techniques (e.g. statistical frequency profiling). This brings us to our second lesson: lexical frequency lists provide a good starting point for much research.

The ability to create lexical lists of high-frequency words for a given language is proving especially useful pedagogically: there is a suggestion, for example, that a non-native speaker of English pursuing higher education could ensure they have an awareness of 85 per cent of the words they are likely to encounter in their academic studies by first learning the most frequent word families on Coxhead's (2000) Academic Word List (AWL).[7] This particular list is based on academic journals and textbooks from arts, commerce, law and natural science, and only includes a word when it has 'occur[red] at least 100 times altogether in the whole academic corpus, at least ten times in each of the sub-corpora and in at least half of 28 more finely defined subject areas, such as biology, economics, history, and linguistics' (Stubbs 2008: 117).[8]

The types of software used to create/generate word frequency lists and concordances can also be used to identify repeated phrases (or n-grams) made up of two or more adjacent words – such as the English n-grams, *you know*, *I think*, *such a lot of*, etc. (Cheng 2011: 102). N-grams are particularly worthy of study because of the functions they perform in a given language. A study by Carter and McCarthy (2006: 834–5) has revealed, for example, that n-grams regularly function as prepositional expressions relating to time in English. But they can also indicate basic relations such as possession, agency, purpose, goal and direction, or impart interpersonal meanings: that is, serve to 'monitor the extent of . . . shared knowledge between participants, hedge assertions and opinions, and express varying degrees of tentativeness'. There are two such example bi-grams above – *you know* and *I think* – but Cheng (2011: 104) provides 4- and 5-gram examples too, including *do you know what (I)* and *I know what you mean*.

2.1 (Descriptive) statistical frequency analysis

Lexical frequencies of a given word or n-gram are often translated into a percentage or normalised figure in CL studies. McEnery and Hardie (2011: 49) provide the example of *Lancaster*. This term occurs 1,103 times in the written section of the BNC, which equates to 0.013 per cent of this sub-corpus. In contrast, its normalised figure (per million words) is 12.55. This is derived by, first, dividing the total number of occurrences of *Lancaster* (1,103) by the total number of words in the *BNC written* sub-corpus (87,903,571), and then multiplying this by the base of normalisation (in this case, occurrences per 1 million words). The usefulness of a normalised figure is that it minimises the problem of comparing corpora of different sizes: assuming that the 'common base' used (in this case, *per million words*) makes sense in respect to both corpora. As McEnery and Hardie (2011: 50–1) go on to note, however, interpreting normalised figures literally can still lead to absurdity:

> For . . . it would be foolish to imagine that, if we chopped the BNC
> into 1-million-word chunks, we would with complete regularity find
> 12.55 occurrences of the word in each chunk . . . [Rather], we would
> probably . . . find lots of instances bunched together in a small number
> of texts where . . . Lancaster is an important topic.

As such, it is important to keep in mind that normalised figures tend to abstract from, and simplify, the reality of 'what's there' in a given corpus. For this reason, researchers adopting CL methods often include raw frequencies of a given lexical item alongside their normalised frequencies.

2.2 (Significance) statistical frequency analysis

Several CL techniques are not merely descriptive in design: rather, they test the *significance* of any differences observed. However, as the features that are usually measured 'are subject to a certain amount of "random" fluctuation', these techniques must allow for the possibility of a given occurrence being 'due simply to chance' (McEnery and Hardie 2011: 51). Two of the most frequently used significance techniques, within CL, are (1) the keyness method (i.e. the identification of key words, key semantic fields or key parts of speech) and (2) collocation identification/extraction.

Collocation extraction involves researchers determining the likelihood of two co-occurring words within a text being a statistically meaningful pairing – according to, for example, the chi-square test, the t-test, the mutual information (MI) test or the log likelihood (LL) test[9] – based on what we know about their individual frequencies. Having mentioned the AWL previously (section 2), it is worth noting work by Durrant (2008) here, which suggests that a native English speaker's ability to retain/use collocations appropriately might be a feature which sets them apart from the prototypical adult language learner. Durrant is thus among a growing number of researchers – and teachers – who are advocating that adult language learners be given repeated exposure to high-frequency n-grams/collocations as part of the learning process. Durrant further advocates the development of a list of frequent 'academic collocations' (which, he argues, should go beyond two-word listings). (Critical) discourse analysts and stylisticians tend to share the applied linguist's interest in collocations. In their case, however, they often investigate how the company kept by a particular word – for example, *Muslim* in British newspaper texts – might serve to colour people's worldviews (see, for example, Baker et al. 2013). I will pick up on this particular characteristic of collocates in section 6.

The second significance technique – keyness – equates to the creation and comparison of two lists, A and B, using a tool such as Wmatrix (Rayson 2008),[10] thereby allowing the researcher to discover the most statistically significant items within list A when compared with list B (in addition to the most frequent items). As several of the following sections will reveal, these items can be statistically key words or statistically key semantic field categories – as well as statistically key parts of speech (POS). There are several tools which enable keyword analysis – including WordSmith Tools (Scott 2012). But Wmatrix is the only tool to enable keyword, key POS or key semantic field analysis. The

Wmatrix system's default measure when assessing the level of keyness of a given item is LL. Social science studies which have drawn on Wmatrix tend to use an LL score of 3.84 per cent or higher: this equates to a 95 per cent confidence of statistical significance. Within linguistics, it is common for researchers to use higher LL scores of 6.63+ and even 15.13+ (thereby allowing them to claim a confidence of significance rate of 99–99.99 per cent or higher).

Although the keyness approach is a sophisticated technique when compared to the lexical frequency list approach, it tends to be much more 'user friendly' than some other approaches, as will become clear (in section 3 below). This said, it has been criticised by some for being somewhat 'blunt' with respect to both potentially 'exaggerat[ing] what differences are present' and also 'fail[ing] to distinguish between quite distinct phenomena' (Blaxter 2014: 169). As such, this CL technique – like all of those mentioned above – should be used with care. I have advocated, for example, that, while the keyness approach and similar data-mining procedures might identify (linguistic) items which are:

- *likely* to be of interest in terms of a given text's *aboutness* (Phillips 1989) and structuring, that is its genre-related and content-related characteristics and
- *likely* to repay further study – by, for example, using a concordancer to investigate collocation, etc.

such techniques remain a way of *mining* texts: that is to say they provide the researcher with a *way in* to more detailed textual analysis as opposed to replacing him or her as analyst. For s/he must still determine whether (even statistically meaningful) results identified by such CL techniques are in/significant to them (and others) in the final instance (Archer 2009: 3–4).

With these caveats in mind, the following sections outline a selection of studies which have used CL techniques successfully/sensitively, beginning with genre analysis.

3. GENRE ANALYSIS USING CL TECHNIQUES

Genre analysis is the study of the different variety of texts found within (or across) cultures – scientific writing, science fiction, letters, press periodicals, conversation, etc. – such that they can be identified/distinguished according to certain (linguistic) characteristics. One of the best-known approaches to genre analysis is multi-dimensional analysis (MDA). Although originally developed by Biber (1988) – as a means of comparing written and spoken registers in English – MDA has since been used to analyse the diachronic evolution of genres, as well as to study different languages and even authorial styles (see, for example, Biber 1995; Biber and Finegan 1994a, 1994b; Reppen et al. 2002). Biber's MDA – or a development of it – involves the assessment of a given genre/register/authorial style according to the following seven dimensions:

1. Informational versus involved production: assessed via, for example, first- and second-person pronouns, THAT deletion, contraction, discourse markers and perception verbs (*believe*, *think*).
2. Narrative versus non-narrative concerns: assessed via, for example, past-tense verbs, third-person pronouns, perfect aspect verbs, present participial clauses and what Biber (1988: 92) calls 'public' verbs (*agree*, *report*, *say*).
3. Explicit versus situation-dependent reference: assessed via, for example, wh- relative clauses, phrasal coordination, nominalisation and time/place adverbials.
4. Overt expression of persuasion: assessed via, for example, prediction modals (*will*, *shall*), necessity modals (*ought*, *should*, *must*), conditional subordination and suasive verbs (*ask*, *beg*, *propose*).
5. Abstract versus non-abstract information: assessed via, for example, conjuncts, main/subordinate passive constructions and adverbial subordinators.
6. Online informational elaboration: assessed via, for example, demonstratives (*this*, *that*), *that* (relative clauses or verb and adjective complements).
7. Academic hedging: assessed via *seem/appear*.

A dimension score of a particular text is achieved by adding together the scores for all linguistic features relating to that particular dimension. A dimension score for a genre, in contrast, is achieved by calculating 'the mean of the factor scores of the text within the genre' (Xiao and McEnery 2005: 6). Xiao and McEnery (2005) have found, for example, that conversational texts taken from the Santa Barbara Corpus of Spoken American English (SBCSAE), speech texts taken from the Corpus of Professional Spoken American English (CPSA) and academic prose representative of both the hard and soft sciences taken from Freiburg-Brown Corpus of Standard English (FROWNJ) differ from each other along the first, third and fifth dimensions in particular (see above). More specifically, they found that the SBCSAE data was the most 'oral' of the three genres and that the FROWNJ was the most 'literate'. The latter also made more use of explicit text-internal referencing as well as being 'much more technical and abstract than [both] speech and conversation' (ibid.: 67).

As Xiao and McEnery (2005: 67) found that 'the process of extracting linguistic features and computing factor scores ... [is] very time-consuming and computationally/statistically demanding', they sought to determine whether similar results to the above might be achieved using the keywords methodology highlighted in section 2.2 (following Tribble 1999). And they found that (key) keyword analysis[11] did, indeed, provide a 'low effort' alternative to MDA. Both approaches were able to tease out the 'most significant difference[s] between conversation and speech' (Xiao and McEnery 2005: 76) – even though the (key) keyword approach did not allow for as fine-grained an analysis as MDA. As such, although (key) keyword analysis 'requires little expertise to undertake and can be undertaken swiftly', Xiao and McEnery advocate that it works best when used to evaluate a genre 'against Biber's dimensions' (ibid.: 77). That is to say, looking for evidence among the (key) keywords which suggests the predominance of a particular dimension within a given data set. For example, the authors were able to use key keywords to suggest similarities between the conversation and spoken genres, as well as differences. A key keyword for conversation but not the spoken genre, for example, was DO. When Xiao and McEnery interrogated the concordance results for DO they found that it tended to appear in its negated form (*do not, don't*), as well as appearing as part of special and general questions and as the pro-verb *do* in the present tense – all of which are features that point to MDA Dimension 1 (see above). Key keywords for the spoken genre (but not conversation) – SO and THAT – in contrast, pointed to Dimension 6 (that is, to a marked degree of online informational processing).

4. USING KEYWORDS AS PART OF EDISCOVERY

The sphere of electronic discovery (henceforth ediscovery) provides us with a second example of how the keyword approach is being proffered as a 'low-effort' alternative to other computational processes (Hietala 2014). The core aim of ediscovery is to identify, collect and produce electronically stored information (ESI) – usually in respect to a request for production in a law suit or investigation – in order to produce a core volume of evidence for litigation. Such ESI might relate to emails, documents, presentations, databases, social media, websites – and even voicemail and audio/video files. Once such materials have been identified, they are placed under a legal hold (to ensure they cannot be modified, deleted, erased or otherwise destroyed). The materials are then analysed, first as a means of segregating anything which is deemed to be irrelevant to the case and then as a means of coding the remaining materials in respect of their actual degree of relevance to the case at hand. Such 'prioritisation' is often undertaken using predictive coding tools. However, as these tools tend to require largish data sets, Hietala (2014: 604) has proposed a cost-effective and time-efficient 'keyword generation protocol' for 'handling midsize productions' (e.g. '40,000 or so documents') – once, that is, the attorney (and team) have first created a *study corpus* and a *reference corpus* from the available ESI (by, for example, identifying relevant materials and irrelevant materials respectively).

Once this first prioritisation step has been achieved, Hietala (2014: 611) advocates that those responsible for analysing the *study corpus* (e.g. the relevant materials) use the keyness approach to study 'a company's internal documents relative to' the 'predefined reference corpus' as a means of understanding 'the differences between the words used by [the] company' (as captured within the study corpus) and those used within the reference corpus. The 'first-pass list of terms', produced by the keyness methodology – especially those with high LL values – can then be used by the 'attorney to craft more useful Boolean [i.e. ediscovery computer] searches' (ibid.: 613). When creating these ediscovery searches, Hietala (2014: 617) suggests, further, that it might be profitable to compute the keyness of word pairs and larger n-grams in addition to individual words within the study corpus.

Although Hietala accepts there are some potential problems and issues with adopting such an approach (including the keyness methodology highlighting potentially misleading or unhelpful key terms), he suggests that it is a better option than – and, indeed, has the potential to protect lawyers 'from the risks associated with' – their searching for 'their own preoccupations' (2014: 619).

5. DETERMINING AUTHORSHIP ATTRIBUTION USING CL TECHNIQUES

Ediscovery can sometimes entail authorship attribution. Authorship attribution, broadly defined, is the study of the linguistic style of a given text or texts as a means of determining the creator(s) of that text or texts. As tools such as Turnitin demonstrate, tools to detect plagiarism (and hence engage in authorship attribution) are now quite commonplace. These tools seek to match word-strings to other (available) data sets to gauge the extent of commonality or overlap. More sophisticated approaches to authorship attribution, in contrast, will draw on lexical, orthographic, morphological and syntactic information contained within a given text (or texts). This might involve identifying and extracting 'style markers' and/or applying a classification procedure that assesses the richness of the vocabulary vs. frequency of common word-use. Such style markers might include average word length, average sentence length, proportion of open-class and closed-class categories, etc.

Given that such evidence is *internal*, i.e. from the text itself (or texts, if more than one is available), many researchers argue that, in order to satisfy standards of proof, a sample (whose provenance is doubtful) needs to be of sufficient length and there also need to be sufficient samples for comparison in similar text types by candidate writers.[12] This said, work by Guzmán-Cabrera et al. (2008: 166) suggests that bi-grams might offer a solution when it comes to working with small text sizes. Vogel (2007: 189) also believes in the evaluation of n-grams: in this case, because an author's orthographical choices (and, in particular, their spelling) can often function as an 'unconscious fingerprint' (given how difficult they are to consciously manipulate). Indeed, bi-grams, in particular, are thought to be the most reliable thing to count 'if forensic analysis of texts using corpus linguistic techniques is to satisfy the Daubert test of admissibility of expert testimony in criminal court' (Vogel 2007: 190; see also Chaski 1997). Vogel and his team of researchers have been experimenting with letters, words and also n-grams of POS tags. They seem to be finding that letter uni-grams and bi-grams have the most predictive potential when it comes to authorship attribution. They were able to correctly assign texts of 'Eamon de Valera, Franklin Roosevelt, Gerry Adams, George W. Bush, Huey P. Long and Margaret Thatcher . . . using letter unigrams', for example, 'but only Dick Cheney and de Velara had that status using word unigrams' (Vogel 2007: 193). Several texts were also wrongly assigned: for example, 'Bertie Aherne's texts were assigned entirely incorrectly to John Hume, and the texts of George W. Bush were assigned to Dick Cheney, Bill Clinton and G.W. Bush' (ibid.). As Vogel points out, this is not too surprising given that 'politicians rarely author their own speeches and many have multiple speech writers' (ibid.). I wonder, too, whether the (local) political climate might be serving as an influence such that politicians in the same political sphere respond to – and, in so doing, have the potential to 'echo' – each other (both at the conscious and subconscious level)? Vogel does not raise this as a potential issue but he does point out that the temporal dimension needs to be factored into authorship attribution studies based on n-grams. By this he means that there is a need to study any potential diachronic effects in order to fully appreciate whether/how a person's language usage – and, hence, their style markers (including any orthographical habits which are suggestive of an idiolect) – change over time. This, in turn, points to the debate over the very possibility that individuals have a (fixed) linguistic fingerprint (see, for example, Olsson 2008).

6. IDENTIFYING IDEOLOGICAL STANCE USING CL TECHNIQUES

A number of researchers are increasingly using the kinds of CL techniques discussed above – and, in particular, collocation extraction – in order to reveal ideological uses of language (most notably within political texts and newspaper texts). For example, in their study of refugee data made up of British national newspaper stories published between 1996 and 2005, Gabrielatos and Baker (2008) found that *refugee* collocated strongly with *flood* (i.e. co-occurred more frequently than we would expect *refugee* and *flood* to co-occur due to chance[13]). And many of these co-occurrences were as a result of the metaphoric string, *flood of refugees.* The implication of this metaphor, in particular, is that the intake of refugees into a given country is akin to an unwanted natural disaster so that refugees are potentially understood by readers to pose a similar possible danger to society.

In a more recent publication, Baker et al. (2013) have explored collocates of *Muslim* in the British Press, this time using the Sketch Engine tool.[14] They prefer the latter tool when investigating collocates as:

> When a corpus is installed in Sketch Engine, each word is assigned a grammatical 'tag', such as a 'proper noun', 'adjective', 'base form of verb', '-s form of verb', etc. As a result, when Sketch Engine identifies collocates, it also takes into account the positions of the collocates in relation to each other, and the grammatical tags of each collocate, in order to identify grammatical relationships. The collocates of a word are thus grouped together . . . as a word sketch. (Baker et al. 2013: 37)

When Baker et al. (2013) explored *Muslim* within Sketch Engine, for example, five grammatical patterns or frames were discernible. Two of the patterns/ frames (e.g. {*Muslim and/or X*}, {*X and/or Muslim*}) provided an indication of the sorts of people groups that Muslims tended to be associated with – many of which (*Sikhs, Buddhists, atheists*) are notable for being belief-based groups. Two additional patterns/frames identified *Muslim* with a verb in either the subject position or the object position (e.g. {[verb] + *Muslim*], {*Muslim* + [verb]}). Some examples of such patterns included *Muslim was beheaded, Muslim was recruited* and *Muslim was suspected*. These examples – in conjunction with the fifth pattern/frame highlighting the modification of *Muslim* using adjectives and nouns – point, in turn, to 'a way of representing an aspect of the world' which may be ideologically slanted (Baker et al. 2013: 39). For, according to the authors, collocates such as '*behead, suspect, arrest, accuse* and *jail* suggest that' *Muslim*, when used in the object position in particular, 'carries a negative *discourse prosody* . . . related to criminality' (Baker et al. 2013: 39; italics as in original). This aspect of criminality seemed to overlap with an identifiable war frame – hence the collocates *militia, plot, prisoner, protestor, terrorist* (among the adjectives and nouns modifying *Muslim*) which, in turn, overlapped with a frame relating to (level of) belief, especially in respect to collocates such as *fanatic, fundamentalist, fanatical, hardline, extremist* and *firebrand* (among the adjectives modifying *Muslim*). The result was that 'Muslims' were associated with 'having strong (sometimes dangerously strong) beliefs' (ibid.: 42).

The (potential) *othering* of a particular ethnic or religious group – such that an evil, harmful or threatening 'enemy' in need of collective resistance or expurgation is constructed (Thompson 1990: 65) – is not peculiar to the British media. Indeed, Adegoke (1999) found similar discourse frames relating to criminality and war as well as additional frames (relating to economic crisis, civil unrest and riots) within South African media texts in the 1990s such that:

> African foreigners in South Africa [were] often represented in the
> South African press as burdens and criminals or as victims of crime.
> They 'flood[ed]' the country and use[d] up resources, creating a social
> and economic burden for South African taxpayers. Thousands of them
> c[a]me in 'illegally', some 'obtaining citizenship fraudulently'. African
> foreigners [were] behind major crimes in South Africa such as drug
> dealing . . . [and e]ven where a report represent[ed] foreign Africans
> as victims of crime [what was accentuated was their being] in the
> environment or scene of a crime – 'found dead or injured'. (Adegoke
> 1999: 107)

It is not surprising that such *stance*-related studies – in considering attitudinal and evaluative expressions – will regularly refer to (issues of) criminality, politics and morality.[15] As will become clear, however, collocates are not the only CL technique that can help us to investigate (ideological) stance.

7. HIGHLIGHTING *OTHERING* USING CL TECHNIQUES

A third CL-based study which touches on *othering* – but in ways that draw specifically from the academic disciplines of Linguistics and History – is that of Williams and Archer (2013). Williams and Archer opted to use the keyness methodology to study the construction of the *ethnic other* within two children's readers. The readers *Tatar Liberation War* (henceforth TLW) and *Udmurtia Forever with Russia* (henceforth UFR) – detail the history of Russia's relationship with Tatar and Udmurtia respectively. Originally written in Russian,[16] they were published in 2007 and 2008 to celebrate a nationally significant anniversary: in the case of TLW, this was the 450th anniversary of the first Kazan war of independence; in the case of UFR, it was the '450th anniversary of the voluntary entry of Udmurtia into the Russian state structure'.

In terms of their approach, Williams and Archer used Wmatrix, first, to create word and semantic field lists for TLW and UFR and, then, to compare these lists as a means of uncovering words and semantic fields – some of which are shown below in bold – that were unusually frequent in one textbook when compared with the other. This resulted in the identification of 190 key terms.[17] As a third step, the authors then identified a small subset of keywords and key semantic fields from this list according to the statistically relevant key items' *cultural significance* (*pace* Williams 1976): that is, their capturing something about the Tatar and Udmurt experience historically, socially and, especially, culturally.

Archer and Williams' most significant finding was that TLW and UFR deliberately omit and/or background some periods of history – but for different purposes. The author of TLW seems to want to create a distinct Tatar voice, for example, sometimes at the expense of *othering* Russia. The authors of UFR, in contrast, emphasise Udmurtia's 'voluntary union' with Russia, but at the expense of a distinct ethnic voice for Udmurtia. By way of explanation, TLW omits and/or backgrounds two of the three major periods of Russian–Tatar history – the so-called Tatar yoke (up to 1552) and the Soviet era (beginning in 1917) – in favour of focusing on a particularly difficult period in Russian–Tatar relations: the 1552 conquest of the Kazan Khanate by Ivan the Terrible to the 1917 revolution. Significantly, its author (Garif 2007) suggests that TLW has been written in a way that allows readers to rethink 'the lessons of history' in terms of its *'times of peace'* and its *'times of mutual enmity and hostility'* (my italics). However, the keywords – **rebels, uprising, resistance, siege, independence, revolt, defenders, liberation, conquest, colonisers, oppression**, etc. – hint at its real focus: Tatar resistance to Russian colonialisation. So strong is this particular frame, in fact, that it accounts for many of the key semantic fields in TLW, including **Warfare, Defence and the Army; Violent/Angry** and **Hindering; Damaging and Destroying**. For example, the children's introduction to 'the conquest of the **Khanate** of **Kazan**' is framed within a discussion of 'the people of the Middle **Volga** region and especially the **Tatars**' being 'put under harsh conditions which demanded *the maximum mobilisation of their will to survive*' (Williams and Archer's italics). The repeated co-occurrence of **Kazan, Khanate, conquest, fall**, etc., in TLW then is meant to trigger a negative view not of the Kazan Khanate, but of the Russian enemy. Additional examples which frame Russia as the *other* include: Russians being characterised by self-serving greed; being otherwise dishonest and unscrupulous; and of enforcing Christianity onto the Muslim Tatars. In terms of orientation to difference then the focus overall is one of accentuating difference (with key semantic fields such as **Not Allowed, Violent/Angry** and **Damaging and Destroying** containing terms such as *suppress(ion)*, *banned/ banning, forbidding*, and ethnic *intolerance, aggression, unrest, violence, wounding, threats, attack(s), fierce, brutal, destroy(ed), slashing, broken* and *demolition*). This proactive stance, however, means that the Tatar people (as well as other ethnic groups such as Udmurts) are depicted as being both the recipients and, importantly, also the agents of violence, especially when it comes to their continuing resistance to Russia's 'policy of aggression'.

In contrast to TLW, most of the keywords within the statistically significant cultural word-subset relating to UFR support the presupposition within its title: for the emphasis is very much upon the **voluntary union** of the Udmurts and Russians – hence the repeated co-occurrence of this phrase in the text. This frame of a 'friendly' joining together of the two people groups is constructed so as to begin in **ancient times**, moreover, and children are meant to infer that it has been mutually beneficial too – especially as regards trading and language borrowing (Bobodzhanova et al. 2008: 14, 27). Yet the suggestion of a voluntary union between Udmurtia and Russia – and, more importantly, the notion of a mutually beneficial shared experience, from the past through to the present – is only made possible by omitting or glossing over periods of conflict in their joint histories. This includes the omission of Southern Udmurts' opposition to Russia after the fall of Kazan (1552–87), major Udmurt uprisings in 1581–4 and 1615, Udmurt support for the Pugachev revolt (1753–5) and, more recently, much of the Soviet period, including the purges of the Udmurt intelligentsia in the 1930s (but excepting the Great Patriotic War, which is mentioned in the children's reader). The authors of UFR might claim that such omissions are necessary, given the age of the intended target audience: the preface states, for example, that the aim is 'to familiarise' pre-school and junior-school children with 'historical stages of [Udmurtia's] development', but in a way that does not 'overload children with information'. Yet, as we have seen, similar children's readers – including TLW – have not omitted the bloodier parts of history. The UFR's decision to omit certain aspects of Udmurt history, then, is probably shaped more by their primary stated objective of 'help[ing] to fulfil the . . . laying down [of a] foundation of tolerance and patriotism' than by the age of the target audience.

Having alluded to patriotism, it is worth noting that all five occurrences of **patriotic** within UFR relate to the Great Patriotic War, when the 'fierce and powerful enemy – fascist Germany' attacked the USSR. This emphasis is one of only two examples of *othering* in the textbook – the other being the depiction of the 'evil and cruel Batyi Khan'. What unites both examples is their depiction of bringing 'war to the Russian land' (ibid.: 26) which allows the authors, in turn, to signal that 'Udmurt people together with other peoples' heroically came 'to the defence of their Motherland' (ibid.: 55). But notice the effect here: patriotic feelings are clearly aligned with Russia as opposed to Udmurtia. The mention of the Mongol ruler, in particular, affords the authors a second, albeit related opportunity: emphasising how Russia and Udmurtia fared badly when there was a lack of unity between Russian princes, and indeed only succeeded when 'Udmurts, Maris and other peoples together revolted against the Golden Horde on the side of the Russian army'. According to Williams and Archer, it is this repeated promotion of (national) cohesion, via the construction of a shared past and present, which not only brackets/suppresses difference but also leads to a 'voice' in URF which is more Russia-inclined than it is Udmurtia-inclined.

8. STUDYING THE LANGUAGE OF PSYCHOPATHS USING CL TECHNIQUES

Our final study – Hancock et al. (2013) – also combines linguistics with another academic discipline: in this case Psychology. Once again, the authors use Wmatrix, but they do so in conjunction with a dictionary-based tool called the Dictionary of Affect in Language (or DAL).[18] Hancock and colleagues are especially interested in determining whether there is anything distinctive about the language of psychopaths. This has led them to compare the language of a group of psychopaths – who (at the time of the study) were serving prison sentences, having been found guilty of murder – with other inmates who were also serving prison sentences for murder but not considered to be psychopaths.

Significantly, this study builds on several hypotheses. The first is 'that subtle patterns in word choice can reveal underlying cognitive and emotional responses, largely because of the automatic and non-conscious operation of language production that is tightly coupled with basic psychological states and dynamics' (Hancock et al. 2013: 102–3). The second hypothesis is that psychopaths appear to view the world (as well as others) instrumentally, that is as being 'theirs for the taking' (Porter and Woodworth 2007; Mokros et al. 2008). In an experiment which made use of the Prisoner's Dilemma scenario, for example, Mokros and colleagues found that psychopaths predominantly displayed selfish, goal-driven non-cooperation. This led Hancock and his fellow researchers to question whether tools like Wmatrix could help to pick out particularly salient language features which were indicative of such behaviour. They hypothesised, for example, that it might be worth looking out for a relatively high use of subordinating conjunctions such as *because, since, as* and *so that*, in the belief that they might point to cause-and-effect statements. Hancock and colleagues also hypothesised that the unique drives and socio-emotional needs of the typical psychopath might result in particular linguistic patterns. In particular, following Maslow (1954), they believed the psychopath's tendency to focus on basic or material needs might result in an underuse of semantic categories relating to higher level needs – like love, family and spirituality – and an overuse of semantic categories relating to food, drink, clothing, sex, money, etc.

Psychopaths are also believed to be deficient when it comes to interpreting and experiencing emotion (see Patrick 2007). Automatic content analysis tools like Wmatrix cannot help when it comes to identifying someone's difficulties in identifying (subtle) emotional expressions, of course. But Hancock and colleagues hypothesised that tools like DAL and Wmatrix (together) can help when it comes to the identification of emotional words and concepts. In respect to Wmatrix, for example, they wanted to determine whether the tool might help them to identify whether psychopaths typically (1) produced fewer, less intense emotional words; (2) produced more disfluency markers (such as 'uh' and 'um'); and (3) produced language which has been shown to reflect increased social distancing. Here, Hancock and colleagues were drawing on the research of people such as Pennebaker and King (1999), who have suggested that psychological distancing is associated with a higher rate of the past-tense forms (and a reduced number of present-tense forms).

Some of the more significant findings of this study suggest that the psychopaths did, indeed, linguistically frame their homicides as more in the past than the control group, while also using more psychologically distant terms, even though there was no difference in respect of the timing of the homicides across the two groups.[19] The psychopaths also indicated a cause-and-effect relationship more than participants in the control group: which was taken as evidence that they viewed their crime as a logical outcome of a plan more so than the latter did (that is, as something that 'had' to be done to achieve a goal). They were also found to have used twice as many words related to basic physiological and self-preservation needs – *eating*, *drinking* and *money* – within their crime narratives. In essence, this meant that their descriptions tended to be delivered in a 'cool, detached manner' and in terms of the basic physiological needs their crimes met at the time of being committed, but in a way that suggested little relevance to their current status and with little or no remorse or empathy for the victim or his/her family. Based on such findings, Hancock et al. (2013: 112) felt able to conclude that tools such as Wmatrix (in conjunction with DAL) not only provide the researcher with a potential means of 'open[ing a] window into the mind of the psychopath', which enables them to understand how 'the psychopath's world view' might differ 'from the rest of the human species', but also alert them to those stylistic differences 'beyond conscious control' which seem to support the view that the psychopath is operating at 'a primitive but rational level'.

9. CONCLUDING COMMENTS

This chapter outlines several CL techniques, and how these techniques have been used by researchers and – in the case of Hietala (2014) – legal professionals to distinguish phenomena as diverse as (1) the similarities and differences between different types of genres, (2) relevant materials for the purposes of litigation (as part of ediscovery), (3) authorship attribution indicators, (4) the author's ideological stance, (5) the construction of *othering*, and (6) the language characteristics of psychopaths. Some of the highlighted studies point, in turn, to the advantages of using a number of CL methods simultaneously, and even a number of tools when investigating the same data set(s). The approach adopted by Hancock et al. (2013), for example, points to the usefulness of enhancing results from Wmatrix with DAL (and vice versa). One potential downside of the Hancock et al. (2013) study, however, is that the psychologists did not work with linguists: as such, some of their linguistic analyses were not as detailed as they might have been.

The Williams and Archer (2013) study is an example of researchers working together across disciplines – as a means of enabling an analysis that was simultaneously statistical (*pace* Rayson 2008) and cultural in emphasis (*pace* Williams 1976) when it came to keywords and key semantic fields. Aware that they were working with translations, Williams and Archer were careful to ensure that their findings were based on key semantic fields more so than keywords: for the same semantic fields were likely to be key within both the Russian originals and the English translations.[20] Their study could be strengthened further, however, by a more detailed discussion of the collocations of the most culturally meaningful statistical keywords/semantic fields. Unfortunately, to date, it is only possible to engage in such a study – via Sketch Engine in conjunction with Wmatrix – if our focus is keywords. But Rayson and colleagues are exploring ways of making (detailed) collocation studies of statically key semantic fields possible.[21]

Several of the other studies mentioned here also drew on the keyness methodology. In so doing, they provide us with timely examples of the positive aspects of this method: namely, that it is a user-friendly and often time-effective means of analysing larg(ish) data sets in ways that make researchers' lines of reasoning transparent and – most importantly – replicable and therefore non-/verifiable (see, for example, Xiao and McEnery 2005; Hietala 2014). The keyness technique is particularly renowned (1) for detecting patterns that might go un-noticed were researchers reliant on close-reading alone (Hietala 2014) or, alternatively, (2) for providing a user-friendly means of finding/(in) validating a set of pre-defined criteria (Xiao and McEnery 2005). However, in light of the criticism that the keyness method – and, indeed, other CL techniques – can sometimes exaggerate what differences are present (Blaxter 2014), it is important for researchers to think of ways of ensuring their evaluations of the data findings are as systematic, as valid and as nuanced as possible. In the case of Xiao and McEnery (2005), for example, this involved using the keywords methodology as a means of searching for linguistic features characteristic of Biber's (1988) seven MDA dimensions.

Ensuring that CL techniques help as opposed to hinder the researcher(s)'s evaluations of the data set(s) can be equally problematic when making sense of the collocation results relating to, for example, media reportage (see, for example, Gabrielatos and Baker 2008; Baker et al. 2013). This is because a collocation result for a particular node word can arise due to its high occurrence in a particular text. One way of combating this is to focus on consistent collocates (c-collocates) only. This can be as simple as separating a data set into years and only discussing those collocates which appeared in each year, year on year, thereby ensuring that the findings are suggestive of prototypical representations (as opposed to being coloured by a particular event or events in a given year). What this might lose, though – when it comes to media reportage – are the differences which particular regional, national and global events can make to such reportage, and hence the different nuances of the various media (re) presentations within a given period and what may be helping to shape them (in the world at large). The best means of ensuring that the kinds of CL techniques discussed here help – rather than hinder – the researcher, in the final instance, is to take seriously Archer's (2009) suggestion that such techniques provide a way of *mining* the data only. For, ultimately, it must always be the researcher who decides what is (and is not) meaningful, based on all available data.

NOTES

1. The frequency profiling method helps users to discover the most frequent words in a text or texts, or the statistically key words which differentiate that text (or those texts) from other texts (see sections 2.1 and 2.2).
2. Concordancing provides a means of grouping the uses of a given word or phrase in a text or texts along with its immediate co-text, such that a user is able to discern patterns of 'typical' usage.
3. From a CL perspective, collocations equate to sequences of words which co-occur more often than would be expected by change, with the result that their *measure of association* is statistically relevant (see sections 2.2 and 6).
4. N-grams are contiguous sequences of a *N*umber of items, be it phonemes, letters, words, etc.
5. Examples taken from frequency lists for the 100-million-word British National Corpus (BNC), made available by Kilgariff at <ftp://ftp.itri. bton.ac.uk/bnc/>.
6. The UCLan team consists of medical professionals as well as linguists. The aim of the project is to improve society's awareness of cancer symptoms such that they are identified as early as possible (thereby improving prognoses).
7. The actual recommendation is to learn 570 word families, for which see: <http://www.uefap.com/vocab/select/awl.htm>.
8. The AWL is but one example of a range of practices involving corpus comparison, in which researchers diachronically and/or synchronically compare (as a means of analysing) registers, genres, languages and even translations (see, for example, Biber 1995; Mair 2006; Teich 2003). To be

possible, in the first place, corpus comparison necessitates corpus processing – including, in many cases, the development of annotation schemes
and appropriate statistical measures for interpreting quantitative data (see,
for example, Gries 2006).

9. Chi-square, t-test, MI and LL equate to different means of assessing
statistical significance – and hence our level of confidence in being able to
accept a given hypothesis (out of 100 per cent) in respect to an observed
phenomenon. Most social scientists agree that for a phenomenon to be
statistical (as opposed to being due to chance) any such test should achieve
a score of 95 per cent confidence or higher.

10. Wmatrix can be accessed from <http://ucrel.lancs.ac.uk/wmatrix/>.

11. A key keyword denotes a keyword which has been found to be particularly
frequent in multiple texts in a corpus. Key keyword analysis is thus a good
way of ensuring that one text – within a given set of texts – does not overly
influence the results (and hence the analysis).

12. Note that this assumes that writers have a sort of 'authorial fingerprint'
that can be detected in their writings (Juola 2008: 7).

13. As we discovered when discussing n-grams (section 2), some function/
grammatical words have a strong tendency to co-occur, but collocates
such as *flood* and *refugee* will not tend to co-occur regularly, generally
speaking. As such, when they do co-occur, they are deemed to be meaningful in some way.

14. For details of Sketch Engine, see <http://www.sketchengine.co.uk/>.

15. Englebretson (2007: 13) found such an association (in 1990s Britain), as
captured by collocates of *stance* in the BNC.

16. Williams and Archer use English translations in their study: Williams is
fluent in Russian, and thus was able to check the accuracy of the translations.

17. One hundred and thirteen keywords and 33 key semantic fields were identified in TLW; 146 keywords and 45 key semantic fields in UFR. These
190 key items had LL scores of between 6.65 and 211.88, giving them a
'confidence of significance' rating of upwards of 99.9 per cent.

18. DAL assesses emotional properties of language along the affective dimensions of (pleasantness) evaluations, activation and imagery.

19. All prisoners were interviewed a decade after the crime, generally speaking.

20. Key semantic fields, in addition, have been found to not only 'refine'
keyword results but also highlight 'patterns that one might not have
noticed looking solely at the words' or keywords alone (Culpeper 2014:
62).

21. Although it is possible to examine key word semantic collocation using
Wmatrix, in 2015 key semtag-semantic collocation is not yet possible.

REFERENCES

Adegoke, R. I. (1999) *Media Discourse on Foreign Africans and the Implications for Education*. Master's thesis. Johannesburg: University of Witwatersrand.

Archer, D. (2009) 'Does frequency really matter?', in D. Archer (ed.), *What's in a Word-list? Investigating Word Frequency and Keyword Extraction.* Farnham: Ashgate, pp. 1–16.

Baker, P., Gabrielatos, C. and McEnery, T. (2013) *Discourse Analysis and Media Attitudes: The Representation of Islam in the British Press.* Cambridge: Cambridge University Press.

Biber, D. (1988) *Variation Across Speech and Writing.* Cambridge: Cambridge University Press.

Biber, D. (1995) *Dimensions of Register Variation: A Cross-linguistic Comparison.* Cambridge: Cambridge University Press.

Biber, D. and Finegan, E. (1994a) 'Multi-dimensional analyses of authors' style: some case studies from the eighteen century', in D. Ross and D. Brink (eds), *Research in Humanities Computing 3.* Oxford: Oxford University Press, pp. 3–17.

Biber, D. and Finegan, E. (ed.) (1994b) *Sociolinguistic Perspectives on Register.* New York: Oxford University Press.

Blaxter, T. (2014) 'Applying keyword analysis to gendered language in the *Íslendingasögur*', *Nordic Journal of Linguistics*, 37: 2, pp. 169–98.

Bobodzhanova, N. G., Andreeva, T. S., Gertiy, Y. N. and Zubkova, N. A. (2008) *Udmurtiia naveki s Rossiei [Udmurtia Forever with Russia].* Izhevsk: Udmurtiia.

Carter, R. and McCarthy, M. (2006) *Cambridge Grammar of English.* Cambridge: Cambridge University Press.

Chaski, C. (1997) 'Who wrote it? Steps toward a science of authorship identification', *National Institute of Justice Journal*, 233, pp. 15–22.

Cheng, W. (2011) *Exploring Corpus Linguistics: Language in Action.* London: Routledge.

Coxhead, A. (2000) 'A new academic word list', *TESOL Quarterly*, 34, pp. 123–238.

Culpeper, J. (2014) 'Developing keyness and characterization: annotation', in D. L. Hoover, J. Culpeper and K. O'Halloran (eds), *Digital Literary Studies: Corpus Approaches to Poetry, Prose and Drama.* New York: Routledge, pp. 35–62.

Durrant, P. (2008) 'High frequency collocations and second language learning'. PhD thesis. Nottingham: University of Nottingham.

Englebretson, Robert (2007) 'Stancetaking in discourse: an introduction', in R. Englebretson (ed.), *Stancetaking in Discourse: Subjectivity, Evaluation, Interaction.* Amsterdam: John Benjamins, pp. 1–26.

Gabrielatos, C. and Baker, P. (2008) 'Fleeing, sneaking, flooding: a corpus analysis of discursive constructions of refugees and asylum seekers in the UK press, 1996–2005', *Journal of English Linguistics*, 36: 1, pp. 5–38.

Garif, Nurulla (2007) *Osvoboditel'naya voina Tatarskogo naroda [Tatar Liberation War]*. Kazan: Tatarskoe knizhnie izdatel'stvo.

Gries, S. T. (2006) 'Exploring variability within and between corpora: some methodological considerations', *Corpora*, 1: 2, pp. 109–51.

Guzmán-Cabrera, R., Nordström, B. and Ranta, A. (2008) 'A web-based self-training approach for authorship attribution', in *Advances in Natural Language Processing*, Proceedings for the 6th International Conference, GoTAL2008, Gothenburg, Sweden, 25–27 August. Dordrecht: Springer Science and Business Media.

Hancock, J. T., Woodworth, M. T. and Porter, S. (2013) 'Hungry like the wolf: a word-pattern analysis of the language of psychopaths', *Legal and Criminological Psychology*, 18, pp. 102–14.

Hietala, J. R. (2014) 'Linguistic key words in e-discovery', *American Journal of Trial Advocacy*, 37: 603–20.

Juola, P. (2008) *Authorship Attribution*. Boston: Now Publishers.

McEnery, T. and Hardie, A. (2011) *Corpus Linguistics: Method, Theory and Practice*. Cambridge: Cambridge University Press.

Mair, C. (2006) *Twentieth-Century English: History, Variation and Standardization*. Cambridge: Cambridge University Press.

Maslow, A. H. (1954) 'A theory of human motivation', *Psychological Review*, 50, pp. 370–96.

Mokros, A., Mennr, B., Eisenbarth, H., Alpers, G. W., Lange, K W. and Osterheider, M. (2008) 'Diminished cooperativeness of psychopaths in a prisoner's dilemma game yields higher rewards', *Journal of Abnormal Psychology*, 117, pp. 406–13.

Olsson, J. (2008) *Forensic Linguistics*, 2nd edn. London: Continuum.

Patrick, C. J. (2007) 'Getting to the heart of psychopathy', in H. Hervé and J. C. Yuille (eds), *The Psychopath: Theory, Research and Social Implications*. Hillsdale, NJ: Lawrence Erlbaum Associates, pp. 207–52.

Pennebaker, J. W. and King, L. A. (1999) 'Linguistic style: language use as an individual difference', *Journal of Personality and Social Psychology*, 77, pp. 1296–312.

Phillips, M. (1989) *Lexical Structure of Text*. Birmingham: University of Birmingham.

Porter, S. and Woodworth, M. (2007) '"I'm sorry I did it . . . but he started it": a comparison of the official and self-reported homicide descriptions of psychopaths and non-psychopaths', *Law and Human Behaviour*, 31, pp. 91–107.

Rayson, P. (2008) 'From key words to key semantic domains', *International Journal of Corpus Linguistics*, 13: 4, pp. 519–49.

Reppen, R., Fitzmaurice, S. and Biber, D. (eds) (2002) *Using Corpora to Explore Linguistic Variation*. Amsterdam: John Benjamins.

Scott, M. (2012) *WordSmith Tools*, version 6. Liverpool: Lexical Analysis Software.

Stubbs, M. (2001) *Words and Phrases: Corpus Studies of Lexical Semantics*. Oxford: Blackwell.

Stubbs, M. (2008) 'Language corpora', in A. Davies and C. Elder (eds), *Handbook of Applied Linguistics*. Chichester: John Wiley & Sons, pp. 106–32.

Teich, E. (2003) *Cross-linguistic Variation in System and Text*. Berlin: Walter de Gruyter.

Thompson, J. B. (1990) *Ideology and Modern Culture*. Oxford: Basil Blackwell.

Tognini-Bonelli, E. (2001) *Corpus Linguistics at Work*. Amsterdam: John Benjamins.

Tribble, C. (1999) *Writing Difficult Texts*. PhD thesis. Lancaster: Lancaster University.

Vogel, C. (2007) 'N-gram distributions in texts as proxy for textual fingerprints', in A. Esposito, M. Bratanić, E. Keller and M. Marinaro (eds), *Fundamentals of Verbal and Nonverbal Communication and the Biometric Issue* Amsterdam: IOS Press, pp. 189–94.

Whissell, C. M. and Dewson, M. R. J. (1986) 'A dictionary of affect in language: iii. analysis of two biblical and two secular passages', *Perceptual and Motor Skills*, 62, pp. 127–33.

Williams, C. and Archer, D. (2013) 'Constructing the "ethnic other" in two history school books: re-colonialisation (Udmurtia) versus de-colonialisation (Tatarstan)', *East/West Journal* (Scholarly Journal for History and Culture), 16–17, pp. 323–40.

Williams, R. (1976) *Keywords: A Vocabulary of Culture and Society*, London: Flamingo.

Wulff, S., Gries, S. T. and Davis, M. (2010) 'Introduction', in S. T. Gries, S. Wulff and M. Davis (eds), *Corpus Linguistic Applications: Current Studies, New Directions*. Amsterdam and New York: Rodopi, pp. 1–6.

Xiao, Z. and McEnery, A. (2005) 'Two approaches to genre analysis', *Journal of English Linguistics*, 33: 1, pp. 62–82.

CHAPTER 6

Reading Twitter: Combining Qualitative and Quantitative Methods in the Interpretation of Twitter Material

Stefan Gelfgren

INTRODUCTION

This chapter will discuss the use of quantitative methods in relation to qualitative methods when reading, interpreting and analysing discussions emerging on Twitter. The main question is: what can you find and achieve by applying quantitative methods such as statistics and network analysis to a Twitter discussion, compared to not doing so? What is the added value of applying a more quantitative approach to the material? The answer might be fairly obvious to someone used to and skilled in digital methods and tools, but not necessarily for someone without a 'digital mindset'. I will argue that statistics and network visualisation are appropriate and complementary methods which generate new patterns and new interpretations of, in this case, a Twitter debate, but a similar approach can be applied to any other networked debate.

Twitter material provides an easy and straightforward example of how to understand and interpret a discussion with both quantitative and qualitative methods. While a qualitative reading focuses on the actual content of what is said in the debate and by whom, a quantitative approach adds the possibility of detecting and visualising the relations between the different actors and their individual impact and influence within the conversation – something that is difficult to detect with traditional, non-digital methods. This chapter focuses on the added value of using quantitative methods with the aid of digital tools for network analysis and visualisation.

I write this chapter in a rather personal tone, grounded in my experiences of coming from a traditional, hermeneutic discipline within the Humanities and moving into the field of digital humanities while trying to keep a foot in each camp. My home discipline is History of Science/History of Ideas, and my PhD (Gelfgren 2003) dealing with a nineteenth-century Swedish confessional revivalist movement is, in a British context for example, situated at the intersection between Church History and History. In short, the discipline is about hermeneutic contextualisation, about putting ideas and practices into a longitudinal and a latitudinal context. One main question is the relation between the ideas studied and previous intellectual and societal traditions, and how these ideas and practices relate to their contemporary context. The discipline is traditionally rather text-oriented, and computerised methods and digital tools are, generally speaking, scarce.

The cases dealt with here concern two Twitter debates: the first is a debate which took place during a live streamed event with a fairly controversial American televangelist and healer (Gelfgren 2013), and the other case deals with a discussion in relation to a fake archbishop's Twitter account (Gelfgren 2015). In both cases, network analysis and statistics provided new, additional interpretations and insights, which were useful in helping us understand the events. In both cases, I am interested in how social media (Twitter in these cases) are and can be tools for negotiating religious authority, an often highlighted theme within the field of what is called digital religion (Cheong and Ess 2012; Cheong 2012). The aim of the two articles I wrote about these cases was to see how power was negotiated and exercised in practice, and who the actors involved were. It was not an aim in itself at the beginning of the work, but the hypothesis that social media undermine established religious (as other) structures had to be qualified. One way of developing the discussion on social media and (for example religious) authority beyond rhetorical claims was to use quantitative methods, as will be discussed and illustrated below. These examples are quite minor and limited in their extent but serve to illustrate the use of a combination of research methods and tools.

TWITTER METHODS: AN OVERVIEW

In recent years, 'big data' (see Chapter 11 by Tobias Blanke and Andrew Prescott in this volume) have come to the fore. Through the easy access to huge amounts of data, with the possibility of combining different data sets, and the development of computational power and new software, it is now possible to carry out data-driven research that was not possible before. Nowadays it is, for example, easy to access user-created content through various forms of social media or metadata on large collections of books, music, archival material and so on. This gives researchers the possibility to analyse and interpret our individual and collective behaviour, and it is also possible, for example, to see patterns in, and to analyse large volumes of, text (see, for example, Liddle 2012; Manovich 2012; Moretti 2005).

Social media (and Twitter among those media) have, I would say, become an easy-to-access source of information for researchers trying, for example, to map discussions, patterns of people's behaviour and distributions of ideas through geography and networks. Tweets are rather easy to retrieve, store, visualise and in this way analyse on a large scale (if you know the methods and tools). Such work is primarily carried out within the social sciences. There are many examples of how specific phenomena or events are dealt with and interpreted through social media, for example crises such as school shootings, natural disasters and revolutions (see, for instance, Markham and Lindgren 2014 for an overview and introduction). Institutions such as the police and intelligence services use tweets and other content from social media for surveillance and to study undesirable behaviour on a large scale (Bauman and Lyon 2013).

The possibility of working with big data has raised a debate about the pros and cons of such methods, although in this specific chapter it is not possible to go into detail regarding this debate (Boyd and Crawford 2011; Kitchin 2013). Still, there are obvious advantages in combining methods to analyse 'big data' (Mayer-Schönberger and Cukier 2013) with 'small data' (Abreu and Acker 2013). For example, Markham and Lindgren (2014) criticise a rather positivistic approach to big data (and social network analysis in their particular case) and argue for a combination of the two strands, coming from a social sciences point of view. They claim that 'if we look closely at the component parts (elements of focal points) of a network analysis approach, we begin to notice sensibility that resonates strongly with the complexity of computer or internet-mediated, networked culture' (9). From their social scientists' perspective Markham and Lindgren argue for a more qualitative approach to data, while I argue from a humanist's perspective for a more quantitative approach. In the following text, through the two case studies chosen, the aim is to develop an argument for combining the two methodologies.

THE TELEVANGELIST DEBATE AND THE FAKE ARCHBISHOP: TWO CASES

The televangelist

During the spring of 2010 it became publicly known that the Swedish charismatic denomination Word of Life (*Livets Ord*) had invited the controversial American pastor Benny Hinn to their conference – controversial because of his theology, his way of dealing with finances, an alleged love story and dubious healings (whether he really is controversial or not is beyond the scope of my work).

Soon after this a discussion about whether or not it was appropriate to invite Hinn took off in the Christian press in related commentator fields, on Christian web portals, on blogs, Facebook and Twitter. Articles in the press were commented on by different people on the websites of the papers such as *Dagen* (2010a, 2010b, 2010c, [approx. *The Day*], associated with the Pentecostal movement) and *Världen idag* (2010a, 2010b, 2010c, [approx. *The World of Today*], associated with The World of Life). Hinn's invitation, and the actual event, was discussed and scrutinised from diverse angles – and both positive and negative comments were made. On one forum related to the Swedish secularist movement (*Forum för vetenskap och folkbildning* [approx. Forum for Research and Adult Education]), attention was drawn to this event, and one person asked the forum if anyone was willing to go to Uppsala to participate in the event. Hinn was going to attend the conference and the official Twitter hashtag was set to #ek10 (ek because of the name of the conference, Europakonferensen (Europe conference), and 10 because of the year 2010). On Twitter an unofficial hashtag, #hinn10, was established for the purpose of discussing Hinn and the event. Blogposts and tweets were posted prior to the event, but it was Hinn's meetings that really spurred the debate.

He held three meetings during the course of a weekend, one on Saturday evening and two on Sunday. During the first meeting, Hinn conducted a theological exploration, considered as rather doubtful in more 'orthodox' or traditional contexts. The main leader and founder of the Word of Life, Ulf Ekman, went on stage and asked people to ponder what had been said, and the following day Ekman also commented on the meeting through his blog and his video blog. So when the meetings started the day after, people sat prepared at home, by their computers, ready to scrutinise what was happening in Uppsala. Some people, both among the advocates and from the scrutinising side, so to speak, were on site, tweeting and blogging as well. People seemed curious and slightly critical. Nothing much happened during the morning meeting.

Later that evening, people were ready in front of the livestream again. The meeting started with some theological teaching and preaching, but after about one and a half hours the meeting turned into a healing session. Hinn started to call people on stage and healed them from different diseases and disorders – people were healed from illness, crutches were left on stage and prophesies were delivered. Most of the tweets were written in a sceptical and openly critical tone about what they saw, and the positive voices were scarce, even though some praised Hinn and Jesus Almighty for what was happening. All this was commented on by the viewers. Some theologians, an illusionist, a couple of journalists, a former Word of Life adherent and some sceptics/secularists, among others, were online watching and commenting on the livestreamed event. In the tweets there were links to sources online in order to strengthen arguments and reference different perspectives. After about an hour and a half, more people from the secularist movement appeared. By the end of the event, the hashtags #hinn10 and #ek10 trended on Twitter and even more people started to stumble on the livestream, often expressing their surprise and some dismay over what they saw taking place on stage. After two and a half hours the meeting ended, Ulf Ekman went on stage, thanked Hinn and said, among other things, that so much had happened that not even the social media could keep up.

The Twitter archive from this event, retrieved through a web-based service for archiving tweets called *twapperkeeper.com*, comprises 757 tweets (missing out the first meeting) from 133 different Twitter users, using the 'hinn10'-tag. The top 10 twitterers (7 per cent) accounted for 65 per cent of the tweets. In addition, there was other online material such as blogposts, news articles and online comments on blogs and articles.

The Archbishop

During the London Olympic Games in the summer of 2012, the Archbishop of the Church of Sweden (the former state church, disestablished in 2000) suddenly appeared on Twitter with his own Twitter account. Instantly, he had an increasing group of followers who welcomed him and applauded his recent social media engagement. The positive responses applauded his initiative, honoured its symbolic value and thereby hoped for a new and more dialectical approach from the Church to the people. The Archbishop tweeted in a rather humorous, tongue-in-cheek style, but also wrote about, for example, Swedish athletics and the need for the Church to communicate. There was one problem, however – noticed by the Church's national Department of Communication – it was not the Archbishop himself who was tweeting. It was someone else, seen to be a fraud against whom the Department took countermeasures. The Department made an appeal to Twitter Inc. and got the account closed down just a few days after it opened. Subsequently, a debate took place on Twitter over the course of a few weeks under the rather humorous hashtag #biskopsriot (humorous since one can hardly describe it as a riot). People debated whether or not it was right and appropriate to close down the account and that the Church was now showing its true hierarchical face. People discussed who the imposter was, how the Church could benefit from a more dialogic approach to the people compared to its usual communicative style, and so on. Some people considered the initiative, even though a fake, to be something positive, while some saw it as a violation of the Archbishop's personal integrity. The discussion also took place mainly in blogs (see, for example, Scharffenberg 2012; Sunnliden 2012; Varg Thunberg 2012) and within the Christian press (for example, *Dagen* 2012; *Kyrkans tidning* 2012). One person claimed the Church was not ready for the new paradigm, and the contemporary conditions which the Church has to live under. How the whole Twitter affair was dealt with proved the Church to be badly equipped to face the reality that people want relations and dialogue rather than one official and monologic voice from the institution.

Some weeks after the initial tweet, the 'fake' archbishop revealed his identity. He was an information officer working locally in a diocese, who, on his own initiative, wished to encourage the real Archbishop to tweet and to be more active on social media. He wanted to hand over the account to the Archbishop at a ceremony a little later, as did in fact occur. The discussion spurred different opinions, but there was definitely a bias toward a critical approach to the Church, its attitude to the social media and how it handled the whole discourse surrounding the Twitter account.

The Twitter archives contain 190 tweets from the fake archbishop's account gathered directly from Twitter, approximately 700 tweets related to his account and about 800 tweets related to the hashtag #biskopsriot, archived through the aforementioned *tweetarchivist.com* service. The top 20 Twitterers posted 74 per cent of the tweets and the top Twitterer alone posted 22 per cent of the tweets – the person behind the archbishop's account. I also used blog posts, news articles, online comments on blogs and articles, and I conducted two interviews with the two main proponents in the discussion.

Common denominators in the two cases

Both cases can be seen as part of a negotiating process over power within the Church in relation to the use of social media and the distribution of power in this. In both cases, the ongoing discussions on Twitter referred to here had a clear tendency to a negative approach to the institutions discussed – both toward the Word of Life and the Church of Sweden. The Word of Life was criticised for the decision to invite Hinn, and Hinn was studied, scrutinised and criticised through the live stream provided by the Word of Life. By giving access to a previously closed arrangement, the event was given distribution and opened up the discussion about Hinn. The activities, including worship, preaching and healing, became public. Not many in the Twitter feed defended what took place there during the actual event and the official voice of the Word of Life was almost completely absent. The leadership replied through their own social media channels and through blogposts and papers, without entering into the debate.

In the example of the fake archbishop and how it was handled on Twitter, one also gets the impression that there was a strong bias against the Church of Sweden, since most twitterers reacted against what were seen as established structures. There was a strong unitary voice arguing for a better, more intense use of social media within the Church and among its representatives. Among the top layer of twitterers were three people with positions in the Church's central office; these were among the few who actually defended the stance of the Church against the majority of twitterers. But, since the active defenders were mainly appointed by the official church, one gets the feeling that the question about the tweeting archbishop was really one of the relationship between the establishment and the people.

In both cases, the established institutional interpretive prerogative was challenged through a multitude of voices given space in online discussions. People were talking to each other, scrutinising and challenging the power of the institutions from a variety of perspectives and positions. This was also in line with how the social media are interpreted as a means for transforming power in a democratising way – seen on a large scale, for example, when talking about the so-called Arab Spring as a 'Twitter revolution' (Howard and Hussain 2011). That is the impression one might get from following the discussions on Twitter, reading it as a text with tweets from different, equal actors. In similar ways as the 'Twitter revolution' has been questioned (Christensen 2011; Lindgren 2013), one might question the idea of a transformation or a democratising participation in public debates in relation to the two cases I deal with here. It is in the context of this question that one can productively contrast a qualitative reading of the tweets with a more quantitative reading.

MATERIAL AND METHOD

The empirical material for the archbishop case (Gelfgren 2015) contains, as mentioned above, approximately 200 tweets posted from the archbishop's account and 700 tweets in total in relation to his account. These tweets were retrieved through the Twitter feed related to that particular account. It is, therefore, a little messy since it is difficult to get all the tweets structured in an orderly way, and also difficult to know if this encompasses the complete list of tweets. In addition, there is an archive containing about 800 tweets related to the #biskopsriot hashtag, which were retrieved through using a web-based service called *tweetarchivist.com*, at the cost of a few dollars per archive. Through *tweetarchivist.com* you get all the tweets listed in an Excel spreadsheet with separate columns for sender, time and date, and the actual content of the tweet in one column with receiver, mentions, tweet text and possible links included. My research material also included twenty blog posts, thirty online newspaper articles (with comments) and two interviews – one with the fake bishop and one with the Program Director for National Communication at the Church of Sweden.

When it comes to the Benny Hinn case (Gelfgren 2013), the material comprises 757 tweets related to the #hinn10 hashtag and some thirty blog posts and newspaper articles with comments. The tweets were compiled in an Excel spreadsheet archive through the *twapperkeeper.com* service. I used two different services, *twapperkeeper.com* and *tweetarchivist.com*, to compile the archives, but tweets can be harvested in other ways, depending on the tools available, one's own competence and so on. The tools available change over time, often depending on regulations imposed by Twitter, for example in 2015 *twapperkeeper* is no longer in use (it closed down in January 2012) but the *tweetarchivist* is. At the time of these studies, it was not possible to retrieve tweets older than about a week, so when there was an ongoing event that you wished to create an archive from, you had to be alert. This has changed as well. Today there are other possibilities, but there are also other regulations, and these are likely to change in the future. But as long you find tools and methods to collect, access and create an archive, you will be able to do what is described in the following. This is just one example of a method.

The tweets are first read qualitatively/hermeneutically as a text with different individual and related replies. Apart from being aware of the actual content, you also get a sense of who is involved, who is speaking to whom and the intensity of the different Twitterers. But it is almost impossible, or at least really difficult, to measure factors such as possible sub-networks and the impact of individual Twitter users with qualitative methods. Therefore, it is important to complement the qualitative reading with a quantitative approach in order to obtain a fuller picture.

In the case of the tweets related to the archbishop's account, I only had the tweets as presented in the Twitter account, and I downloaded the page as a web page-file while I knew it was publically available – a method not really recommended but which was available to me at that time. Such a download makes the archive quite messy, with no stringent and coherent order in the relation between tweets, replies and re-tweets. Therefore, the archbishop's account cannot be used, for example, for a network analysis, but only for a qualitative content analysis based on text.

For the network analysis, I used a tool called *Textometrica* (Lindgren and Palm 2011), freely available at <http://textometrica.humlab.umu.se>.[1] I used it for both the archbishop and the televangelist case. *Textometrica* has been developed for text analysis to detect and show co-occurrences within text blocks. It had not been previously used for Twitter network analysis, but I found it useful for that purpose, since I was interested in how and to what extent twitterers interact with each other – in other words to what degree senders of tweets mention other twitterers as receivers or as re-tweets (how they co-occurred within the tweets).

However, first I used a rather simple statistical approach, making lists and counting each person's frequency of tweeting (automatically done by the *Tweetarchivist*). The top twenty twitterers on #biskopsriot posted 74 per cent of all the tweets while 22 per cent (one-fifth or, more precisely, 178 tweets) was posted by the one person behind the fake account. The seven next most active twitterers posted between twenty and forty-two times. Then I wanted to see who the twitterers were. Among the top twenty, there were fifteen people who in their biography described themselves as having a professional interest in communication and ICT, thirteen who worked with communication within the Church of Sweden, of which three worked for the Archbishop's Office (those who defended the stance taken by the Church). Only three of the top twenty twitterers were members of the clergy, but of these one was also an active and well-established twitterer within the community as well as a satirist and artist. In other words, very few in the discussion represented the established hierarchical structure of the Church. Two people, as far as can be gleaned from the Twitter biographies, could be labelled as 'ordinary people' – meaning that they did not work within the Church or in communications. If we consider the active accounts in relation to the archbishop's account, a similar pattern emerges. Those active in the discussion were mainly people working within the Church or who had a specific interest concerning communication. Only a few theologians or clerics were involved in the discussion regarding the importance of the tweeting archbishop and the need for a more communicative, social media-active Church.

When turning to *Textometrica* for a network analysis, other aspects of the discussion became visible. The aim in using *Textometrica* was to detect how the different actors interacted ad how they related to each other, and also to measure, or at least to get an indication of, how influential they were in the discussion. *Textometrica* shows how different words co-occur with each other – and in one tweet, with a sender, how the sender co-occurs with, for example, the receiver, mentions and re-tweeted senders. In that way, you know whether senders co-occur with other accounts. In order to differentiate between senders, receivers/mentions and re-tweets I added the suffix s_ to senders, nothing to receivers/mentions and rt_ to the re-tweeted senders.

This made it possible to see to what extent someone sent tweets addressing another specific account. If, for example, one person sends many tweets addressing others, but is rarely mentioned by others, one might assume that this account is a fairly weak node in the network. But, if someone is mentioned and re-tweeted to a high degree, one can talk about that particular node as influential in the network. Someone with a large number of tweets that are never mentioned or re-tweeted is someone who might be listened to but not considered worth re-tweeting or being answered.

In the analysis process, someone who tweets frequently and then mentions others (since *Textometrica* is about co-occurrences) is given larger dots (see Figure 6.1 here and Figure 6.4 below), but this does not say much about their influence. Someone who is mentioned but never responds also shows up as a node. For example, accounts such as Benny Hinn, Ulf Ekman and even God are mentioned through receiving tweets, under the #hinn10 tag, but they never respond.

As shown in Figure 6.1 based on the #hinn10 tag, the whole cluster was centred on a few central twitterers who, in other words, were influential within the network. Most other twitterers were, as shown, distributed as nodes around the central core, indicating their rather low level of influence and activity. What is also noticeable is a few smaller clusters 'floating' around on the outskirts of the centre, indicating that these accounts mainly communicated with each other on Twitter.

Textometrica creates the visualisation itself (which was used for the #hinn10 case). The program also creates a .net file which in its turn can be visualised in another program. For the #biskopsriot case, I used quite a simple online visualisation tool called *MapEquation*, freely available at www. mapequation.org, to visualise the different networks (see Figures 6.2 and 6.3). There is more elaborate software for adjusting and modifying visualisations such as *Cytoscape*, *Gephi* or *Pajek*. In my case *MapEquation* was good enough – and, not least, easy to use. The size of the nodes indicates the frequency of the activities and the thickness of the lines between the nodes indicates the strength of the links between the nodes. That is large dots indicate high levels of activity (tweets, mentions and re-tweets) and thick lines indicate high levels of co-occurrences.

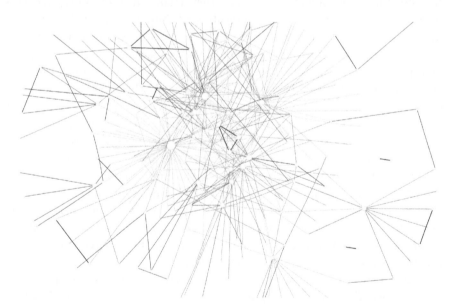

Figure 6.1 The #hinn10 network visualised and anonymised in Textometrica
(Source: The author)

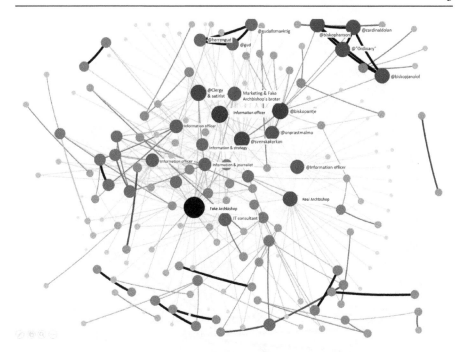

Figure 6.2 The network with merged categories, visualised with MapEquation
(Source: The author)

In Figure 6.2 about #biskopsriot, the different categories of tweets are merged together so that if someone appears frequently – senders, with mentions, or re-tweets – the node is visualised as larger and hence appears to be more active, but this does not say much about influence. The top twitterer, and the one behind the archbishop's account, appears of course as the largest node.

Among the central accounts, we find individuals working on the archbishop's staff. We see some active accounts that do not appear in the statistics, and that are, for example, a few accounts owned by other regional bishops, which seem to be really active. It also seems as if God is an active twitterer (with a few different accounts), but if we assume God does not tweet Himself, we understand that this diagram does not show us an accurate picture of the situation – God is in this case a mere recipient of tweets or is mentioned in tweets. Therefore it is relevant to differentiate the categories of tweets in order to be able to make a comparison.

If one compares the first network diagram (Figure 6.2) with a diagram where the different categories of tweets are separated (Figure 6.3), a different picture appears. For example, the person behind the fake archbishop is a large node in all categories and so are the people working for the real archbishop – even though they have larger receiving nodes than their sender categories. The two largest 'sender nodes' were related to the main individuals in this debate – one

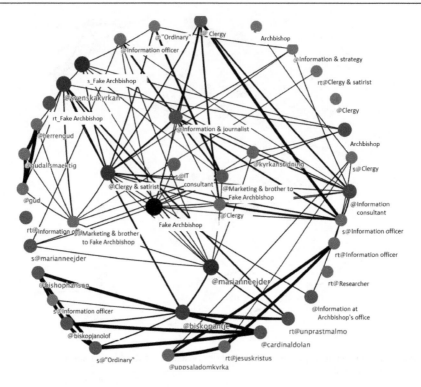

Figure 6.3 The network with separated categories, visualised with MapEquation
(Source: The author)

was the person behind the fake archbishop and the other was the Head of
Communication of the Church of Sweden. The different bishop accounts do
not show up at all as senders but as fairly large nodes in the receiver category;
official representatives of the Church of Sweden received tweets but did not
send, and the same was true for the journal of the Church of Sweden and for
the different God accounts. Twitterers address, for example, the bishops, but
the latter are not active in the discussion. The other active Twitterers show up
as different nodes of different sizes. Some accounts have significantly larger
mention nodes than senders, and the reverse is also true. Through comparing
the different categories of tweets one gets a sense of how active, and in what
ways, different actors in the Twitter discussion are.

CONCLUSIONS FROM THE QUANTITATIVE MATERIAL

The question is how and to what extent do a quantitative reading and the
visualisation of the material benefit the interpretation of Twitter discussions?
Can one not read and interpret the conversations just as texts? The answer

is, yes and no. Of course, it is possible to read and acquire an understanding of the discussions based on a qualitative reading of the tweets, but then a few important things are probably missed out. Statistics show, for example, in the archbishop case that the discussion was kept alive and going by a fairly small number of people, even though the total group of people contributing to the discussion was considerably larger. From the statistical material, I went to the Twitter biographies in order to see who the most active twitterers were, and there it was obvious how this discussion (on Twitter) engaged mainly people with a profession closely related to communications, information technology and the Church. That does not come as a complete surprise, but when people in the Twitter discussion refer to what was going on on Twitter as proof that it is important for the Church to be online, they are talking to the already converted (to use religious terminology). It was clear that it was mainly people working with questions related to communication who thought that the Church should communicate to a greater extent through social media. This raises questions about the negotiation of power within the Church, between the established hierarchies and the communication departments. The statistics illustrated that the people who thought Twitter and social media are important were already working with these media channels (compare with Hindman, 2008). Twitter is, in that sense, a small pond where the already initiated, the big fishes, see and emphasise the importance of the tool.

The false 'archbishop' had the outspoken aim to spin the web and encourage the Church to have a more elaborate web presence when he started up and activated the account. In the discussion, it was also apparent how people viewed the contemporary societal situation as a paradigmatic turning point. One of the participants in #biskopsriot claimed that 'it is a paradigm shift we are seeing', and another said 'it is a revolution!' – and that was meant to be something positive, as long as the Church was ready for this situation, which allegedly it was not.

In a similar way, we see in the #hinn10 case how the discussion was rather one-sided, although there were many different actors with different experiences and opinions. There were, however, very few comments in favour of Benny Hinn or *Livets Ord*, and almost none from any of the officials. It is, however, noteworthy, and visible in the visualisation of the network, how the secularists formed a kind of a sub-network centred on one of their 'own' twitterers among the top ten. Almost all traffic in the conversation from the secularists went through, and was related to, that particular person. If we read the tweets in chronological order as text, at first glance we are inclined to think that the secularists were involved in the general discussion and interacting in the same way as everybody else. However, the visualised network shows that this was not the case (see Figure 6.4).

The #hinn10 network is what can be called a centralised network (for

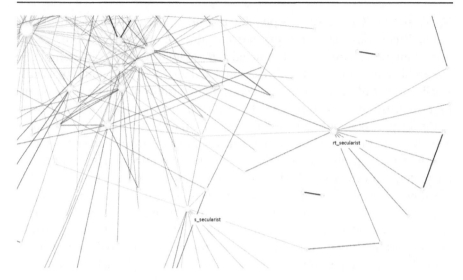

Figure 6.4 The #hinn10 network visualised with Textometrica, with the secularist sub-network in focus, sender and receiver nodes
(Source: The author)

networks see Barabási 2003). In other words it was closely linked to a core of actors. At the core, with a high degree of impact, were two journalists, which is interesting when talking about the relation between offline and online authority. Authority online is often intertwined with authority offline (see, for example, Cheong 2012; Hindman 2008). *Twirus.com* shows and visualises trends on Twitter, and there both #hinn10 and #ek10 trended, while the two most influential Twitter users that weekend were the two journalists who are well known within the Swedish Christian press. One of them initiated the unofficial #hinn10-tag and the other (also an active social media proponent) was on site live-tweeting and blogging.

In both cases, we see how the core of the networks, literally, and hence the most active and influential actors, consisted of people working with the media and who were skilled at writing and using social media to get their ideas out. They also had a significant group of followers who could and wanted to share their ideas and messages. It is often claimed that social media undermine and negotiate established and traditional structures (for the field of digital religion, see for example Campbell 2010; Cheong and Ess 2012; Cheong 2012), but these cases suggest that such un-nuanced claims have to be balanced. We see, indeed, how voices other than the official voices from within the established structures are heard, but on the other hand, these voices that we hear have a platform from which they can work (Campbell 2010). There are journalists and information officers already working within the Christian sphere who are still the most influential participants in the networks, neatly visualised through the network diagrams. Other voices are by comparison on the outskirts of the networks and the discussion. The ability to know and therefore to be able to spin the web and to have an established audience is of course of great importance when it comes to social media and Twitter.

CONCLUSION

There are several different aspects that are highlighted and made visual through the use of quantitative methods and network visualisation which are rather difficult to detect using qualitative methods alone. The most productive research combines the two different methods – to obtain an overview and context with quantitative methods, and the actual content through a qualitative reading of (in this case) the tweets.

Through counting tweets, the number of actors and the activity of each twitterer one gets a sense of what the network might look like. But through the use of, in this case, the co-occurrence software *Textometrica*, one also gets a sense of and can measure the importance and the impact of each individual twitterer. Through differentiating between senders, receivers and re-tweets, one can see what the pattern looks like in the different categories. Someone who is an active sender without receiving tweets is someone who tweets without an audience. And, according to the same Twitter-logic, someone who is re-tweeted is someone who is distributing his/her ideas and messages beyond his/her own group of followers. This understanding results from a comparison of the different diagrams.

After the core twitterers are identified, one can continue to examine the role and interest of each of these to see who is tweeting and, in the light of the identity of the actors, one can say something about their viewpoint. It is also possible to see the absence of certain groups – if you are familiar with, and have a qualitative understanding of, the discussion. In the cases discussed in this chapter the official voices from the Church of Sweden and Word of Life were to a large degree absent. This was also the case for other actors in defence of each institution. One can consider the formation of the core of the networks, and consequently whether there are any sub-networks. In the #hinn10 case, it became obvious that one group of twitterers formed their own group, centred on one person who in his turn was among the core twitterers.

A large number of the twitterers, especially in the #hinn10 case only popped into the discussion because the tag trended; they then asked what it was all about, maybe saw the live stream and tweeted something without addressing anyone. This group does not show up in the co-occurrence diagrams but in the list of tweets, which is another reason for reading the tweets quantitatively. However, in order to interpret the nuances of all this, one has to have an understanding of the cases as a whole, an understanding of the details and also the content of the tweets. Otherwise one only has figures. The interesting part is therefore to move between qualitative and quantitative interpretations. And that is the real strength of such a dualist methodological approach.

NOTE

1. The software was developed at HUMlab, Umeå University, by Simon Lindgren, Professor in Sociology, and Fredrik Palm, Research and Development Coordinator at HUMlab.

REFERENCES

Abreu, A. and Acker, A. (2013) 'Context and collection: a research agenda for small data', in *iConference 2013 Proceedings*, Fort Worth, TX, 12–15 February, pp. 549–54.

Barabási, A.-L. (2003) *Linked: How Everything is Connected to Everything Else and What It Means for Business, Science, and Everyday Life*. New York: Plume.

Bauman, Z. and Lyon, D. (2013) *Liquid Surveillance: A Conversation*. Cambridge: Polity Press.

Boyd, D. and Crawford, K. (2011) *Six Provocations for Big Data* (SSRN Scholarly Paper No. ID 1926431). Rochester, NY: Social Science Research Network, at <http://papers.ssrn.com/abstract=1926431> (last accessed 29 May 2015).

Campbell, H. A. (2010) 'Religious authority and the blogosphere', *Journal of Computer-Mediated Communication*, 15: 2, pp. 251–76.

Cheong, P. H. (2012) 'Authority', in *Digital Religion: Understanding Religious Practice in New Media Worlds*. New York: Routledge, pp. 72–87.

Cheong, P. H. and Ess, C. (2012) 'Introduction: religion 2.0? Relational and hybridizing pathways in religion, social media, and culture', in P. H. Cheong, P. Fischer-Nielsen, S. Gelfgren and C. Ess (eds), *Digital Religion, Social Media and Culture: Perspectives Practices and Futures*. New York: Peter Lang, pp. 1–21.

Christensen, C. (2011) 'Twitter revolutions? Addressing social media and dissent', *Communication Review*, 14: 3, pp. 155–7.

Dagen (2010a) 'Benny Hinns mirakel är svåra att bevisa . . . och Ulf Ekman vill inte försvara hans lyxliv' ['Benny Hinn's miracles are difficult to prove . . . and Ulf Ekman does not want to defend his luxurious life'], 22 July, at <http://www.dagen.se/dagen/article.aspx?id=219648> (last accessed 2 December 2011).

Dagen (2010b) 'En irrlärare på Livets ord' ['A heretic at Livets Ord'], 28 July, at <http://www.dagen.se/dagen/article.aspx?id=220211> (last accessed 2 December 2011).

Dagen (2010c) 'Sjöberg: Hinn är ledsen över sina uttalanden' ['Sjöberg: Hinn is sorry about his statements'], 29 July, at <http://www.dagen.se/dagen/article.aspx?id=220452> (last accessed 2 December 2011).

Dagen (2012) 'Anders Wejryds namn "kidnappat" på Twitter' ['Anders Wejryd's name "kidnapped" on Twitter'], 14 August, at <http://www.dagen.se/anders-wejryds-namn-kidnappat-p%C3%A5-twitter-1.117395> (last accessed 29 May 2015).

Forum för vetenskap och folkbildning (2010) Forum thread 'Europakonferensen 2010' – Forum för vetenskap och folkbildning, 20 July – 14 September, at <http://www.vof.se/forum/viewtopic.php?f=38&t=13051> (last accessed 2 December 2011).

Gelfgren, S. (2003) *Ett utvalt släkte: väckelse och sekularisering: Evangeliska fosterlands-stiftelsen 1856–1910. [A Choosen People: Revivalism and Secularisation – Evangelsiska Fosterlands-Stiftelsen 1856–1910]*. Skellefteå: Norma.

Gelfgren, S. (2013) 'A healer and televangelist reaching out to the secular Swedish public sphere', *Temenos*, 49: 1, pp. 83–110.

Gelfgren, S. (2015) 'Why does the Archbishop not tweet? How social media challenge church authorities', *Nordicom Review*, 36: 1, pp. 109–23.

Hindman, M. (2008) *The Myth of Digital Democracy*. Princeton: Princeton University Press.

Howard, P. N. and Hussain, M. M. (2011) 'The role of digital media', *Journal of Democracy*, 22: 3, 35–48.

Kitchin, R. (2013) 'Big data and human geography: opportunities, challenges and risks', *Dialogues in Human Geography*, 3: 3, 262–7.

Kyrkans tidning (2012-07-31) 'Kyrkokansliet reagerar på falsk Wejryd' [Church of Sweden's secretariat reacts against fake Wejryd], 31 July, at <http://www.kyrkanstidning.se/inrikes/kyrkokansliet-reagerar-pa-falsk-wejryd> (last accessed 29 May 2015).

Liddle, D. (2012) 'Reflections on 20,000 Victorian newspapers: "Distant reading" *The Times* using The Times Digital Archive', *Journal of Victorian Culture*, 17: 2, pp. 230–7.

Lindgren, S. (2013) 'The potential and limitations of Twitter activism: mapping the 2011 Libyan uprising', *tripleC: Communication, Capitalism and Critique. Open Access Journal for a Global Sustainable Information Society*, 11: 1, pp. 207–20.

Lindgren, S. and Palm, F. (2011) *Textometrica Service Package*. At <http://textometrica.humlab.umu.se/> (last accessed 29 May 2012).

Manovich, L. (2012) 'Trending: the promises and the challenges of big social data', in M. K. Gold (ed.), *Debates in the Digital Humanities*. Minnesota: University of Minnesota Press, pp. 460–75.

Markham, A. and Lindgren, S. (2014) 'From object to flow: network sensibility, symbolic interactionism, and social media', in M. D. Johns, Shing-Ling S. Chen and L. A. Terlip (eds), *Symbolic Interaction and New Social Media*. Bingley: Emerald Group, pp. 7–42.

Mayer-Schönberger, V. and Cukier, K. (2013) *Big Data: A Revolution That Will Transform How We Live, Work, and Think*. New York: Houghton Mifflin Harcourt.

Moretti, F. (2005) *Graphs, Maps, Trees: Abstract Models for a Literary History*. London: Verso.

Scharffenberg, M. (2012) 'Kyrkan överreagerar?' ['Is the Church overreacting?'], 31 July, at <http://wien.scharffenberg.eu/kyrkan-overreagerar> (last accessed 29 May 2015).

Sunnliden, J. (2012) 'Jag kommer ut! #biskopsriot' ['I am coming out! #biskopsriot'], 16 August, at <http://sunnliden.se/?p=2958> (last accessed 29 May 2015).

Varg Thunberg, S. (2012) 'Kyrkan behöver förnyas II' ['The Church needs to be renewed'], 21 August, at <http://samuelvargthunberg.se/2012/08/21/kyrkan-behover-fornyas-ii-om-jacobsunnliden-och-sociala-medier> (last accessed 29 May 2015.

Världen idag (2010a) 'Ulf Ekman kritisk till Benny Hinns predikan' ['Ulf Ekman critical about Benny Hinn's preaching'], 26 July, at <http://www.varldenidag.se/nyhet/2010/07/26/Ulf-Ekman-kritisk-till-Benny-Hinns-predikan> (last accessed 2 December 2011).

Världen idag (2010b) 'Teologisk analys efterlyses' ['A theological analysis is wanted'], 28 July, at <http://www.varldenidag.se/blogg/2010/07/28/Teologisk-analys-efterlyses> (last accessed 2 December 2011).

Världen idag (2010c) 'Benny Hinn inser felformulering' ['Benny Hinn realizes his miswording'], 29 July, at <http://www.varldenidag.se/nyhet/2010/07/29/Benny-Hinn-inser-felformulering> (last accessed 2 December 2011).

Chapter 7

Reading Small Data in Indigenous Contexts: Ethical Perspectives

Coppélie Cocq

INTRODUCTION

This chapter is concerned with reading digital data from an ethical point of view by focusing on the use of online media in communities with few individuals. It describes and discusses the research process from the selection and collection of data to participant involvement and dissemination of the results, based on a study of the use of hashtags[1] by Sámi speakers[2] on Twitter[3] conducted in 2013. The methodological questions raised in the process include ethical considerations when working with online communities that overlap with identified local groups. The entwining of online and offline networks requires a research approach that can capture the dynamism and specificity of network building by geographically localised communities in an ethically appropriate manner.

This discussion brings together two strains of ethical debate: one from indigenous research and the other from Internet research. In both cases, concepts and approaches from ethnography can be applied in order to find an ethically adequate mode of conducting research using online data. With a background in folklore studies, a sub-field of ethnology in Sweden, and Sámi studies, I have worked with qualitative data such as ethnographic fieldwork notes, archives, printed and oral sources, and interviews. Ethical aspects are an integral part of my research, from source criticism (Cocq 2010) and positionality in research (Cocq 2008, 2014) to critical perspectives on the field of Sámi studies (Cocq 2013, 2015b). Over the last few years, my research focus has shifted to digital modes of expression and the use of the Internet and digital technologies for knowledge production. This present chapter finds its source in a study of social media use by linguistic communities where I had to reflect upon my role and position as a digital ethnographer.

The study in point (Cocq 2015a) investigated the advantages and limits of social media by examining collective hashtags created by Sámi users on Twitter that enhance the Sámi languages. It was part of a larger project that examines modes of knowledge production in a contemporary context. The ten Sámi languages are today endangered and Sweden has been repeatedly criticised by the European Council for the lack of implementation of the European Charter for Regional or Minority Languages; resources in terms of teaching materials and trained teachers are insufficient. In this context, folk initiatives contrast with institutional shortcomings, and efforts of language and cultural revitalisation are taking place in several areas (Magga and Skutnabb-Kangas 2001; Scheller and Vinka forthcoming), including digital media.

ETHICAL CHALLENGES IN SÁMI RESEARCH AND DIGITAL HUMANITIES

Sámi research is an interdisciplinary field and an established research area at a few universities in Norway, Sweden and Finland. In an international context, it is closely connected to research fields known as indigenous studies, native studies and minority studies. One of the aims of the field is to settle accounts with a heritage of colonial ideologies (Cocq 2015a), and today it is oriented toward decolonising methodologies and community-based research. From this perspective, the role and position of the researcher is an aspect under constant investigation.

In the contemporary Scandinavian academic context, discourses about ethical matters in relation to indigenous research have gained more and more attention over the last few decades. Many Sámi scholars that scrutinise the status of indigenous research in a Scandinavian context have suggested the need for better methods in the documentation of traditional knowledge (cf. Nordin-Jonsson 2010), the need for community influence and participation (cf. Porsanger 2004) and the need for improved relationships between academics and Sámi communities (Kuokkanen 2000, 2008).[4] These insights underscore the need to problematise and recontextualise Sámi research, the importance of ethical sensitivity and the relevance of scholarly works for the communities. This development follows an international discussion where indigenous perspectives take the lead in shaping the contemporary research landscape and raise standards in requirements for collaboration, dialogue and restitution (cf. Kovach 2009; Mihesuah 1998; Smith 1999). In addition, discussions within the field emphasise the implications of a lack of adequate formal ethical guidelines in the humanities in general and for Sámi research in particular.

The development toward increased participation of indigenous people in research follows various patterns and paces that differ not only between countries and geographical areas, but also between disciplines. For instance, in cultural anthropology – a field that has had to deal with and process a heritage of colonisation and ethnocentrism (Christophe et al. 2009) and must examine its sometimes questionable work in the past – much attention is paid to codes of ethics (e.g. AAA Committee on Ethics,[5] AFS Statement on Ethics[6]). Since the late 1900s, the concept of reflexivity (Babcock 1980; Ehn and Klein 1994) – the researcher's self-consciousness in relation to the focus of research and his or her implication in the process as part of what is being observed and studied – has been a matter of course when discussing the role of the researcher and consequently the role of the 'other' in a research process. Contemporary approaches in anthropology take an insider's view and use field methods with a focus on participation and relationships with participants (Geertz 1973; Hannerz 1992; Ortner 2006).

From a different angle, the role and position of the researcher has been discussed in Internet research. A discussion about research ethics is also of immediate importance for scholars reading digital data and conducting fieldwork in digital environments. A blurred distinction between the notions of private and public, along with an alleged inadequacy of established methods such as participant observation, call for a readjustment of traditional approaches. Also, humanities scholars in Internet research have to deal with and take into account the ethical questions implied by an increased access to data (for instance, Hudson and Bruckman 2004; Ikonomidis Svedmark and Nyberg 2009). In relation to Sámi studies, this brings to the fore questions of ownership, anonymity, confidentiality and restitution when reading small data.

The range of ethical issues that scholars meet can vary depending on their approach to the Internet as 'a social phenomenon, a tool, and also a (field) site for research' (Markham and Buchanan 2012: 3). These three aspects are often intertwined, and each of them entails a set of ethical problems that needs to be addressed in relation to the research questions while taking into account the participants. Principles identified as fundamental to an ethical approach to Internet research include the obligation of the researcher to minimise harm to the community and the participants, the application of practical judgement that is attentive to the specific context (phronesis), the need to consider principles related to research on individuals because 'all digital information at some point involves individual persons' and the need to balance the rights of subjects (as authors, as research participants, and as people) with the social benefits of research and the researchers' rights to conduct research (Markham and Buchanan 2012: 4–5). Rather than considering ethics primarily as regulations, an approach based on these principles advocates a mode of conduct that considers ethics to be based on decision-making processes (for instance, Ess

2013). This chapter examines such ethical issues applied to digital data from a geographically localised indigenous community.

SMALL DATA, HYBRID NETWORKS AND ENDANGERED LANGUAGES

This present chapter was developed out of a study about the use of hashtags on Twitter. Hashtags, labels marked with the hash character (#), are a type of folksonomy, i.e. categories created by users in order to organise web content, for instance in social media such as Instagram, Twitter, Flickr, BibSonomy, Delicious, etc. Hashtags function as keywords, and they are a way to filter, categorise, organise and share. These emic categorisations give us an angle of approach to alternative voices compared to traditional media, and this has been highlighted in previous research (see, for instance, Bronner 2009; Jung 2011; Lin and Chen 2012; Mika 2007). Unlike hierarchical and exclusionary taxonomic systems, folksonomy is a 'bottom-up classification of resources by users and is a result of using personal tagging to form a data structure' (Nair and Dua 2012: 310).

In my study, the hashtags emerged from initiatives by Twitter users with a common interest in learning, teaching or promoting Sámi languages. The data consisted of tweets tagged with #gollegiella, #sámegiella and #åarjel[7] collected during a three-month period.[8] These hashtags were selected after a period of coverage of tweets using Sámi keywords and were identified as the most used hashtags in this context. A total of 109 tweets by 41 different authors tagged with one or more of the hashtags were archived.[9] Conversations, i.e. 'replies' to tweets, were included in the corpus, whereas messages 're-tweeted' without comments were excluded.[10] This provided us with a corpus of short messages that reflected the multi-lingualism of the Sámi area.

The digital data collected based on hashtags give us insight into processes of cultural expression and knowledge production and are a valuable source of information about topics of importance from an emic perspective. The Internet is a global phenomenon in many aspects, and it is therefore important to investigate how practices specific to a group come to be expressed. In the case of Sámi folksonomy on Twitter, these include language use, modes of communication and network and social aspects. Folksonomies illustrate the empowering potential of Twitter for the continuity of cultural practices and vernacular expressions, and participatory media open new modes of knowledge production for indigenous people in terms of mediation.

The case study that was the basis for this chapter also gave indications of the use of languages and of networking practices for ethnolinguistic identification. Ethnolinguistic identity is a key for building or reinforcing a language community (Giles and Johnson 1987; Tafjel and Turner 1979; Vincze and Moring 2013), and it is a reason for affiliating with a group through a hashtag. Such social media practices create and maintain networks that, in turn, contribute to strengthening group identity. The relationship between practices illustrated by the digital data and identity issues enhances the necessity to take into consideration ethical aspects when reading small data. Concerns to be specifically addressed include questions of the accessibility of the data, the nature of privacy, informed consent, dissemination and restitution.

ETHICAL CHOICES

A message or a post on a social media site is often not just a line of text; it can be a contribution to a conversation or a debate, it can be aimed at a specific reader or a specific audience, or it can be written with the ambition of going viral. We can assume that in most cases messages on Twitter are not written and published with the intention to produce research data for scholars.

The researcher's role and degree of participation is related to his or her position in the context of the study, in this case as part of the audience on Twitter. Because following an account on Twitter is not a mutual engagement, the audience can be described as visible, inferred or abstruse (Cocq 2015a). A participatory audience consists of followers who are a visible part of the network and can interact with the author of a tweet, whereas an inferred audience is addressed through hashtags and is not necessarily known by the author of a tweet. More distant from the author is an indistinct abstruse audience, an unknown readership whose presence is allowed by the publicity of the posts on Twitter. In the case of the study discussed in this chapter, I was in some instances part of the participatory audience, in other cases part of the inferred audience and sometimes part of the abstruse audience. Online social networks tend to replicate offline social networks (Ellison et al. 2007; Kirschenblatt-Gimblett 1996) and, in the case of geographically localised minority groups, a Twitter network is very likely to overlap to a great extent with already existing offline networks. Such overlap between online and offline networks was no exception in my case, and my degree of acquaintance with the people behind the data influenced my degree of presence in the audience. However, I was never the primary addressee of the tweets of interest for the study. For that reason, I found it essential to respect the confidentiality of the Twitter users behind the data set.

Perceptions and definitions of privacy might vary individually and in cultural contexts (Markham and Buchanan 2012: 6). Therefore, any attempt to make a distinction between private and public data should be problematised in terms of in what context, how and to whom information is made public, and in terms of expectations of privacy rather than in terms of accessibility. Ethical considerations impose themselves when attempting to identify the relationship between the ability to access and the right to access, between the right to access and the right to use, and between the right to use and the right to disseminate. Even if it is out there, am I, as a researcher, entitled to use the data and to what extent? And if so, does the right to access give me the right to use it in my analysis and, for instance, to quote it? A further distinction needs to be made between the right to use and the right to disseminate. Especially when it comes to small data related to specific communities, confidentiality is hard to guarantee.

In communities with few individuals, it can be easy to recognise participants in various debates and discussions. Focusing on the use of Twitter among Sámi speakers means that the number of people from the Sámi community involved in these practices is too small to guarantee the anonymity of the Twitter users by solely removing names. Languages and language learning in indigenous contexts can be a delicate subject, and this has been observed in Sámi contexts (see, for instance, Juuso 2013). My ethical considerations resulted in the decision not to refer to the author by username, ethnolinguistic group, age or gender.

In addition to the data collected on Twitter, I also conducted interviews and had a few personal communications with Twitter users whose messages were included in the data set. They were contacted by e-mail or private message on Twitter and Facebook. Not all persons contacted replied, and in one case an interview was not possible. This choice to supplement the online data with interviews was intended not only to get more material, but also to discuss and reflect on my research with the participants. Interviews thus included a form of participant involvement, information about the project and a request for consent. They were also a means for contextualising the digital data.

One central issue in ethics is informed consent, a principle related to issues of insight and transparency. From the perspective of the researcher, this gives rise to several questions, including whom one should inform about what one is doing and when and how they should be informed. In the early phases of a project, fieldwork can include collection of data that will not necessarily be included in the project after the first stage. Also, there are reasons for not sharing information about ongoing research. Among these are ethical reasons such as the risk of negatively influencing certain practices, acting as a trigger or counteracting an activity, as has been discussed for instance in research about mental health (Johansson 2010; Svedmark 2012).

The question of whether or not informed consent is needed has to be addressed at an early stage of every project. A researcher might choose to opt for transparency and set as a condition that any data that have not been approved for dissemination will not be used. In the case of my study, I determined that informed consent was ethically and morally appropriate and was a critical first step for involving participants. This choice entailed practical issues of how to identify and contact a person behind a source. The completion of the study was thus dependent on informed consent from the participants. In cases where I did not receive explicit permission to use the data, I decided not to quote the messages as they appeared on Twitter. At most, I referred to them in paraphrases and in translation. In cases where I was able to make direct contact with the author of a tweet, I informed them about my project and asked for permission to use the data and to quote the tweet(s) in a publication. In all cases, they agreed. Attitudes toward the status of their tweets as private or public differed somewhat – one participant compared messages on Twitter with newspaper articles whereas the first reaction of another was that the messages were not primarily intended for research but the author approved of the topic of the study (the role of social media for language revitalisation). Participants were informed of the process of anonymisation. Although not all of them considered it necessary to be anonymised, none of the participants wished to be referred to by name.

Reading digital data from an ethical perspective should also include considerations about sharing the data and about the dissemination of results. To what extent is it legitimate to use the tweets in a research publication? On the one hand, we have a blurred distinction between public and private data and between contextual and cultural perceptions of privacy. On the other hand, I, from the perspective of Sámi research, have opted for an approach where informed consent, participant involvement and transparency in research are core values. The criterion of informed consent can be further developed toward the notion of entitlement, a concept that problematises the 'use of a particular story beyond the context of the experience it represents' (Shuman 2006: 3) and how this happens. The process by which a story is transferred is complex and has many meanings. However, according to Shuman, 'Stories must travel beyond their owners to do some kind of cultural work' (2006: 18–19). From that perspective, the concept of entitlement can fruitfully be borrowed from narrative research and applied to the process through which an account is transferred from participant to researcher (Cocq 2014) and back to the community.

The case study based on hashtags on Twitter resulted in a research article to be published in a scientific journal. For communication and dissemination of results, a draft of the article was sent to the participants who had been interviewed and with whom I had discussed my project. They were invited to comment on the use of the material and the presentation of results and to provide more general comments – although the study, its analysis and its outcomes were my sole responsibility. I received a few comments, approval and encouragements. The results of this study were also presented in an open lecture[11] and participants were contacted and asked for permission to quote their messages in the context of the lecture. I considered this aspect necessary because the participants had agreed on their tweets being quoted in an article in English and to being published in an academic journal. Their consent, therefore, did not include a presentation in Swedish, but they had no objection that I quoted their messages in a new context. Reading digital data may imply recontextualising the data, e.g. by getting at or engaging with the subjects/ participants behind the data.

Ethical discussions in research often focus primarily on risks of harm, concern for property and protection of rights. Here, I suggest taking the issue of the implications of research one step further: ethical considerations should include reflections about the ways in which research can lead to benefits for the community and not just be about preventing possible harm. The ethical rec-ommendations of the Association of Internet Researchers (AoIR), for instance, remind us how maximisation of benefits is 'one of the basic tenets of central policies in research ethics such as the UN Declaration of Human Rights, the Nuremberg Code, the Declaration of Helsinki, and the Belmont Report' (Markham and Buchanan 2012: 4).

From the perspective of Sámi research, dissemination of outcomes is a sig-nificant part of the research process. On a deeper level, it is the researcher's entitlement to share information as 'the distribution of knowledge' (Shuman 2006: 29). This standpoint is related to questions about whom research is for, who owns it and who benefits from the research (Smith 1999). Therefore, the question to be addressed is not how to 'protect' people from our research, but what role a study/project has for the community and what benefits there are outside of an academic context.

I can say without hesitation that my study of hashtags on Twitter by Sámi speakers did not cause any harm. But what were the benefits for the Sámi lan-guage communities? Participants were interested in the study and stressed the importance of studying different aspects of the effects and uses of social media. As for the relevance and significance of my study beyond the participants, it might be too early to evaluate the possible impact.[12] A research article in an international journal is not the best way to reach a non-academic readership and a broader audience. The published article will be disseminated through a blog[13] to a broader audience along with a Swedish summary. Open lectures are other appropriate ways to restitute knowledge. Workshops with digital media users can be yet another method for enhancing reciprocal appropriation where community members define the goals, needs and strategies in research.

FURTHER REFLECTIONS

Ethical aspects such as respect for privacy, informed consent and research benefits require careful consideration and scrutiny of methodologies and perspectives and, entwined with these, careful consideration of the role of the researcher. This comes to a head when reading digital data based on indigenous media use and that constitute a unique and valuable but potentially sensitive data set.

Decision-making occurs at every step of the research process, from the design of the study to the dissemination of the results, and requires an attitude to research similar to the one recommended in indigenous methodologies that emphasises dialogue, knowledge exchange and reciprocity as core values in research (see, for instance, Kovach 2009; Smith 1999). Community-based participatory research similarly calls for consideration of more specific issues such as 'ethics of partnership working, collaboration, blurring of boundaries between researchers and researched, community rights, community conflicts and democratic participation' (Banks et al. 2013: 1).

The principal ethical challenges that arose in my study of folksonomy on Twitter were related to the data set. The process of working with small data differs from the collection of big data (Mayer-Schönberger and Cukier 2013) and this raised other ethical questions. Small data are collected purposefully in defined settings and data collection is local. The relation to the community is therefore often based on individuals rather than on larger patterns. As Abreu and Acker emphasise, data collection follows disciplinary and community standards as well as standards for ethics in data collection (Abreu and Acker 2013).

As a folklorist and ethnologist, searching for the emic perspective is a 'modus operandi'. This implies that the focus is on the perception and account of a member of a group or a community – in contrast to the perception of the observer (Harris 1976; Lundberg and Ternhag 2002). Digital data are interesting specifically because they represent the accounts, utterances and productions of individual persons. The people behind the data are what are relevant. The implications of working with small data therefore call for a need for ethical and moral considerations from the perspective of the participants. Issues touched upon in my research, and not least in the specific case study referred to here, include identity issues and questions of human rights from a minority/indigenous perspective. The central significance of these aspects motivated the critical importance of ethical considerations.

CONCLUSIONS

Ethical considerations and choices have, obviously, implications for the ends and results of a study. For instance, my choice to use data only upon consent from the participants, together with the difficulty in contacting authors of tweets, limited the fraction of the data set that I could quote or explicitly refer to in my analysis. Also, anonymisation by removing the authors' user-names and the ethnolinguistic group, age and gender of the authors inevitably implied a loss of information. My main concern was the impossibility to fully highlight the empowering use of the Sámi languages on Twitter because the anonymisation process implied that the languages themselves could only be visible to a limited extent when presenting the results.

Sámi research that includes online data brings ethical matters to a head. Increased accessibility to information, an overlap between online and offline networks, and online communities that are geographically delimited in the physical world require a rethinking of the concepts of privacy, participation and benefits in research when reading digital data. Based on my experience and evaluation of previous work with communities with few individuals, I summarise suggestions for scholars working with similar data and meeting similar challenges. First, we cannot rely on ethical rules and approval by ethical review boards – often received prior to the conduct of the research – in order to ensure ethically appropriate research. A processual approach to ethics, i.e. as a set of issues and challenges that emerge, evolve and need to be addressed in research, is necessary and should include the perspective of the participants. Ethics are not simply about following rules and principles, but rather they are an approach based on careful considerations, continual reflec-tions and conscious choices at every step of the project: when collecting digital data, in the dissemination of results, etc. More importantly, ethical concerns are not merely an academic matter but rather a central and sometimes deci-sive issue for research participants. Second, community-based participatory research can be developed to include online communities. Collaboration and engagement between researchers and participants should be encouraged. Methods that combine online and offline fieldwork and data collection should be considered in order to contextualise the digital data and grasp the rela-tionship between online and offline practices from an emic perspective, and should incorporate reciprocal and collaborative work between researchers(s) and participants in various phases of the project. Third, reflexivity should be a central tool for reading digital data in an ethically appropriate manner. By critically reflecting upon and evaluating the researcher–participant relation-ship and the researcher's positionality in the field, one can prevent deficiency, shortcomings and negligence that might result in inappropriate ethical deci-sions or lack thereof. This implies ethical sensitivity (Banks et al. 2013: 6) and responsibility in research. In most cases, the question of protecting people from our research is not a primary concern in the humanities and social sciences. Therefore, I want to suggest that we, to a greater extent, turn the question of how our research can benefit people into a primary focus of our research.

NOTES

1. Hashtags are words marked with the symbol # in order to enhance, add or emphasise an aspect in a message or a post.
2. The Sámi are the indigenous people of Fenno-Scandinavia. The traditional Sámi area, which comprises northern Norway, Sweden, Finland and the Kola Peninsula in Russia, presents a complex heterogeneity in terms of languages, livelihoods and living conditions.
3. Twitter is a micro-blogging service used for information sharing, communication or interaction. By choosing to 'follow' someone, one receives his or her updates. One can also track a hashtag regardless of who the author is. Tweets – short texts of a maximum of 140 characters – are public by default and a user can only see who 'follows' him or her, not who reads the messages.
4. Indigenous methodologies comprise a variety of theoretical and methodological approaches and perspectives with the common aim to foreground the roles, rights and epistemologies of indigenous people in research. In this chapter, indigenous methodologies are applied at a general level in order to implement ethical perspectives in line with these methodologies, and this constitutes the frame of reference in contemporary Sámi research.
5. <http://ethics.aaanet.org/category/statement/>
6. <http://www.afsnet.org/?page=ethicsandterms=%22ethics%22>
7. #gollegiella, meaning 'golden language' in North Sámi, enhances the value given to the language; #sámegiella, for 'Sámi language', was applied to several of the Sámi languages; #åarjel, 'South', is meant for South Sámi.
8. By using the application *Flipboard* and subscribing to the hashtags, every new tweet containing at least one of the hashtags was saved into a category created for that purpose.
9. The messages were written in North Sámi, South Sámi, Swedish, Norwegian, English, a few in Lule Sámi and one in Finnish. Several contained more than one language.
10. However, the re-tweets were taken into account in terms of interaction with the audience.
11. The lecture was given at the Sámi Week festival in Umeå in 2014 and was broadcast on television by the Swedish Educational Broadcasting Company.
12. The article based on this study has not yet been published and was in press at the time this present chapter was being written (May 2015). Therefore the impact of the study cannot yet be fully evaluated.
13. Since 2011, I have used a research blog for giving information on my research and spreading its outcomes. Blog posts can be linked to through other blogs or social media platforms.

REFERENCES

Abreu, A. and Acker, A. (2013) 'Context and collection: a research agenda for small data introduction: what big data leaves behind', in *iConference 2013 Proceedings*, Fort Worth, TX, pp. 549–54.

Babcock, B. A. (1980) 'Reflexivity: definitions and discriminations', *Semiotica*, 30: 1/1, pp. 1–14.

Banks, S., Armstrong, A., Carter, K., Graham, H., Hayward, P., Henry, A. and Strachan, A. (2013) 'Everyday ethics in community-based participatory research', *Contemporary Social Science*, 8: 3, 263–77, pp. 1–15.

Blank, T. J. (ed.) (2009) *Folklore and the Internet: Vernacular Expression in a Digital World*. Logan: Utah State University Press.

Bronner, S. J. (2009) 'Digitizing and virtualizing folklore', in T. J. Blank (ed.), *Folklore and the Internet. Vernacular Expression in a Digital World*. Logan: Utah State University Press, pp. 21–66.

Christophe, J., Boëll, D.-M. and Meyran, R. (2009) *Du folklore à l'ethnologie* [*From Folklore to Ethnology*]. Paris: Editions de la Maison des sciences de l'homme.

Cocq, C. (2008) *Revoicing Sámi Narratives: North Sámi Storytelling at the Turn of the 20th Century*. Umeå: Sámi Dutkan, Umeå University.

Cocq, C. (2010) 'Forskningshistoriskt perspektiv på insamlingen av samiskt arkivmaterial' ['Research historical perspective on the collection of Sámi archives'], *Svenska Landsmål Och Svenskt Folkliv* [*Swedish Dialects and Folklife*], 336, pp. 121–56.

Cocq, C. (2013) 'Savoirs traditionnels et traditions de recherche: Le folklore comme instrument politique et arme idéologique' ['Traditional knowledge and research traditions: folklore as a political tool and an ideological weapon'], in K. Andersson (ed.), *L'image du Sápmi 2*. Örebro: Örebro University, pp. 170–90.

Cocq, C. (2014) 'Att berätta och återberätta: intervjuer, interaktiva narrativer och berättigande' ['To tell and retell: interviews, interactive narratives and entitlement'], *Kulturella Perspektiv: Svensk Etnologisk Tidskrift* [*Cultural Perspectives: Swedish Journal of Ethnology*], 23: 4, pp. 22–9.

Cocq, C. (2015a) 'Indigenous voices on the web: folksonomies and endangered languages', *Journal of American Folklore*, 128: 509, pp. 273–85.

Cocq, C. (2015b) 'Traditionell kunskap och forskningstraditioner. Samisk folklore som politiskt verktyg och ideologiskt vapen' ['Traditional knowledge and research traditions: Sámi folklore as a political tool and ideological weapon'], in K. Andersson (ed.), *Sápmi i ord och bild* [*Sápmi in Words and Pictures*], Örebro: Humanistica Oerebroensia, pp. 170–83.

Ehn, B. and Klein, B. (1994) *Från erfarenhet till text: om kulturvetenskaplig reflexivitet* [*From Experience to Text: On Scientific Reflexivity*]. Stockholm: Carlsson.

Ellison, N. B., Steinfield, C. and Lampe, C. (2007) 'The benefits of Facebook "friends": social capital and college students' use of online social network sites', *Journal of Computer-Mediated Communication*, 12: 4, pp. 1143–68.

Ess, C. (2013) *Digital Media Ethics*. Cambridge: Polity Press.

Fjell, T. I. (2005) 'Offentliggjort, men inte offentligt? Några tankar om bruket av Internetkällor' ['Published, but not public? Some thoughts on the use of Internet sources'], in C. Hagström and L. Marander-Eklund (eds), *Frågelistan som källa och metod* [*The Question List as Source and Method*]. Lund: Studentlitteratur, pp. 177–91.

Geertz, C. (1973) *The Interpretation of Cultures*. New York: Basic Books.

Giles, H. and Johnson, P. (1987) 'Ethnolinguistic identity theory: a social psychological approach to language maintenance', *International Journal of the Sociology of Language*, 68, pp. 69–99.

Hannerz, U. (1992) *Cultural Complexity: Studies in the Social Organization of Meaning*. New York: Columbia University Press.

Harris, M. (1976) 'History and significance of the emic/etic distinction', *Annual Review of Anthropology*, 5, pp. 329–50.

Hudson, J. M. and Bruckman, A. (2004) 'Go away: participant objections to being studied and the ethics of chatroom research', *Information Society*, 20: 2, pp. 127–39.

Ikonomidis Svedmark, E. and Nyberg, A. (2009) 'Om det privata i publika och digitala rum' ['About privacy in the public and digital spaces'], in *Se mig: Unga om sex och internet* [*See Me: Youth About Sex and the Internet*]. Stockholm: Davidsons Tryckeri AB, pp. 354–83.

Johansson, A. (2010) *Självskada: En etnologisk studie av mening och identitet i berättelser om skärande* [*Self-harm: An Ethnological Study About Meaning and Identity in Stories About Cutting*]. Umeå: H:ström.

Jung, J. J. (2011) 'Discovering community of lingual practice for matching multilingual tags from folksonomies', *Computer Journal*, 55: 3, pp. 337–46.

Juuso, J. (2013) *Mov gielem bååstede vaaltam: Jag tar tillbaka mitt språk*. [*I Take Back My Language*], ed. S. Sparrok. Kiruna: Sametinget.

Kirschenblatt-Gimblett, B. (1996) 'The electronic vernacular', in G. E. Marcus (ed.), *Connected: Engagements with Media*. Chicago: University of Chicago Press, pp. 21–66.

Kovach, M. (2009) *Indigenous Methodologies: Characteristics, Conversations, and Contexts*. Toronto: University of Toronto Press.

Kuokkanen, R. (2000) 'Towards an indigenous paradigm: from a Sami perspective', *Canadian Journal of Native Studies*, 20: 2, pp. 411–36.

Kuokkanen, R. (2008) 'From research as colonialism to reclaiming autonomy: toward a research ethics framework in Sápmi', in *Ethics in Sámi and*

Indigenous Research. Report from a Seminar in Kárášjohka, Norway, Nov. 23–24, 2006. Kautokeino: Sami Institute, pp. 48–63.

Lin, C.-S. and Chen, Y.-F. (2012) 'Examining social tagging behaviour and the construction of an online folksonomy from the perspectives of cultural capital and social capital', *Journal of Information Science*, 38: 6, pp. 540–57.

Louis, R. P. (2007) 'Can you hear us now? Voices from the margin: using indigenous methodologies in geographic research', *Geographical Research*, 45: 2, pp. 130–9.

Lundberg, D. and Ternhag, G. (2002) *Musiketnologi: En introduktion [Music Ethnology: An Introduction]*. Hedemora: Gidlunds förlag.

Magga, O. H. and Skutnabb-Kangas, T. (2001) 'The Saami languages: the present and the future', *Cultural Survival Quarterly*, 25: 2, at <http://www.culturalsurvival.org/publications/cultural-survival-quarterly/saami-languages-present-and-future> (accessed 9 June 2015).

Markham, A. and Buchanan, E. (2012) *Ethical Decision-Making and Internet Research Recommendations from the AoIR Ethics Working Committee (Version 2.0)*, at <http://aoir.org/reports/ethics2.pdf> (accessed 9 June 2015).

Mayer-Schönberger, V. and Cukier, K. (2013) *Big Data: A Revolution that Will Transform How We Live, Work, and Think*. London: John Murray.

Mihesuah, D. A. (ed.) (1998) *Natives and Academics: Researching and Writing About American Indians*. Lincoln, NE: University of Nebraska Press.

Mika, P. (2007) *Social Networks and the Semantic Web*. New York: Springer.

Nair, V. and Dua, S. (2012) 'Folksonomy-based ad hoc community detection in online social networks', *Social Network Analysis and Mining*, 2: 4, pp. 305–28.

Nordin-Jonsson, Å. (2010) *Árbediehtu: samiskt kulturarv och traditionell kunskap [Árbediehtu: Sámi Cultural Heritage and Traditional Knowledge]*. Uppsala: CBM; Sametinget.

Ortner, S. B. (2006) *Anthropology and Social Theory: Culture, Power, and the Acting Subject*. Durham, NC: Duke University Press.

Porsanger, J. (2004) 'An essay about indigenous methodology', *Nordlit*, 15, pp. 105–20.

Scheller, E. and Vinka, M. (forthcoming) 'The Saami languages', in M. O. (ed.), *The Barents Encyclopedia*. Oslo: Pax Forlag.

Shuman, A. (2006) 'Entitlement and empathy in personal narrative', *Narrative Inquiry*, 16: 1, pp. 148–55.

Smith, L. T. (1999) *Decolonizing Methodologies: Research and Indigenous Peoples*. London: Zed Books.

Svedmark, E. (2012) 'Att skydda individen från skada: En forskningsetisk balansakt' ['To protect the individual from harm: a research ethics balancing act'], in H. Kalman and V. Lövgren (eds), *Etiska dilemman: Forskningsdeltagande, samtycke och utsatthet [Ethical Dilemmas: Research*

Participation, Consent and Vulnerability]. Malmö: Gleerups Utbildning AB, pp. 101–13.

Tafjel, H. and Turner, J. C. (1979) 'An integrative theory of intergroup conflict', in W. G. Austin and S. Worchel (eds), *The Social Psychology of Intergroup Relations*. Monterey: Brooks/Cole, pp. 33–47.

Vincze, L. and Moring, T. (2013) 'Towards ethnolinguistic identity gratifications', in E. Haf Gruffydd Jones and E. Uribe-Jongbloed (eds), *Social Media and Minority Languages: Convergence and the Creative Industries*. Bristol: Multilingual Matters, pp. 47–57.

CHAPTER 8

Knowing Your Crowd: An Essential Component to Crowdsourcing Research

Gabriel K. Wolfenstein

'But there is such a crowd already in the house tonight as there hasn't been for long enough. It never rains but it pours, we say in Bree.'

J. R. R. Tolkien (1954: 150)

Crowdsourcing, or community sourcing (different terms for what I define broadly as the same thing),[1] is, at its most basic, a mode of research, knowledge-gathering and analysis, whereby a researcher engages a community to provide answers to questions or solutions to problems or analysis of material. The relationship between researcher and crowd can range from simple (or not so simple) data collection to involvement in the direction of the research.[2] There are many different forms of crowdsourcing, but they are all linked by the idea that a large group of people can offer solutions to research questions and data analysis that would be unavailable to the individual or small group. Because of the possibilities of wider engagement, crowdsourcing offers opportunities to advance humanistic work within and beyond the walls of the academy. It is important to note, however, that crowdsourcing is a complicated and time-intensive process. Those looking to crowdsourcing as a way to get work done quickly, or who do not take the time to lay the groundwork for a successful crowdsourcing project, may end up disappointed or frustrated. We tend to hear about the successful crowdsourcing projects (both in the humanities and beyond); we rarely hear about the ones that failed, or those that never even got off the ground. It is with these two topics in mind – the potential for crowdsourcing and being aware of how complex it is to do it successfully – that this chapter is written. It is not a comprehensive study of crowdsourcing by any means. Rather, it aims to ask potential crowdsourcers to consider their crowds before and as they proceed with any crowdsourcing study.

At Stanford's Center for Spatial and Textual Analysis (CESTA),[3] we[4] have been engaged in an Andrew W. Mellon supported project to study the question of whether crowdsourcing is useful for humanities research. To do so, we have been conducting three simultaneous crowdsourcing projects: *The Year of the Bay*, *Living with the Railroads* and *The Emotions of London*. Each project is engaged with different kinds of crowds and asks different questions. And each, in different ways, is exploring the value for academics of partnering with non-academic media bodies. In the case of all three sub-projects, our partner is Historypin, 'a global community collaborating around history',[5] which offers users a web-based platform where memories (in the form of digital images and audio/visual materials) can be pinned to a map, locating the material in both time and space, as well as providing metadata and commentary.

Though in a longer format I would detail each project, their research results, and their full narratives, this chapter will discuss what I see as one of the major challenges of crowdsourcing: knowing your audience. It is one of the earliest issues you need to explore if you want to engage in crowdsourcing. While it is tempting to prioritise one's research question, one must consider the crowd or community with which one wants to engage. Crowdsourcing for the humanities, and this chapter, offer arguments to that point. In each instance we engaged different crowds as part of this study – the general community of San Francisco Bay Area interested people, the expert community of railroad enthusiasts and the mostly anonymous community of Amazon's Mechanical Turk – and there were challenges associated with each. So as not to make the message a mystery, here is the key takeaway: though these communities are unique, with their own challenges and rewards, one of the key lessons learned thus far from these projects is that in order to undertake successful crowdsourcing, you must be able to answer this fundamental question: what does your crowd want? And creating, or engaging with, this community will require more leg work than the popular idea of crowdsourcing as a free and quick way to do tasks suggests. However, if you are willing to put in the work, crowdsourcing offers communities and data that were unreachable before the advent of the twenty-first-century information age.

CROWDSOURCING FOR THE HUMANITIES

The overall project, supported by a generous grant from the Andrew W. Mellon Foundation, was undertaken with the assumption that crowdsourcing offers opportunities to advance humanities research, and that although there have been numerous crowdsourcing projects, there has not yet been enough systematic study that can offer analyses and best practices to those who might want to engage in such research.[6] Though this is definitely not the place to enter into a discussion of the role of the humanities in the twenty-first-century information society, it is worth saying that we hoped that crowdsourcing, like other digital humanities projects, would highlight the way that we can use modern tools to continue to ask, and advance, humanities research.

More specifically, the project had two related questions. First, we wanted to explore whether the power of the crowd could be used to help researchers obtain, tag (that is add metadata) and analyse varieties of documents. Second, we wanted to see if, by engaging in crowdsourcing projects, we could better engage the public in humanities research. Through crowdsourcing, can the public become more engaged in humanities research, and can researchers, by moving beyond the walls of academe, better engage with the public? Most broadly, is crowdsourcing useful for humanities research? These were the primary questions that motivated the study.

Rather than doing a complex literary review or explore all the crowd-sourcing projects that had a humanities bent we instead sought to test these questions by engaging in crowdsourcing ourselves. This would allow us to both better understand crowdsourcing for the humanities in a practical way, as well as to be able to offer best practices (both things to do and things not to do) for others looking to explore similar projects and/or methodologies. Led by CESTA Director Zephyr Frank, the three projects we settled upon parlayed the strengths of the Principal Investigator (PI) researchers, allowing us to come up with original questions that let us test crowdsourcing while at the same time having the possibility of advancing the PIs' research questions. Thus, the *Year of the Bay*'s PI, Jon Christensen, was interested in the chang-ing San Francisco Bay, physically, environmentally and socially, over the last 150 years. Living with the Railroads sought to help PI Richard White better understand the impact of the railroad on the American West in the late nine-teenth century. And the Emotions of London (originally called Tagging 500 Novels), sought to help PI Franco Moretti create and explore the emotional map of Victorian London as understood through its contemporary literature.

In all three of these projects we partnered with a London-based non-profit, We Are What We Do (now Shift Design), specifically to use and work with them to help further develop their Historypin platform. The Historypin plat-form was particularly well suited to our goals. What it offers is an engaging web platform whereby users can upload pictures and other digital materials to a Google basemap, allowing for the geolocation of the materials as well as the ability to locate them chronologically, and add metadata as to the content of the images. Their ideology, that by sharing our history we can not only preserve it more effectively, but create community as well, fit the goals of the sub-projects to both generate community and gather material. For two of the projects, the Year of the Bay and Living with the Railroads, the Historypin platform was used to engage with the community through data and material gathering. For the third, the Emotions of London, the Historypin platform offered us a way to display our research results to the wider community.

Why three projects under the same roof? If the goal were only to advance the research aims of the PIs, each could have proceeded on their own. But our goal from the beginning was to conduct three simultaneous crowdsourcing projects, so that we could connect the things that we learned across the projects and thus be able to say something broader about the utility of crowdsourcing for humanities researchers. What we ended up with was an experiment that involved academic researchers, non-academic web media bodies, as well the community at large, with each project looking at a different aspect of crowdsourcing to explore how it could contribute to academic learning as well as to community engagement.

The following discussion focuses on the crowds that we sought to engage with, highlighting the strengths and challenges of working with it. Though readers will get a flavour of each project, of necessity I will be glossing over the major research questions and results in order to say something about the process by which we determined who the crowd was and how to best interact with it.

THE YEAR OF THE BAY: THE COMPLEXITY OF THE LARGE CROWD

The Year of the Bay, 2013, in the San Francisco Bay Area, allowed us to test how to engage a broad, public audience by tying the sub-project to a regional event that had both public and media opportunities. Broadly speaking, the intent was to get people to upload and annotate materials on Historypin. The year 2013 was significant for the Bay Area, both historically and in terms of major events. It saw the America's Cup sailing race, as well as the opening (eventually) of a new span of the Bay Bridge. It was also the 150th anniversary of the Port of San Francisco and the opening of a new home for the Exploratorium on the bay, and it saw exhibitions at the California Historical Society and the Oakland Museum of California focused on the bay. These various happenings were commemorated by a number of events and exhibits at cultural and historical institutions in the area, including museums, libraries and newspapers. As we were exploring the possible project it became clear that there were groups who were interested in the possibility of mobilising the crowd to help rectify maps, identify images, place historical photographs and documents geographically, and identify the people, places and things in those photographs. It was out of this space that the Year of the Bay project was born. Its ultimate goal was to generate new data sets that would become a crowdsourced collection of objects that would be both geolocated and located in time, that would allow the PI, Jon Christensen, to address questions in environmental history and historical ecology.

In terms of crowd engagement, the goal here was twofold. First, our Historypin site would have material from cultural heritage partners, giving the public material to explore.[7] Second, we would provide a space for the community to upload their own material, limited only in the sense that it had to have some connection to the Bay, understood as the San Francisco Bay Area writ large. The hope was that through these two prongs, new materials would be added and metadata would be uploaded, enriching materials already available. Together, this process would create an active community engaged with the site, returning often to explore new material in addition to using the site as they saw fit.

Rather than identifying a specific crowd to engage with this project, the scope of the community was left deliberately open. This allowed for the testing of the two questions: if you created the space, could you ride the coat-tails of media exposure to generate materials; and second, could a new crowd, a new community be formed out of this process? The testing of the open crowd is important, because studies show that more people interact and engage with projects superficially than the number of people who engage more deeply. People who study this phenomenon often use the metaphor of the funnel as a way to visualise the engagement.[8] The amount of information/work/ data available at the top of the funnel far outweighs what is left as the funnel narrows, or so the idea goes. Our experiment with the Year of the Bay, then, was to create a space with a low bar to entry so that we could widen the funnel as much as possible. By collabourating with museums, libraries, archives and media organisations, we hoped to bring people to our Historypin site (yearofthebay.org), to engage with materials and add their own.

How successful was this engagement? The answer here is both very successful and not very successful, as the explanation which follows will suggest. The initial thought process associated with the crowd engagement for this project was built around the idea of, if you build it, they will come.[9] This is not to say that our hope was if we create a website, the crowd will magically start to engage with it; far from it. Here, the 'it' was both the website, but also the publicity created by various heritage and media partners on the project. Bodies like the California Historical Society for instance, who have significant media contacts and well established track records of both community engagement and public events, would help create the publicity that would bring people to the site.

What became clear after the launch of the site in 2013, however, was that much more work would have to be undertaken if the project was going to achieve some level of success. That is, simply advertising the site through digital, print and in-person events would not be enough to generate content and interest, as we came to understand. It was at this point that one of the important things we learned as part of the project became apparent: getting to your crowd is not just something that takes place prior to project launch; it is an ongoing process that requires you to be nimble in terms of research design and goals, as we will see.

What we found in the early phase of the project was that people would check out the site, but any engagement with it would be limited, and return visits were more, rather than less, rare. It was here that a Community Outreach Officer, Kerri Young, was added to the project. For anyone seeking to engage with the public in a crowdsourcing project, this is a very important role to have filled. Without someone in this position, it is unlikely that you will achieve much in the way of active participation.

The crowd of people interested in the Bay Area was too amorphous, which made it difficult to target them. Where we did begin to achieve success was when we engaged with niche groups, like local history bloggers, local history societies and community groups. This is not to say that there were no other participants – in a project like this one, cultural heritage sites will be your best partners. Indeed, large chunks of our content came from museums and organisations that were already on board with the mission of preserving and disseminating historical material. But successful community crowdsourcing will take a lot of time and effort from someone who is on the ground, meeting people, going to events and gatherings, and actively making contacts and showing people how your project will benefit them.

This raises *the* central question you have to ask yourself if you are engaging with crowdsourcing: what does your community want? That question was a particular challenge with the Year of the Bay, because there were a myriad of communities, all with different goals. While we tried to anticipate this in the planning of the project, to at least some degree there was no way to be able to answer this question until the project got going. This meant that the Year of the Bay sub-project turned out to have a series of sub-sub-projects which required the focus and attention of the community outreach officer, as well as research assistants (RAs) and other project members.

Generating those contacts and increasing community interest was a long and intensive process. It began both through broad outreach efforts, like press releases and magazine articles aimed at general audiences, as well as through directed outreach to individuals and organisations. The former required constant focus on social media efforts, both to get the knowledge of our project out to the public as well as to maintain its profile. This meant regularly engaging with Facebook and Twitter and following up stories on the various websites with comments and other forms of digital engagement, all in order to build up the community of people interested in the Year of the Bay and to maintain their interest in it. This is a significant challenge that anyone engaging with crowdsourcing needs to be aware of. For example, after the release of stories about the project from the Stanford News Service, from the Associated Press and from weekly calls to visit the page from a popular blogger, the average number of home page views rose between five hundred and a thousand more than the daily average.

But for all the interest generated by these online mentions, actual use of the site (use defined as the uploading of material or the adding of metadata) remained low for the general public. Many people either did not respond to outreach efforts or expressed an interest but did not follow it up. For some, the requirement to have a Gmail, Facebook or Twitter account to join Historypin (this is no longer the case, as you can now join with an e-mail), acted as a deterrent. In addition, the older population, who were most likely to have new material or be able to add metadata to existing material, were often not comfortable enough with a computer to create an account, not to mention scanning and uploading their own materials. We were, in fact, requiring quite complex engagement with the site. Still others were concerned about rights issues, how copyright metadata would appear on the site and how their materials would be protected. These are only some of the challenges that faced us in this project. But, again, I want to emphasise that many of these issues only emerged through running the project. This is why being nimble is important: not only do you have to learn what the crowd wants, you have to be able to shift gears when necessary to provide it.

We achieved our greatest success in two ways. The first was through social media, through highlighting pieces of content already pinned, thereby spotlighting the work of specific pinners. Sharing examples of what others contributed within the project was both valuable in demonstrating to others what they could pin, but also in encouraging people who had already pinned to either pin again or at least remain engaged with the project. Though it is true that highlighting material around big events – the San Francisco Earthquake of 1906, the opening of the Golden Gate Bridge, etc. – generated the most traffic to the site, excellent material was added through the engagement of a few users around more locally based stories.

The second way of achieving success, however, was through personal contact with smaller historical societies and neighbourhood groups. It was through this understanding of what our crowd wanted – local, small group, personal contact – that greater success in terms of public use of the site was achieved. Kerri Young attended numerous meetings and gatherings, sometimes as a guest, sometimes to present the site, sometimes to use the site as part of the event to gather material or metadata. And it was these groups, among the public, that were the most active pinners and users of the site. Here we were able to use the Mysteries aspect of the site (a functionality Historypin created to highlight materials and create specific asks about them – see Figure 8.1), developed in part in response to the needs of the project to engage this

Figure 8.1 Mysteries aspect of Historypin
(Source: <https://www.historypin.org/project/22-yearofthebay/>)

crowd, to engage with local groups. Asking questions like 'Can you identify the location?', 'Can you tell us when this picture was taken?' or 'Do you know the person in the picture?' allowed us to target specific communities and engage them directly. However, rather than simply putting mysteries up to be solved as we had initially done, we put up mysteries aimed at specific neighbourhoods, and asked the neighbourhood groups to help solve them. This generated much more useful material.

The challenge, then, was not only in driving traffic to the site, but also in generating engagement. And it is for this issue that the question of what your community wants is so vital. In the case of the Year of the Bay, we had numerous communities, and serving them all was a challenge. Heritage partners want secure sites for their material, the protection of that material through some sort of copyright, and to make sure their contribution is highlighted. Neighbourhood groups want material targeted at them. Individuals want either high-value items – earthquakes, the World Series, etc. – or materials specific to them or their community. Each of these needed to be addressed if we wanted the project to be a success. And even addressing all these did not guarantee success. Though our heritage partners uploaded large amounts of material, others either uploaded less or ultimately provided material that did not necessarily address the PI's research questions (this, of course, is one of the things that goes hand in hand with trying to make use of the wide part of the funnel). So you can ask these questions, and still not necessarily achieve success.[10]

Generating project engagement is often a slow and labour-intensive process. Before people will engage, they have to be interested in the project and, just as importantly, what it can offer their project in turn. This is particularly challenging when you are trying to generate a community where one did not exist before. In this sense, the wide part of the funnel is the greatest challenge. Because this project did not have a specific ask, a large amount of leg work needed to be done to engage with the people and groups likely to be able to contribute material. Moreover, it is likely that the most successful engagement happened not on the website, but in the person-to-person contacts. When we left material on the site, hoping people would engage, this was far less successful than promoting the material on social media and in person. It was through on-the-ground interactions that we were able to learn what the community wanted.

LIVING WITH THE RAILROADS: ENTERING THE EXPERT COMMUNITY

Unlike the Year of the Bay, Living with the Railroads sought to interact with a more specific crowd: the railfan community.[11] And while this alleviated some of the challenges associated with the Bay project (namely the complexities associated with the non-specific crowd and the non-specific ask), working with expert communities brings a different set of challenges. Though you do not have to identify the crowd, finding both what the community wants and what you can offer to it is more complex. This is because the community already exists and has a set of practices and a modus operandi already in place. Put another way, since you are not bringing the community into existence and since it is already well functioning, it does not obviously need you. So gaining entrée, as we will see, requires laying a different kind of groundwork than that associated with the Year of the Bay.

Following the work of PI Richard White, Living with the Railroads seeks to use crowdsourcing to learn more about the social, cultural and environmental impact of the development and expansion of the railroads in the American West, and hopefully across the United States (White 2011). The goal is to collect, tag and interpret the thousands of photographs of railroads, trains, stations and depots in the United States. Here, photographs are particularly important, as they are an unparalleled source of information about the impact of the railroad on the environment. The possibility of pairing nineteenth-century photos with both modern photos as well as images from the intervening century offers the potential to tell the story of the railroad in a novel way.

The genesis of this sub-project began well before the Mellon grant to study the question of crowdsourcing. White commissioned a preliminary proof-of-concept study in 2009 to see if repeat photography could offer a lens to document the changes wrought by the railroads. Here, Alfred Hart's famous photographs of the birth of the railroad were re-shot from as close to the same point as possible.[12] This project was successful, but only to a certain point. Though it certainly demonstrated the change, and lack of change, in the environment, it was both a time- and labour-intensive project and offered little about the actual process of change that took place between then and now.

It is here that the project of crowdsourcing this process emerged. By engaging with a community that has unparalleled knowledge of the railroads and unmatched resources in terms of images and other documents, the project hoped to generate a database that would allow for researchers to look at changes in the landscape, both physical and social, over time. Though railroad buffs and local historians are sometimes dismissed as antiquarian, Living with the Railroads instead saw this as a community with deep knowledge. Moreoever, the focus on photographs played to the strengths of our partnership with Historypin. The results, though data collection remains ongoing, can be seen in the project page on the Historypin site.[13]

But gaining access to this community was a challenge, as we learned from the outset. The railfan community is vast, spanning the United States. And it ranges from isolated individuals who are not publicly minded about their interests to large regional organisations like the Southern Pacific Historical and Technical Society which has annual meetings, publications both book and article in nature, newsletters, websites, message boards, etc. Thus this is not a community that you can simply walk up to (virtually or otherwise) and ask them to contribute to your project. If you try to simply extract data from them, as you would from an archive, you would gain no traction. Before even launching the Historypin site, then, groundwork had to be laid.

Drawing on connections from both Historypin and CESTA, starting in April 2013 we began to have regular meetings with our Crowdsourcing Trains Advisory Board (initial meetings had taken place in the autumn of 2012). The actual site did not launch until 2014, so this should already give an idea of the lead time it took to get this project off the ground. The group itself consisted of CESTA staff, undergraduate RAs, Historypin, and three or four local railroad enthusiasts. What this group was able to do was help the project leaders better understand the community we were hoping to engage with, as well as to help guide us as to how to interact with them and give suggestions as to what kinds of tools and materials they would be interested in. That is, they helped us to start to answer the key question of what the community would actually want and/or need. Without asking this question, the project would have been doomed from the start.

Two things emerged from these meetings. First, some people would be interested in partnering with Stanford and Historypin if their data would be secure and available to them after input. They did not want Stanford to simply take their material and hide it away in the Ivory Tower. We would, in fact, learn that while for some affiliation with Stanford was a positive, others were sceptical of academic researchers, if not downright hostile. The second thing we learned was that if we did not approach the community as partners and as people also interested in trains at least in some way as they were, we would have a hard time entering their world. Crowdsourcing with expert communities requires establishing trust. One way to generate that trust was to have materials already on the site when it launched, to 'have skin in the game' so to speak.

We could not just offer a blank map and ask them to fill it in. Before launching the site, CESTA RAs did significant amounts of work over the spring and summer of 2013 collecting materials so the site could be pre-populated when it launched. In addition, RAs generated databases of museums and railroad societies, started a test blog to improve outreach and began to participate in railfan message boards and communities. The goal of the blog, run for a month between June and July of 2013, was to get a better sense of what kinds of material railfans would be interested in and what kinds of questions we could ask to generate productive discussion. In addition, the RA in charge of the blog, Sophia Paliza-Carre, sought to see what types of photographs would generate most interest: landscape or people oriented, famous pictures or more anonymous images, older images or ones of more recent vintage? One thing was particularly key here: we were able to have a member of our Advisory board – a member of the railfan community – send it to the various community message boards of which he was a part. This helped legitimate our effort and was invaluable in generating interest in it. Indeed, it was his sanctioning of our work that led to the 924 page views from 274 unique visitors over the one-month trial period. Comments on the images, however, suggested the difficulty we would have if we were to focus the question as to the environmental changes which the PI was most interested in. As one commentator stated: 'Hmmm---what are fences usually used for? Does it really matter if the plants are native---as long as they have a green card, what does it matter?'[14] The most interest was in more recent photos and in images they had not seen before.

These early attempts at outreach emphasise that a key to success in crowdsourcing is getting to know your community. In this case, what we learned, or what we had to do, were three things. First, we had to present ourselves not as experts, but as facilitators. Second, we had to get a sense of how the crowd would engage with the material we wanted to offer to them. And, lastly, we needed to give them something, whether the platform we had created or material that they did not already have access to. More specifically, we began to understand that if we wanted to meet our goals, we would have to figure out how to get our questions as a secondary result, not as the primary. But for all the work we did laying this groundwork (which we placed great emphasis on based on what we had already learned from the Year of the Bay), after we launched the project, community engagement became perhaps even more important.

The complexity of this process was demonstrated to us when we went to present the preliminary project at the Southern Pacific Historical and Technical Society meeting in October of 2013. We saw attending the meeting as an important part of community engagement and an ideal space to launch the site. There we were able to interact with railfans through attending panels, walking through the exhibit room and purchasing some material for use in the project and, of course, our presentation. It was there that we learned that there was some animosity toward Stanford due to the perception that much of our archival materials on the Southern Pacific was limited in terms of access. Though this turned out not to be the case (it might have been at one time when the archives were first deposited at the university, but before they were properly catalogued), this revealed an important aspect of community expectation we would have to overcome if the project were to stand a chance of success.

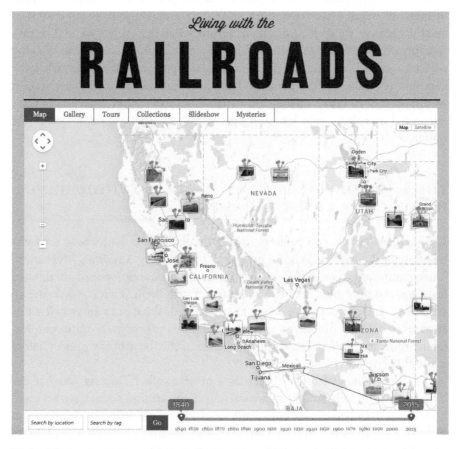

Figure 8.2 A part of Living with the Railroad's Historypin page showing image locations – multiple pins indicate numerous images at that point
(Source: <http://www.historypin.org/project/42-railroads/>)

All of this led to us spending more time on outreach than we had originally planned. Following the meeting, we decided to start a regular Stanford Railfan day. We brought railfans to campus, helped facilitate their access to Special Collections, asked them to present their work and began to demonstrate our Historypin site. This did much to generate goodwill as well as interest on the part of the community. To date, there are 3,421 pins to the site.

Though large amounts of material came from work done by the RAs mining Flickr, significant amounts of material came from connections we made through personal outreach to conferences, museums and historical societies whose goodwill and participation emerged out of continued and new outreach. Learning what your community wants does not have a fixed answer; it is an ongoing, sometimes changing, process.

The point here, however, is that all this took more than a year from preliminary explorations to the launch of the site, and the largest influxes of material began after we began our active outreach, which was only successful because we spent time figuring out what the crowd wanted, rather than prioritising what we wanted. This process should be seen as an ongoing part of a crowdsourcing project. Had we stopped learning about what the community wanted at the point we launched the site, the only content on it would have been ours. This meant expanding our research interests beyond our initial questions in order to engage with issues that are important to the railfans.[15]

THE EMOTIONS OF LONDON: PAID CROWDSOURCING IS NOT ONLY ABOUT BEING PAID

Unlike the previous two projects, the Emotions of London, whose data was based upon the paid crowdsourcing world provided by Amazon's Mechanical Turk community, would seem to offer a more straightforward method of learning who the crowd is and how to interact with them. That is, you come up with tasks, you pay people to do the tasks, the end. What does the crowd want? It wants to be paid. But as you will see, even here the process is more complex, taking time, multiple iterations and a change in the focus of the project before we could generate the data we needed.

The Emotions of London began as a project called Tagging 500 Novels. This project initially sought to answer questions around social networks and how they developed across nineteenth-century novels. Principal Investigator Franco Moretti was interested in analysing traditional literary hypotheses regarding the extent to which social settings correlated with social networks, in terms of density, size and type. The plan was to use Named Entity Recognition[16] and pronoun disambiguation algorithms[17] to tag the novels and then use crowdsourcing to either confirm or correct the results from the algorithmic phase.

What we discovered upon the deployment of our initial human intelligence tasks (HITs)[18] to our own community was that this required the crowd to perform tasks of significant complexity and annotate or check each instance of dialogue for both speaker and recipient. Anaphora resolution (whereby for each pronoun you find its antecendent) proved to be too time-consuming. It was not that the crowd was necessarily incapable of performing the task, but that it would likely not be worth their while to do so. Our research into the Turk community suggested that HITs had to be discrete tasks.[19]

The question became: how could we get at the questions that Moretti was interested in exploring while at the same time asking questions of our community that required no literary expertise and no knowledge of the specific novels they were asked to tag? It was at this point that Moretti transformed the project into one of more limited scope. Instead of exploring the social networks in novels, the project sought to analyse the ways in which the physical spaces of the city and mental constructions of location represented changing understandings of London through the nineteenth century.[20] More specifically, as the project name suggests, the project shifted its focus to better understanding the emotions tied to specific locales. This shift allowed for a viable mapping of emotional spaces in order to search for trends among particular places and potential explanations for those trends.[21]

To be clear, this process took place prior to engagement with the Turker community.[22] As with the previous projects, it was important to understand the relevant community before engaging with them. A great deal of work was done to anticipate what the crowd would be able to do, but even that changed as we began to deploy tasks to the Turkers.[23] Thus, in the spring and summer of 2013, we conducted a series of experiments, deploying passages to the Turkers as to setting, character status and location of process. In order to do this, we went through an iterative process that required us to: develop a template for the HIT; test it ourselves using the Amazon interface; revise the template; deploy the HIT to the crowd of Turkers; and evaluate the responses. It is important to emphasise that we would always run the HITs on ourselves, our community of project leads, graduate students and undergraduate RAs, before sending it out to the Turk community. The Turkers were not the only testers.

This process of refinement allowed us to understand better what our crowd was capable of doing. We were able to determine both a price point (7 cents per HIT, which roughly correlates to minimum wage (in the US $7.25/hour) as well as determine Turker accuracy as to the annotation of passages regarding emotions.[24] Though we originally sought to have them annotate passages using a colour wheel that allowed for complex emotional gradations, testing determined that these gradations of emotion were too subjective (not just for Turkers, it should be noted; we saw this testing among ourselves as well as testing through English PhD students at Stanford). We eventually settled upon asking Turkers to do two things. First, all Turkers were asked whether the placename was the setting of the passage. Second, the Turkers were split, with half of the participants per passage being asked whether the emotion of fear was associated with the place, and the emotion of happiness for the other half.[25]

What I want to emphasise here is that it was only through repeated testing through the Turker community that we were able to determine what kinds of questions would yield usable data. Through analysis of the data (correlating individual Turker responses with the aggregate Turker responses, as well as comparing Turker responses to our responses and analysis) we were able to determine whether the Turkers were doing the tasks seriously, and whether the combination of the complexity of our task combined with the price point made the HITs attractive to the community. Since Turkers are only paid *after* they complete the task and *after* we authorised their work, this encourages honesty in the work. If we did not think that they took the task seriously, we did not have to pay them. In this sense, we constructed tasks that fit the needs of the community as profit maximisers.

But it was only when we began to look carefully at the larger data samples that we learned that Turkers are more than profit maximisers. Initially, we authorised payment for all work done. But as we ramped up the numbers of HITs from the testing and iterative phase, we also began to run tests on Turker responses. Here, we discovered that some Turkers were trying to game the process. For instance, one Turker simply answered 'Yes' to every passage. Others answered using obvious yes/no patterns (see Heuser and Algee-Hewitt 2015: section 3.1). As we started denying payment to some, the previous black box of the Turker world began to open up, as people would e-mail us thereby breaking down the barriers of anonymity.

Some would contact us if we were not quick enough to approve their work. This fitted our basic understanding of Turkers as profit maximisers. But others requested that we either approve their work without paying or demanded that we approve their work because if we did not their reputation on the Amazon Mechanical Turk site could take a hit. This is important because you have some control over what level of Turker has access to your tasks. You can choose to open up your task only to Turkers of a certain reputation (you can also limit by geographic region, though we chose not to exercise this option, language proficiency or your own qualification limits). Further explorations of the Turker world led us to message boards like mturkforum. com. It was here that we learned that Turkers were also reputation maximisers. Though they loved CESTA when we approved all the HITs, the moment that we started rejecting some, our reputation on the forum took a hit. As one poster, CorruptAl125, noted: 'CESTA went from hero to scumbag real quick.'[26] Indeed, there was a lot of anger on the forums on the part of people whose HITs were rejected, as well as from other Turkers sympathising with their compatriots. This also created angst in the community, as the people doing the tasks were concerned about both money and reputation. 'I am freaking out about my CESTAS. GOD GOD GOD GOD GOD GOD GOD', said one poster on the thread about rejected HITs.[27] Sharkl11 raised the reputation issue: 'Holy Moly 127 Rejections and my 99.9% went to 99.5%.........still got lots pending. Here we goooooooooooooooooooooooooooooooooooooooo

*Though they approved 500~' This highlights the fickle, or at least moment-to-moment nature of the Turker community. The concern over reputation – 'my 99.9% went to 99.5%' – overrode the fact that we approved a huge chunk of HITs for this user.

So we learned that Turkers were not just maximising their profit, but were also centrally concerned with maintaining their reputation. Our reputation in the community affected who would do our tasks. The message boards indicated that certain users stopped doing our HITs when we started rejecting some responses.[28] I do not want to paint all Turkers with this brush. Many of the direct communications we received were from people who felt that *they* had made an error and that was the reason for the rejection of the HIT. Many of those whose HITs were rejected offered to re-do them. And some evinced genuine interest in the project, offering suggestions as to how to deploy the

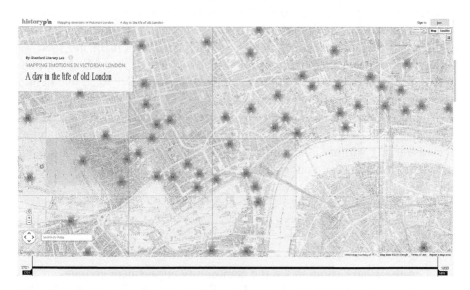

Figure 8.3 The Emotion of London's Historypin page – locations that are neutral with respect to happiness or fear are indicated by the pink dots
(Source: <https://www.historypin.org/en/explore/victorian-london>)

HITs more effectively or wanting to know more about why we were sending these out. Indeed, we ultimately ended up with an excellent data set that let us generate valuable research.[29]

But the main point is that, even in paid crowdsourcing, it is important to try to figure out what your crowd wants and you may not be able to do so until you are in the thick of the process.

CONCLUSION

Crowdsourcing is an art. There is art when you design your project; there is art when you figure out how you are going to interact with the crowd; there is art when you figure out how to respond to the factors that are motivating your crowd so that you can continue to move your research forward. The central point of this short chapter has been that one of the key components to successful crowdsourcing is not just knowing your community, but figuring out what they want. For all three of our projects, this was true in different ways. In the Year of the Bay, we came to understand that community outreach was more important than we had thought after the project had started. Though we had certainly made connections with community, media and heritage groups, it was only once the project was going that we began to understand we needed to see the community we were trying to build as a number of smaller communities if we wanted to gather good data. With Living with the Railroads, despite doing significant research into our community before we launched the project, we found after launch that as we learned more about what they wanted, we would have to modify how we interacted with them and what we offered if we wanted their participation. Finally with the Emotions of London, it took repeated experiments of sending out HITs before we were able to find the sweet spot of what the Turkers were willing and able to do. And even then, we found out that that community was more complex than our research had suggested. Figuring out what your crowd wants is not the only component of crowdsourcing within a humanities (or any other) context. But if you do not prioritise that question, you will make it much harder to engage that community.

NOTES

1. Because I have come to see the community engagement component and new data source aspects of crowdsourcing as important, I am comfortable with understanding crowdsourcing or community sourcing as any project which seeks to engage a large group of people for the purpose of data-

gathering or problem-solving. In this, I agree with Stuart Dunn and Mark Hedges (2012: 3) who define crowdsourcing as 'the process of leveraging public participation in or contributions to projects and activities'. Their work is highly recommended as a starting point for those interested in humanities crowdsourcing.

2. The terms themselves are slippery as fishes, my precious, as Gollum might have said. In his recent book *Crowdsourcing*, Daren C. Brabham (2013: xix) defines crowdsourcing as 'an online, distributed problem-solving and production model that leverages the collective intelligence of online communities to serve specific organizational goals'. Here the important thing to note is that the crowd is neither left to its own devices nor is it used as only a provider of information or mechanical work. Rather, Brabham makes a strong claim that for something to be called crowdsourcing, there must be an almost symbiotic relationship between the organisation (or researcher) and the crowd. This distinguishes 'true' crowdsourcing from things that have come to be called crowdsourcing: Wikipedia, open source software and the like (which are driven bottom up, by the community), or a Mars poll to find a new colour M&M, as control is held completely by the company. Though there is value in this precise understanding of crowdsourcing, I also think that the things that have popularly been called crowdsourcing still count, even if they do not meet these definitional components. Hence my elision of the difference between crowdsourcing and community sourcing. However, one could write a whole paper on the different definitions of crowdsourcing (a Google search as of 23 May 2015 reveals about 8,060,000 results for a search on the term 'crowdsourcing').

3. <http://www.cesta.stanford.edu>

4. My use of 'we' hides the fact that numerous people made this project possible and therefore made this chapter possible. Digital humanities projects are more often than not collaborative, and this one was exceptional in its scope. At CESTA/Stanford: Mark Algee-Hewitt, Matt Bryant, Emma Budiansky, Jon Christensen, Zephyr Frank, Ryan Heuser, Annalise Lockhart, Franco Moretti, Sophia Paliza-Carré, Raina Sun, Daniel Towns, Van Tran and Richard White. At Shift Design: Rebekkah Abraham, Nick Stanhope, Jon Voss and Kerri Young. And from our Railroad Advisory Panel: Robert Bowdidge, Dave Martens and Anthony Thompson. Much thanks are also owed to the Dean of Research at Stanford for supporting CESTA and this project, and the Andrew W. Mellon Foundation for the generous grant that made Crowdsourcing for the Humanities at Stanford possible. Any errors are, of course, my own.

5. <http://www.historypin.org> (last accessed 20 May 2015).

6. See <http://www.humanitiescrowdsourcing.stanford.edu> for more information on this project.

7. See <http://www.yearofthebay.org> to explore the site. The blog posts affiliated with the project can be found at <http://blog.historypin.org/category/yotb/>

8. For an excellent visualisation of the engagement funnel, see the one created by Mark Smickilas (at <http://www.intersectionconsulting.com/2010/the-social-media-engagement-funnel/> (last accessed 20 May 2015)). Though this is geared towards social media, the point is the same. There are lots of people who lurk about on your site/project. The goal is to get as many of them to become brand loyalists/engage in your project more deeply.

9. This is a massive, and maybe unfair, simplification. As you will see, a large amount of groundwork was laid and, once the site was live, increasing efforts were made at community engagement to drive traffic (i.e. people) to the site and to encourage them to be active upon it. The hope, however, was that the site would also sell itself, itself contributing to its success.

10. For a more in-depth discussion by PI Jon Christensen on how the resulting data did not allow him to address the questions he was interested in, see Christensen (2015: 25–7).

11. This is a group of people united by their love of trains and the railroad. The interests of this community span trainspotters, modellers, engineers, former railroad employees, amateur and professional historians, and more. This is a group whose demographics are 50 and older and who are overwhelmingly white and male.

12. <http://www.stanford.edu/group.spatialhistory/Visualizations/Hart/>

13. <https://www.historypin.org/project/42-railroads/>

14. The politics of the rail fan community tends towards the right, as well.

15. It meant that Living with the Railroads needed to be open in terms of time period and material. It led us to a side project on mapping railroad milepost markers, as we were able to parlay our GIS skills to help serve the community. This has generated goodwill in terms of being accepted as part of the community such that people are willing to engage with us. Finally, it led to our semi-regular rail fan days, as what this community desires is in-person interactions. Even the people who are digital friendly are often part of the community for the community component. I should add that joining expert communities brings with it the obligation of maintaining, at least for a time, both the project and the community you have generated. Enthusiast communities can be sceptical of outsiders; they do not want to be used and discarded. And you do not want to damage the possibilities for future researchers.

16. Named Entity Recognition (NER) is a process in Natural Language Processing that, in this case, classifies text into categories. As the Stanford Natural Language Processing Group states: 'Named Entity Recognition

(NER) labels sequences of words in a text which are the names of things, such as person and company names, or gene and protein names' (see <http://nlp.stanford.edu/software/CRF-NER.shtml> (last accessed 31 May 2015)).

17. Pronoun disambiguation algorithms are those digital processes that seek to determine to whom a pronoun is referring, to better identify characters for analysis.

18. Human Intelligence Tasks are any tasks that users of the Mechanical Turk site do. They are single tasks to be performed. These can range from counting the number of mentions of smoking in a magazine article, to writing captions, to telling researchers at Stanford whether a passage from a nineteenth-century novel indicates that a location is a place of happiness or not.

19. The Mechanical Turker community is hard to get a handle on because it is deliberately a black box. Unless the Turkers break the seal and contact the researchers/task creators, researchers have no way of knowing who the community who is answering their HITs actually is. While you can control for certain factors – rating, language skills – you are limited in what you can know about them. That said, we do know something about them in the aggregate. We know they are younger, 'more male, poorer, and more highly educated than Americans generally' (Richey and Taylor 2012). We also know that a significant portion of Turkers are Indian. This was sometimes an issue for our project, where knowledge of English is vital. For more on the Turker community, see Fort et al. (2010).

20. Specifically, the project focuses on the emotions associated with particular urban locales in London during the nineteenth century, where 'the narrative system becomes complicated, unstable: the city turns into a gigantic roulette table, where helpers and antagonists mix in unpredictable combinations' (Moretti 1998: 68).

21. More specific questions were: what areas of London were most represented? Do the spatial representations of the novels correlate to class divisions in the city? Do characters of different genders or classes have different spatial distributions in the geographies of the novels?

22. Here, Turker is used as a shorthand for the individuals who sign up to do tasks through Amazon's Mechanical Turk site, which you can find at <https://www.mturk.com/mturk/welcome>. As the splash page states: 'Mechanical Turk is a marketplace for work. We give businesses and developers access to an on-demand, scalable workforce. Workers select from thousands of tasks and work whenever it's convenient.' The name is meant to evoke in particular an eighteenth-century automaton, a chess-playing device called the Turk. The Turk turned out to be a fraud, though that is a discussion for a different paper.

23. A variety of other tasks also had to take place before the project could move forward. These included gathering a list of urban locations in London that figure prominently in Victorian novels, as well as the text mining of a corpus of over 4,000 novels for passages with place names. The use of a combination of digital humanities tools, combined with a more classic approach to finding locations (research by RAs and post-doctoral fellows into locations in nineteenth-century novels), ultimately resulted in 280 unique locations in London. From there, 'legitimate' passages were determined. These were defined as passages of at least 200 words, containing one of our locations, though they could be longer as determined by sentence boundaries. It is these passages that were ultimately sent out to the Turkers. This short description obviously glosses over a variety of steps. For further description and analysis, see <http://www.humanitiescrowdsourcing.stanford.edu>.

24. We struggled with the issue of how much to pay quite a bit, as well as the question of whether to use a micro-task site like the Mechanical Turk at all. Once we decided it was important to test this mode of crowdsourcing, though, we wanted to make sure we were not being exploitative, within our budgetary constraints. But it is important to note that there are increasing ethical concerns about making use of this kind of labour pool. See, for instance, Marvit (2014).

25. For a more detailed discussion of this process, as well as the results of the research, see Heuser and Algee-Hewitt (2015).

26. <http://mturkforum.com/showthread.php?17725-Can-t-Find-Eye-Pop ping-HITs-7-28-Make-Money-Monday!/page138> (last accessed 28 May 2015).

27. <http://mturkforum.com/showthread.php?17725-Can-t-Find-Eye-Pop ping-HITs-7-28-Make-Money-Monday!/page135> (last accessed 28 May 2015).

28. It is worth noting that we only rejected responses where it was patently obvious that someone was trying to game the system. And the majority of responses were accepted. Moreover, we did not have trouble getting our HITs completed. In this sense, the pushback was a tempest in a teapot. However, had we increased our rejection rate, or chosen not to explain why we rejected them, we might have driven away effective Turkers.

29. Again, see Heuser and Algee-Hewitt (2015) for some of the results of the work. In addition, see our Historypin site (<https://www.histor ypin.org/en/explore/victorian-london/paging/1>) and also Figure 8.3, which shows points of emotion that were neutral as to fear or happiness for a visual representation of the data.

REFERENCES

Anon. (n.d.) 'Amazon Mechanical Turk FAQ', Amazon Web Services, Inc., accessed May 2015.

Brabham, D. C. (2013) *Crowdsourcing*. Cambridge, MA: MIT Press.

Christensen, J. (2015) 'Reporting negative result in crowdsourcing', *American Historian*, May, pp. 25–7.

Dunn, S. and Hedges, M. (2012) 'Crowd scoping study, engaging the crowd with humanities research', at <http://crowds.cerch.kcl.ac.uk/wp-content/uploads/2012/12/Crowdsourcing-connected-communities.pdf> (last accessed 28 May 2015).

Fort, K., Adda, G. and Cohen, K. B. (2010) 'Amazon Mechanical Turk: gold mine or coal mine?', *Computational Linguistics*, 37: 2, pp. 413–20.

Heuser, R. and Algee-Hewitt, M. (2015) 'Mapping the emotions of London in fiction, 1700–1900: a crowdsourcing experiment', in P. Murrieta-Flores, D. Cooper and C. Donaldson (eds), *Literary Mapping in the Digital Age*. Farnham: Ashgate [forthcoming].

Howe, J. (2006) 'The rise of crowdsourcing', *Wired*, 14: 6, at <http://www.wired.com/wired/archive/14.06/crowds.html> (last accessed 28 May 2015).

Marvit, M. Z. (2014) 'How crowdworkers became ghosts in the digital machine', *The Nation*, 24 February, at <http://www.thenation.com/article/178241/how-crowdworkers-became-ghosts-digital-machine> (last accessed 25 May 2015).

Moretti, F. (1998) *Atlas of the European Novel, 1800–1900*. London: Verso.

Richey, S. and Taylor, B. (2012) 'How representative are Amazon Mechanical Turk workers?', at <http://themonkeycage.org/2012/12/19/how-repre sentative-are-amazon-mechanical-turk-workers/> (last accessed 21 May 2015).

Saldanha, F. P., Cohendet, P. and Pozzebon, M. (2014) 'Challenging the stage-gate model in crowdsourcing: the case of Fiat Mio in Brazil', *Technological Innovation Management Review*, September, pp. 28–35.

Tolkien, J. R. R. ([1954] 1994) *The Fellowship of the Ring*. New York: Del Rey.

White, R. (2011) *Railroaded: The Transcontinentals and the Making of Modern America*. New York: W. W. Norton.

CHAPTER 9

Fantasies of Scientificity: Ethnographic Identity and the Use of QDA Software

Anna Johansson and Anna Sofia Lundgren

INTRODUCTION

Largely neglected in methodological debates, software is both a technology and a medium with implications for research. As demonstrated by work in digital media studies and the emerging field of software studies, software is encoded with particular assumptions about the user and about society (e.g. Manovich 2013; Galloway 2012). This is not to say that user practices are determined by software and interface design but it suggests that we need to reflect on the ideological underpinnings of software as well as their implications for research practice and results.

This chapter engages with a specific type of software developed to facilitate qualitative analysis and often referred to as Computer Assisted Qualitative Data Analysis Software (CAQDAS) or simply Qualitative Data Analysis Software (QDAS). Originally programs for annotating textual data and retrieving annotated segments, the features of a QDAS package today typically include a 'coding' tool as well as tools for content search, network visualisation, hyperlinking data segments and querying. Many packages, such as Nvivo, MAXQDA and TAMS Analyzer, allow for analysis not only of textual data but also images, audio and video files.[1]

While there are numerous QDAS packages distributed commercially and through open sources, this chapter focuses mainly on one particular program called ATLAS.ti.[2] Building on experiences from our work as ethnographers and ATLAS.ti users, we aim to discuss the feelings and practices brought on by our encounters with this software. By relating our own experiences to broader debates about the use of digital tools in ethnographic research – historical as well as contemporary – the chapter explores the implications of digital technology use for the ethnographic self-image and also vice versa.

We start out by describing our own encounters with ATLAS.ti. Following that, we situate our experiences by briefly reviewing how ethnographic researchers have previously approached issues of computing and qualitative analysis software. Lastly, we draw on the psychoanalytic notion of 'fantasy' to discuss ethnographic experiences of digital tools. According to Glynos (2008: 283), fantasies name 'a narrative structure involving some reference to an idealized scenario promising an imaginary fullness or wholeness (the beatific side of fantasy) and, by implication, a disaster scenario (the horrific side of fantasy)'. We argue that the concept's potential to describe how people become invested in discourses may shed light on the way scientific identities and methodologies are built around emotionally charged constructs (fantasies) and, hence, why people hold on to certain practices and self-identifications even when confronted with alternatives. We also suggest that the concept of fantasy highlights how and why new technologies may become positioned as the Other of these constructs, identities and practices – as obstacles that hinder the realisation of the imaginary fullness promised by the fantasy.

ENCOUNTERS WITH ATLAS.TI

During 2013, the authors of this chapter were working on two separate research projects that both involved the use of ATLAS.ti for data management and analysis of ethnographic materials. Below, we account for our respective experiences with the software and the feelings and practices provoked in this process.

ATLAS.ti and interview transcripts: the ambiguity of distance

Anna Sofia Lundgren's first encounter with ATLAS.ti was brought about by a research project that involved analysing in-depth interviews with older people in order to deepen the understandings of reproductive choices during the Swedish baby boom in the 1940s and 1950s.[3] Thirty in-depth interviews were carried out with Swedish women who had their reproductive period during the baby boom. Generally, the interviews took the form of life stories where the women talked relatively freely about their experiences. Each interview was transcribed into around 25–50 pages.

The project as a whole involved several different countries around the world and one of the initial hopes was that ATLAS.ti would facilitate international comparisons. The Swedish interviews were carried out by two researchers, which meant that neither had first-hand experience of all of the interviews. We therefore thought that ATLAS.ti would help to structure our material which we perceived to be messy to the point of being overwhelming. One idea that lurked in the background was that ATLAS.ti would somehow assist in controlling this rich material and perhaps help us find unexpected connections in the data that we had trouble finding ourselves. Furthermore, using ATLAS.ti we imagined would provide us with a more explicit methodology. We should also not hide the fact that we probably imagined that ATLAS.ti would lend our study a more widely accepted scientific cachet (e.g. Fielding 2002; Gibbs et al. 2002; Seale 2002); more than once, we had had peer reviewers requesting a more explicit description of methods of analysis by naming different QDAS that we might have used.

Since the project members knew exactly nothing about ATLAS.ti when we started conducting the interviews, the first step was to attend a course. The course was a half-day long and, apart from a one-hour introduction, mainly consisted of hands-on practice, where course participants could explore the functions of ATLAS.ti using their own data. Having got a brief understanding of the program and the kinds of functions it offered, we instantly and enthusiastically got started with the coding. Soon, the first uploaded PDF transcripts were studded with codes. Every little part of the pages was found to contain immense significance and we struggled with how to name and level the codes, whether we were to code for manifest meanings or if we were to be more open to interpreted significance. For a while, we considered simply coding the transcripts for what the project plan had identified as important, leaving us with around five different central codes. However, it did not take long before we were back in what may be called 'the grounded theory mode', coding the transcripts for anything and everything that we could possibly find in them. The software numbered and counted the documents, and as the coding proceeded, the Code Manager[4] indicated to us how many codes we had created and how many times each code had been used. We found ourselves urged to continuously develop more and more fine-grained and detailed codes, perhaps falling into what Gilbert (2002) describes as the 'coding trap'. Regardless of it actually being a 'trap' or not, it was clear that we acted on a fantasy about what ATLAS.ti would be able to do and it resulted in a – for us – changed analytical practice as we shall discuss below.

The very possibility of detailed coding and the software's built-in features for abstracting from the data soon evoked the feeling that the material was graspable and controllable. Because the software encouraged and facilitated management of a large number of codes, as well as their relationships to each other, this seemed to suggest that detailed coding and greater systematics meant better knowledge of the research material. Since our material consisted of in-depth interviews that had the character of life stories, each transcript contained an enormous amount of information. The women talked about the

1940s and 1950s in general, but also about policies, availability and uses of contraceptives, fears of unwanted pregnancies, childcare, loves, complications and sorrows. The option of creating an infinite number of fine-grained codes and linking them through Code-Code Relations seemed to direct our focus to details in a manner that was not necessarily fruitful or even meaningful when analysing and interpreting ethnographic material. In retrospect, it seemed almost as if ATLAS.ti was exercising agency and affecting analytical processes. Our obsession with coding was not so much related to an unwillingness to proceed with the analytical-interpretative process, as Gilbert (2002) has suggested, but rather to the feeling that with the help of ATLAS.ti it would be possible to embrace the whole material in all its details.

A few weeks later, we sat down for coffee and discussed our material in depth, or rather we discussed the codes, new possible codes, and whether certain codes were frequently recurring or not. We realised that we had come to talk about the material in terms of codes where before we had talked about it in terms of individual life stories in which the parts had been made meaningful primarily within the context of either the individual narrative or society. In a way, this movement from the rich narratives to the codes that represented their smallest components was also accompanied by a simultaneous move where the material, the data, had gone from existing in between the transcripts and our almost physical memories of fieldwork to being limited to the text files uploaded in ATLAS.ti. Mea culpa, one may say. But the fact remained: starting to use ATLAS.ti had somehow redirected our focus.

The digitalisation of the material, together with the sudden focus on particularities and the possibility to abstract from them, helped to shed light on similarities and differences within the data. The software allowed for easy retrieval of coded quotations and generated detailed lists and visual displays of, for example, Code Neighbours and Coocurring Codes. But at the same time – and perhaps paradoxically – we felt that it involved the risk of failing to acknowledge the complexity of the material or the way meaning is dynamically produced in specific contexts. While Childers (2014: 819), for instance, claims that '[c]ontrary to the desires for certainty, coding cannot save the researcher from the messiness and complexity of the material world', we experienced the opposite. Childers (2014: 821) describes how her fieldwork experience brought her back 'to thinking–feeling the materiality of fieldwork' during her handling and analysis of data. In our case, not working with pen and paper but within ATLAS.ti, the digitalisation of the material seemed to distance us from our own experiences of fieldwork, yet position us too close to the material (cf. Gilbert 2002). We found this problematic, a feeling that revealed perhaps the way we had internalised the ethnographic notion that there is analytic potential residing in the field experience, and that this was put at risk in the QDAS coding process.

ATLAS.ti and social media materials: the ambiguity of quantification

During the same time period, Anna Johansson worked on a project exploring how blogs are used to negotiate notions of mental illness and identities related to mental health. The project included observations of social media interactions, interviews and analysis of blog content. Like the members of the baby boom project, I was hoping that the program would provide systematicity in the organisation and analysis of the data, which included textual as well as visual elements. Using QDAS, I imagined, would increase the reliability of my findings and allow me to better account for my method of analysis in future publications.

At the start of the project, it took some time initially to figure out the easiest way to archive social media content, and I learnt that ATLAS.ti does not support any smooth import process from web to desktop. After trying out screenshots, videos and plain text documents, I ended up with downloading PDFs of blog posts which were added to the project's Hermeneutic Unit (HU). Two of the leading Swedish mental health blogs were used as a starting point for the study and their current and historical posts were documented by downloading and incorporating them into the project archive. During this process, I began to write tentative memos and as I gradually came to identify recurrent themes I also started the inductive coding of the documents. In parallel, I continued browsing the online blog networks, following links from the two main blogs, carrying out a few interviews, emailing with bloggers and taking field notes. Every new blog I encountered led me to further blogs. I used a bookmarking tool to keep track of them as I attempted to figure out the social life of bloggers and the thematics emerging from blog contents. Fairly soon I had identified twenty blogs that all seemed significant enough to warrant an in-depth analysis and their blog posts were added to the HU.

Meanwhile, I kept on exploring the ever-expanding blog circles: keeping up with new blog posts, clicking links, taking notes and adding to my bookmarks. Two weeks later I found myself following ninety blogs and consecutively putting their complete archives into the HU. Still, I began to feel a nagging sense of my work as meagre. There were infinite amounts of data out there in the blogosphere and the ATLAS.ti software clearly facilitated storage and organisation of the blog posts. But how much data could I possibly engage with as an ethnographer? How many blog posts would it be possible for me to analyse? I easily found another forty relevant blogs that I added to the HU, and then another forty. Details became less and less important, as did contacts with bloggers, reflexive field notes and analytical work itself. What was important was instead the urge to collect a vast and well-managed repository of documents. At 250 blogs – and, hence, many thousands of individual blog posts – I decided to discontinue the collection.

At this point, however, the set of data was already too large to allow for a comprehensive close reading, given the timeframe of the project – a consequence of poor planning, for sure, but also an illustration of how I got lost in the frenzy of collecting *everything*. Evidently, it was the accessibility and infiniteness of blog posts that brought about this urge, together with current trends in the study of digital culture – but the structure of ATLAS. ti itself also contributed to my focus on quantity. One benefit stressed in debates about QDAS is precisely their facilitation of managing large amounts of data (Dohan and Sanchez-Jankowski 1998; St John and Johnson 2000). This might encourage the qualitative researcher to eschew smaller samples in favour of larger ones, especially in contexts where discussions about big data abound. Media scholars Boyd and Crawford (2012: 663) point out that the notion of big data rests on 'the widespread belief that large data sets offer a higher form of intelligence and knowledge that can generate insights that were previously impossible, with the aura of truth, objectivity, and accuracy'. As such, it has profound epistemological implications, and as I experienced in this project, this trend in the study of digital data – enabled by certain technological possibilities such as ATLAS.ti in this case – might lead scholars in traditionally qualitative disciplines to take on more quantitative approaches.

For pragmatic reasons, I eventually decided to code only part of the blog posts we had collected. However, when I wanted to delve deeper into our data using the analytical tools provided by the software, I realised that having a large data set and a large number of coded quotations was a clear advantage. Indeed, none of the features really requires a certain amount of input; ATLAS.ti can generate reports based on as little as one single code in one single document. But numerical dimensions seemed brought to the fore as soon as I tried to create output from the programme. The Word Cruncher feature, for example, transformed data into Excel tables while giving me the options of 'Separate counts', 'Absolute counts', 'Relative counts' and 'Word lengths'. The Query Tool allowed me to search for combinations of codes using operands that could be 'recalculated' while the Code Cooccurrence features displayed numbers arranged in trees and tables.

As a qualitatively trained ethnologist, I found this output in the shape of spreadsheets, the foregrounding of numbers on the screen and the general emphasis on quantity and countability somewhat difficult to comprehend. I was worried that my qualitative analysis competencies were not sufficient to analyse this type of data, but the seeming scienticity of the data output still had a certain allure. When the connections identified as significant by the machine did not correspond to the hunches I had of what was really going on in these blogs, I began to question myself rather than the computer – and my conclusions, hence, seemed to emerge less from my own engagement with the source material and the bloggers and more from the number of co-occurrences that ATLAS.ti presented me with.

In summary, both examples show that we had great hopes for what the technology would do, but we were also hesitant about what it would entail. It was obvious that things happened when we started using ATLAS.ti and that we, to some extent, reacted ambivalently to how the digital tool affected our analyses. Rather than just taking our reactions as a confirmation of the short-comings of QDAS or dismissing them for being the result of ignorance and lack of training, we think there are reasons to reflect on where they came from and what they were about. Therefore, in what follows, we attempt to scrutinise our experiences and contextualise them by delving into what ethnographers before us have said on the matter.

ATLAS.TI IN CONTEXT: ETHNOGRAPHIC RESPONSES TO DIGITAL TOOLS

Ethnographic literature about the use of QDAS indicates that, just like us, others have also found digital tools both useful and unsettling. Early versions of this type of software emerged with the advent of the PC or microcomputer in the 1980s (Seidel and Clark 1984; Richards 2002). These programs have evolved over the decades, but while some uses of computers and, for example, word processors have become incorporated into ethnographic practice to the extent that they are rarely reflected upon, QDAS are still met with scepticism by some scholars. Part of the criticism has focused on the new form of ortho-doxy in data management that renders *coding* the natural or privileged way of handling data. For example, Coffey et al. (1996: §7.6) stress that '[a]nalytic pro-cedures which appear rooted in standardized, often mechanistic procedures are no substitute for genuinely "grounded" engagement with the data throughout the whole of the research process' (see also Bong 2002; Roberts and Wilson 2002; Moss and Shank 2002; Thompson 2002). The emphasis on coding has similarly been described as involving the risk of being distant from or losing closeness to the data (Gilbert 2002; Fielding and Lee 1998: §2.3) and of prompt-ing researchers to adopt a grounded theory methodology (Lonkila 1995).

Other scholars challenge such critical claims and take a more approving stance to QDAS. For example, Lee and Fielding (1996) note that coding 'is a form of data reduction, and for many qualitative researchers is an important strategy which they would use irrespective of the availability of software'. Proponents of QDAS also point to how it fosters reliability and generalisabil-ity (Dohan and Sanchez-Jankowski 1998; St John and Johnson 2000) and how this type of software might enhance researcher reflexivity for scholars who are willing to engage in reflective practice (Woods et al. 2015).

To better understand these divergent attitudes, we argue that they should be situated as part of a longer history of computing in ethnography during which similar approaches have recurred again and again (cf. Seaver 2014). A look in the rearview mirror shows that ethnographers have long searched for ways to systematise collected data, ranging from pre-digital methods such as index cards to today's digital tools. Texts on the use of computers and software in ethnographic research date back at least to the 1960s (e.g. Hymes 1965; Randolph and Coult 1968; Burton 1970; Colby 1966). Accounts from this early period are usually technical in nature and provide detailed instructions on how to design programs and prepare research materials in ways that render them 'computable' (e.g. Lamb and Romney 1965; Garvin 1965). At this point, individual programs had to be written for every new research context. The lack of ready-made solutions meant that digitally inclined ethnographers worked closely together with computer scientists or did some of the programming themselves, and this sparked discussions on how much ethnographers must know about computer operations in order to 'get their hands dirty' and stay in touch with their data (Hymes 1965: 23). Such debates tended to pit the discipline of computer science against that of anthropology, describing the latter as less advanced and less explicit in its theory and methodology. Similar dichotomies have proved to be persistent over the years.

Acknowledging that some anthropologists might oppose the use of computers, Hymes (1965), for example, saw computing as an opportunity for ethnography because it would facilitate systematicity and organisation of data that are otherwise typically seen as big and messy. This dichotomy of order/disorder was also invoked in Weinberg and Weinberg's (1972: 37) report on their study of kinship. Suggesting that '[a]ny anthropologist knows that no two aspects of science could be further apart than the orderly, rational, clean computer and the disorganized, irrational, and dirty job of fieldwork', they argued that ethnographic data quality would benefit from computing because it permits 'more precise and more complete data with less effort and more reliability than any other method' (1972: 39).

As the use of microcomputers spread in the 1980s, scholars could turn to ready-made applications without prior knowledge of programming. Similar to how the relation between computers and ethnography had been conceptualised at earlier stages, proponents of microcomputer use generally stressed the way in which computers would improve the shortcomings of ethnography – by facilitating the handling of large data sets (Podolefsky 1987), making fewer mistakes (Agar 1983) and shortening the time span between and supporting the dialectic process of collection and analysis (Dow 1983). Computers were seen to increase methodological rigour and scientificity by making the ethnographic research process more explicit and transparent (Conrad and Reinharz 1984; see also Dohan and Sanchez-Jankowski 1998; St John and Johnson

2000). This last argument also indicates a perceived opacity of conventional ethnographic methods of analysis, for which Conrad and Reinharz (1984: 6) suggested several reasons:

> Perhaps it is that they [analytic methods] have been seen as private (when one returns from the interaction of the field or the interview, one sits alone, thinks and writes), mysterious (drawing on intuition, cognitive leaps, on patterns or concepts that 'emerge'), idiosyncratic (with each researcher assumed to analyze data her/his own way), and to some degree simplistic (because these procedures are so mechanical and boil down to nothing more than underlining, shuffling paper, rereading, and cutting and pasting). [. . .] With the introduction of personal computers, we should become able to codify exactly how we analyze our data and to reproduce our analytic steps in ways that serve the interests of teaching and communicating to our fellow researchers.

Irrespective of these celebratory accounts, however, digital technology was still recognised as an alien field to many ethnographers – as evidenced by Stuck's claim that the mistaken association of computers with numerical data had left qualitative social scientists 'in the "dark ages" using photocopies, colored pencils, index cards and differently shaped stickers as their tools' (Stuck 1989: 6).

Needless to say, much has happened since the 1960s: many uses of digital technology (e.g. to store data, write, record sound and images, and perform literature searches) have become commonplace in ethnographic research. At the same time, and judging from the critique against QDAS, the debate on computing and ethnography still revolves around a constantly perceived opposition between technology and culture; as anthropologist Nick Seaver (2014) puts it in his discussion about computers and anthropology, 'there are some remarkably persistent debates that keep popping up – about formalism, quantification, and the division of research labor, among others'.

Regardless of whether it is early computing or QDAS that is in focus, the texts discussed here tend to construct the digital as both an opportunity and a risk (cf. Paulus et al. 2013) – an *opportunity* because it provides ethnography with valuable rigour, order and distance (characteristics that are often unreflectively described as the path towards scientificity) and a *risk* because it might compromise precisely such aspects that are traditionally valued in ethnographic research. To sum up, the tension between digital technology and ethnography is formulated in the literature in at least five different ways: as a tension between explicit and less explicit methodologies; between computers as orderly and fieldwork as messy; between analysis as mechanical or computer-driven and manual or human-driven; between quantitative and qualitative analysis; and between distance and closeness to the data. These dichotomies seemingly form the structure and boundaries of what may be conceptualised not only as a fantasy of digital technology but also as an ethnographic fantasy or a fantasy of ethnography that seems to have permeated the field of ethnography at least since the 1960s. When encountering ATLAS.ti we were thus already being positioned in the midst of such conflicting viewpoints. In the next section, we turn to these fantasies in order to discuss what they might tell us about the persistence of ambivalent feelings in ethnographers' encounters with QDAS.

FANTASIES OF SCIENTIFICITY

The feelings and practices evoked in us by our encounters with ATLAS.ti are, just as the reviewed literature, formulated from within and thus conditioned by the field and history of anthropologically influenced ethnography. This means that the critique partly functions as boundary work (Gieryn 1983); it scrutinises the possibilities of new technologies, but this is done from the standpoint that there is something to safeguard, boundaries to uphold, competences to defend. In his text 'Ten Lies of Ethnography', Fine (1993: 267) proclaims that '[i]llusions are essential to maintain an occupational reputation'. While it may be harsh to call it lies, which Fine also admittedly recognises, it is still relevant for our purposes to outline what 'illusions' or, as we will call them, 'fantasies' about ethnography (and digital technology) that are brought to the fore in our own experiences and in the literature.

Ethnography is typically understood as a reflexive process where the research as well as the researcher are inevitably part of the world that is being studied (Hammersley and Atkinson [1983] 2007). The repeated emphasis on 'being there' (cf. Clifford and Marcus 1986) and getting one's hands 'dirty'– a metaphor that has already been cited twice in this text – constitutes ethnography as a very personal and emotional way to go about research. Personal feelings are described as central not only to how fieldwork develops but also to the practice of analysis and writing (e.g. Briggs 1970; Favret-Saada 1982; Cesara 1982; Ehn and Klein 1994; Hammersley and Atkinson [1983] 2007; Coffey 1999). Browsing through the textbooks used in the specific Swedish ethnographic context in which we are trained, creativity, fantasy and empathy are oft-noted qualities of the ethnographic researcher (Ehn and Löfgren 1996, 2001, 2012). Just as fieldwork itself, analytical craftspersonship is typically described as primarily a creative process (Ehn and Löfgren 1982, 2001), difficult to grasp and escaping reproducible models or procedures (Ehn and Löfgren 1996). Fieldnotes are described as secondary to what is in the researcher's head (Arnstberg 1997). This leads Hallberg (2001: 119) to note that for ethnographers, collectable data 'cannot completely replace the kind of experiences that the researcher gains by attending, participating, perceiving moods and interpreting subtexts'. According to this view parts of the data will inevitably continue to be localised within the individual researcher, perhaps not even explicated in field diaries, thus too volatile for the digitisation practice – but still central to ethnographic analyses.

Given that this fantasy of ethnography has partly been formed in relation to a supposedly less reflexive and more objectivist scientific paradigm (Clifford and Marcus 1986; Marcus and Fischer 1986), it is not surprising that many of the functions offered by ATLAS.ti implied more than just neutral options to us. The opportunity of creating a large and well-structured repository was perceived to turn fieldwork into a mere archiving practice, which in turn threatened the 'lived' and creative character of ethnographic research that is so central to the fantasy of ethnography. The opportunity for fine-grained coding and quantifiability, and the ensuing 'datafication' (Markham 2013) that transformed our experiences into pieces of digitised information created a sense of distance in relation to the ethnographic material. Hence, these features also threatened the significance traditionally ascribed to the ethnographer's self as an intrinsic part of the research material. While we certainly believed that the use of software contributed to methodological rigour, it also evoked a feeling that analysis was machine-driven – which we, in turn, perceived as intimidating to the personal approach of ethnography.

The potential bias towards quantification and detachment has partly been rejected as a valid problem by researchers who stress that one does not necessarily have to use all the (quantifying) functions afforded by a specific programme (Paulus et al. 2013; Gilbert 2002). We would argue that this is a simplified way of approaching the issue. Following Drucker (2014), interfaces are performative, enunciative apparatuses that structure subjectivity by encouraging certain practices and restricting others (cf. Stanfill 2014: 2). In our case, not only did the affordances of ATLAS.ti threaten what we perceived to be important scientific values. Engaging with ATLAS.ti also meant being drawn into already established power relations. For example, the opportunity of handling larger samples may seem neutral, but it easily implies that larger samples are better than smaller ones since ATLAS.ti translates the analyses into numbers and figures (and even the qualitative researcher realises that these may lose bearing if the sample is too small). The researcher might of course act in ways other than those suggested by the software, but it still makes a normative-ideological claim and produces a certain ideal (cf. Galloway 2012; Chun 2005; Manovich 2013), which, in this particular case, implicitly threatens to devalue purely qualitative approaches. As Roberts and Wilson (2002) have suggested, the positivist philosophy underpinning computer technology is contrary to the philosophical foundations of qualitative research, a fact that, according to them, not only drastically limits the uses of QDAS in qualitative research, but actually risks harming the process of qualitative data analysis.

Against this backdrop, it is clear that the primary angst in our encounters with ATLAS.ti, as well as in the general ethnographic critique of QDAS, is for the researcher to become separated from 'reality' – from the field, the material or the data – and power relations we were not only drawn into but also subordinated by. Hence, our reactions when working with ATLAS.ti were not primarily about whether or not the software is in fact suitable for analysis of ethnographic materials. They also had to do with our ethnographic identifications and the way these were sustained by investments made in the fantasies of ethnography.

According to Glynos (2008, 2011) every fantasy involves references to a desirable 'imaginary fullness' but also, since according to this Lacanian perspective such fullness can never be entirely realised, to 'obstacles' that can explain why this fullness has not yet been achieved. In this sense, the obstacles tend to transform the ontological impossibility of fullness into a manageable problem that would be possible to solve if only different measures are taken. In the case presented here, we have suggested two sets of fantasies were at play: fantasies of digital technology and fantasies of ethnography. Since both of us work in interdisciplinary research contexts and are positioned in a Swedish humanistic context of increasing pressure for international publications, we had been confronted with intensified demands to communicate ethnographic results to a wider audience and to submit our studies to multi-disciplinary reviews. In light of these demands, QDAS seem to have been drawn into a fantasy of digital technology in which they came to symbolise and promise a fullness to come in the shape of increased scientificity.

CONCLUDING REMARKS

Our investments in fantasies of ethnography were central for how QDAS were perceived – by us, and also by a significant number of ethnographers before us. In fact, we would suggest that QDAS generally have been positioned as either the solution to the perceived problems of ethnography or as an obstacle preventing the fantasy of ethnography from being realised.[5] Although being described – and partly perceived! – as a desirable alternative to the creative but difficult-to-grasp ethnographic methods of analysis, many ethnographers have obviously struggled with the incorporation of this facilitator, choosing sometimes rather to hold on to the ethnographic fantasy and the methodologies and subject positions that come with it.

However, despite being positioned as an obstacle, we would argue that it is not digital technology per se that constitutes the main threat to the fantasy of ethnography. Instead, QDAS, just as many other digital tools before it, have come to symbolise something larger: it is invested 'in properties that far exceed its materiality' (Glynos 2008: 285), namely the scientific philosophy that underpins QDAS technology and that has a history of being antagonistically positioned in relation to ethnography. From this angle, ethnographers' choice to work with QDAS can be viewed as a practice that challenges an old ethnographic self-identity in ways that may suggest change. At the same time, the persistent ethnographic critique against QDAS can be conceptualised as a mobilising force that aims to protect ethnography from perceived threats and that finds support in the fantasy of ethnography and its notion of deep analysis as forever out of reach for stringent and easily reproducible analytic methodologies. QDAS and other digital technologies then become not only obstacles to be overcome, but symbols of this threatening but necessary Other.

The appeal to fantasy in this chapter has helped accessing the structure of desire (and enjoyment) more than it assists in an analysis of whether a belief is 'true' or 'false' (Glynos 2011). In this way, the concept of fantasy may shed light on the desires, identifications and investments that guide ethnographers' reactions and feelings when encountering QDAS, as well as the fantasies attached to QDAS. As we have shown we would certainly argue that ATLAS. ti is (already) performative of a quantifying scientificity, but we suggest that ethnographers' interest in this type of digital tools as well as their reactions to them make visible more than that. Rather than establishing whether the interest and reactions are good or bad and whether they rest on rational or irrational grounds, we suggest that they – as the concept of fantasy has helped us to show – have a potential to shed light on much more than just the potential benefits and risks of QDA software.

NOTES

1. For more information about these packages, see their respective websites: <http://www.qsrinternational.com>, <http://www.maxqda.com/> and <http://tamsys.sourceforge.net/> (accessed 25 May 2015).
2. See <http://atlasti.com/> (last accessed 25 May 2015).
3. The project was carried out with ethnologist Angelika Sjöstedt Landén, Umeå University (see Lundgren and Sjöstedt Landén 2015; Sjöstedt Landén and Lundgren 2016).
4. The Code Manager is a term used to describe one of the features in ATLAS.ti. Familiarity with this and other specific functions mentioned in the chapter is not necessary for comprehending our general argument.
5. Of course, the opposite is also a possible interpretation: that the viable fantasy of ethnography constituted an impediment for the fantasy of digital technology to deliver its promises.

REFERENCES

Agar, M. (1983) 'Microcomputers as field tools', *Computers and the Humanities*, 17: 1, pp. 19–26.

Arnstberg, K.-O. (1997) *Fältetnologi [Fieldethnology]*. Stockholm: Carlssons.

Bong, S. A. (2002) 'Debunking myths in qualitative data analysis', *FQS Forum: Qualitative Social Research*, 3: 2, at <http://www.qualitative-research.net/index.php/fqs/article/view/849/1844> (last accessed 25 May 2015).

Boyd, D. and Crawford, K. (2012) 'Critical questions for big data: provocations for a cultural, technological, and scholarly phenomenon', *Information, Communication and Society*, 15: 5, pp. 662–9.

Briggs, J. (1970) *Never in Anger*. Cambridge, MA: Harvard University Press.

Burton, M. L. (1970) 'Computer applications in cultural anthropology', *Computers and the Humanities*, 5: 1, pp. 37–45.

Cesara, M. (1982) *Reflections of a Woman Anthropologist: No Hiding Place*. London: Academic Press.

Childers, S. M. (2014) 'Promiscuous analysis in qualitative research', *Qualitative Inquiry*, 20: 6, pp. 819–26.

Chun, W. H. K. (2005) 'On software, or the persistence of visual knowledge', *Grey Room*, 18, pp. 26–51.

Clifford, J. and Marcus, G. E. (1986) *Writing Culture: The Poetics and Politics of Ethnography*. Berkeley: University of California Press.

Coffey, A. (1999) *The Ethnographic Self*. London: Sage.

Coffey, A., Holbrook, B. and Atkinson, P. A. (1996) 'Qualitative data analysis: technologies and representations', *Sociological Research Online*, 1: 1, at <http://www.socresonline.org.uk/1/1/4.html> (last accessed 25 May 2015).

Colby, B. N. (1966) 'The analysis of culture content and the patterning of narrative concern in texts', *American Anthropologist*, 68, pp. 374–88.

Conrad, P. and Reinharz, S. (1984) 'Computers and qualitative data: editor's introductory essay', *Qualitative Sociology*, 7: 1–2, pp. 3–15.

Dohan, D. and Sanchez-Jankowski, M. (1998) 'Using computers to analyze ethnographic field data: theoretical and practical considerations', *Annual Review of Sociology*, 24: 1, pp. 477–98.

Dow, J. (1983) 'Communications and conferencing software for anthropology', *Annual Meeting of the American Anthropological Association*, at <http://files.eric.ed.gov/fulltext/ED244853.pdf> (last accessed 25 May 2015).

Drucker, J. (2014) *Graphesis: Visual Forms of Knowledge Production*. Cambridge, MA: Harvard University Press.

Ehn, B. and Klein, B. (1994) *Från erfarenhet till text: Om kulturvetenskaplig reflexivitet [From Experience to Text: About Reflexivity in Cultural Analysis]*. Stockholm: Carlssons.

Ehn, B. and Löfgren, O. (1982) *Kulturanalys* [*Cultural Analysis*]. Stockholm: Liber.

Ehn, B. and Löfgren, O. (1996) *Vardagslivets etnologi* [*Everyday Ethnology*]. Stockholm: Carlssons.

Ehn, B. and Löfgren, O. (2001) *Kulturanalyser* [*Cultural Analyses*]. Malmö: Gleerups.

Favret-Saada, J. (1982) *Deadly Words*. Cambridge: Cambridge University Press.

Fielding, N. (2002) 'Automating the ineffable: qualitative software and the meaning of qualitative research', in T. May (ed.), *Qualitative Research in Action*. London: Sage, pp. 161–78.

Fielding, N. G. and Lee, R. M. (1998) *Computer Analysis and Qualitative Research*. London: Sage.

Fine, G. A. (1993) 'Ten lies of ethnography: moral dilemmas of field research', *Journal of Contemporary Ethnography*, 22: 3, pp. 267–93.

Fisher, E. (2010) 'Contemporary technology discourse and the legitimation of capitalism', *European Journal of Social Theory*, 13: 2, pp. 229–52.

Gallagher, K. and Freeman, B. (2011) 'Multi-site ethnography, hypermedia and the productive hazards of digital methods: a struggle for liveness', *Ethnography and Education*, 6: 3, pp. 357–73.

Galloway, A. R. (2012) *The Interface Effect*. Cambridge: Polity Press.

Garvin, P. L. (1965) 'Computer processing and cultural data: problems of method', in D. H. Hymes (ed.), *The Use of Computers in Anthropology*. New York: Wenner-Gren Foundation, pp. 119–40.

Gibbs, G. R., Friese, S. and Mangabeira, W. C. (2002) 'The use of new technology in qualitative research: introduction to Issue 3(2) of FQS', *FQS Forum: Qualitative Social Research*, 3: 2 at <http://www.qualitative-research.net/index.php/fqs/article/view/847/1840> (last accessed 31 August 2015).

Gieryn, T. F. (1983) 'Boundary-work and the demarcation of science from nonscience: strains and interests in professional ideologies of scientists', *American Sociological Review*, 48: 6, pp. 781–95.

Gilbert, L. S. (2002) 'Going the distance: "closeness" in qualitative data analysis software', *International Journal of Social Research Methodology*, 5: 3, pp. 215–28.

Glynos, J. (2008) 'Ideological fantasy at work', *Journal of Political Ideologies*, 13: 3, pp. 275–96.

Glynos, J. (2011) 'Fantasy and identity in critical political theory', *Filozofski vestnik*, 32: 2, pp. 65–88.

Hallberg, M. (2001) *Etnologisk koreografi: Att följa ett ämne i rörelse* [*Ethnological Choreography: Following a Discipline on the Move*]. Nora: Nya Doxa.

Hammersley, M. and Atkinson, P. ([1983] 2007) *Ethnography: Principles in Practice*. London: Routledge.

Hymes, D. H. (ed.) (1965) *The Use of Computers in Anthropology*. New York: Wenner-Gren Foundation.

Lamb, S. M. and Romney, A. K. (1965) 'An anthropologist's introduction to the computer', in D. H. Hymes (ed.), *The Use of Computers in Anthropology*. New York: Wenner-Gren Foundation, pp. 37–90.

Lee, R. and Fielding, N. (1996) 'Qualitative data analysis: representations of a technology: a comment on Coffey, Holbrook and Atkinson', *Sociological Research Online*, 1: 4, at <http://www.socresonline.org.uk/1/4/lf.html> (last accessed 25 May 2015).

Lonkila, M. (1995) 'Grounded theory as an emerging paradigm for computer-assisted qualitative data analysis', in U. Kelle (ed.), *Computer-aided Qualitative Data Analysis: Theory, Methods and Practice*. London: Sage, pp. 41–51.

Lundgren, A. S. and Sjöstedt Landén, A. (2015) 'Struggling with choice: narrating reproductive practices in Sweden, ca. 1940–1960', in L. Karlsson et al., *Ageing: Culture and Identity*. Umeå: Umeå University, pp. 65–92.

Mangabeira, W. C. (1996) 'CAQDAS and its diffusion across four countries: national specificities and common themes', *Current Sociology*, 44: 3, pp. 191–205.

Manovich, L. (2013) *Software Takes Command*. New York: Bloomsbury.

Marcus, G. E. and Fischer, M. M. J. (1986) *Anthropology as Cultural Critique: An Experimental Moment in the Human Sciences*. Chicago: University of Chicago Press.

Markham, A. N. (2013) 'Undermining "data": a critical examination of a core term in scientific inquiry', *First Monday*, 18: 10, at <http://firstmonday.org/ojs/index.php/fm/article/view/4868/3749> (last accessed 25 May 2015).

Moss, C. M and Shank, G. (2002) 'Using qualitative processes in computer technology research on online learning: lessons in change from "Teaching as International Learning"', *FQS Forum: Qualitative Social Research*, 3: 2, at <http://www.qualitative-research.net/index.php/fqs/article/view/860/1868> (last accessed 25 May 2015).

Paulus, T. M., Lester, J. N. and Britt, V. G. (2013) 'Constructing hopes and fears around technology: a discourse analysis of introductory qualitative research texts', *Qualitative Inquiry*, 19: 9, pp. 639–51.

Podolefsky, A. (1987) 'New tools for old jobs: computers in the analysis of field notes', *Anthropology Today*, 3: 5, pp. 14–16.

Randolph, R. R. and Coult, A. D. (1968) 'A computer analysis of Bedouin marriage', *Southwestern Journal of Anthropology*, 24: 1, pp. 83–99.

Richards, T. (2002) 'An intellectual history of NUD*IST and Nvivo', *International Journal of Social Research Methodology*, 5: 3, pp. 199–214.

Roberts, K. and Wilson, R. W. (2002) 'ICT and the research process: issues around the compatibility of technology with qualitative data analysis', *FQS Forum: Qualitative Social Research*, 3: 2, at <http://www.qualitative-research.net/index.php/fqs/article/view/862> (last accessed 25 May 2015).

St John, W. and Johnson, P. (2000) 'The pros and cons of data analysis software for qualitative research', *Journal of Nursing Scholarship*, 32: 4, pp. 393–7.

Seale, C. F. (2002) 'Computer-assisted analysis of qualitative interview data', in J. F. Gubrium and J. A. Holstein (ed.), *Handbook of Interview Research: Context and Method*. Thousand Oaks, CA: Sage, pp. 651–70.

Seaver, N. (2014) 'Computers and sociocultural anthropology', *Savage Minds: Notes and Queries in Anthropology*, at <http://savageminds.org/2014/05/19/computers-and-sociocultural-anthropology/> (last accessed 25 May 2015).

Seidel, J. V. and Clark, J. A. (1984) 'THE ETHNOGRAPH: a computer program for the analysis of qualitative data', *Qualitative Sociology*, 7: 1–2, pp. 110–25.

Sjöstedt Landén, A. and Lundgren, A. S. (2016) 'Intergenerational interviewing: exploring the silences of female experiences', in G. Griffin (ed.), *Cross-Cultural Interviewing: Feminist Experiences and Reflections*. London: Routledge, pp. 208–24.

Stanfill, M. (2014) 'The interface as discourse: the production of norms through web design', *New Media and Society* [online], pp. 1–16.

Stuck, M. F. (1989) *The 'How To's' of Using Word Processors and Database Managers with Qualitative Data: A Primer for Professionals*. Presented at joint session of IACE (International Association for Computing in Education) and AERA (American Educational Research Association), San Francisco. At: <https://archive.org/details/ERIC_ED311878> (last accessed 25 May 2015).

Thompson, R. (2002) 'Reporting the results of computer-assisted analysis of qualitative research data', *FQS Forum: Qualitative Social Research*, 3: 2, at <http://www.qualitative-research.net/index.php/fqs/article/view/864> (last accessed 25 May 2015).

Weinberg, D. and Weinberg, G. M. (1972) 'Using a computer in the field: kinship information', *Social Science Information*, 11: 6, pp. 37–59.

Woods, M., Macklin, R. and Lewis, G. K. (2015) 'Researcher reflexivity: exploring the impacts of CAQDAS use', *International Journal of Social Research Methodology*, May, pp. 1–19.

CHAPTER 10

Digital Network Analysis: Understanding Everyday Online Discourse Micro- and Macroscopically

Robert Glenn Howard

INTRODUCTION: MOTHERING DISTRUST

In a large online forum, *Mothering.com*, dedicated to what is termed 'natural family living', I have been tracking expressions of distrust and hostility to institutional medicine and its practitioners. On this forum, the idea that individual doctors are corrupt is linked to the expression of distrust for the institutional structures that empower them. This is common in discussions of the 'birth industry', circumcision and elsewhere. But it is maybe most prevalent in the discussion of vaccines. One user exemplifies the attitude that vaccines are 'unnatural' when she stated that: 'I believe that all vaccines are 100% harmful and 100% ineffective and have always been a big scam. Vaccines are blood poisoning and are completely toxic garbage and do not belong in the human bloodstream' (MyLilPwny 2009). The idea that vaccines are a 'big scam' is a common one. Another user linked the medical field's avocation of vaccines to a fundamental misunderstanding of human biology: 'Most people in the health field, buy into Germ Theory' (MyLittleWonders 2006). By far the most common explanation for doctors buying into 'Germ Theory' found in these forums is something like: 'IMO, it's all about the pharm industry. Hmmm . . . how do we get people to buy stock in the company that produces Tamiflu(sp?)? Scare people!' (NaomiLoreli 2006).

In the most extreme assertions I have found, this distrust of medicine evolves from questioning the expertise of institutional structures to a belief in a broad conspiracy between medical practitioners, pharmaceutical companies, media institutions and governments. When the 2009 H1N1 flu pandemic never materialised, for example, the forum exploded with rumours that the pharmaceutical industry pays kickbacks to ensure the purchase of vaccines. A user wrote: 'Because of the politics involved, it makes me even more sure that our kids shouldn't be injected with any vaccine because it's all just money, greed, politics, and disregard for human life' (AllyRae 2009). The specific allegation that viruses are being manufactured by drug companies is often repeated. Another user wrote: 'Personally, not to look for the black helicopters or anything, but I think [avian flu] is a man-made strain, tested overseas to see what would happen on a population too uneducated to realize what was going on' (Grahamsmom98 2005). These kinds of discussions often lead to worries that the government will force individuals to take vaccines in the future. One user reported that her husband 'learned today that the state of MA has legally deputized doctors and dentists in preparation for mass vaccinations. [. . .] I sometimes sound like a conspiracy theory nut but my state is sure passing a lot of laws about it lately for some reason' (laohaire 2009).

In this chapter, I use these online discussions about vaccines to demonstrate how a computational 'macroscopic' method can augment online ethnographies of media users. Engaging this discussion accomplishes four things. First, it demonstrates how the concept of 'vernacular authority' can help reveal the power of informal and everyday communication occurring in participatory media. Second, it suggests that, while irreplaceable, ethnographic methods are necessarily limited in their ability to discern the large-scale processes of vernacular discourse that give everyday communication online its power. Third, I outline a computational method I have developed to address this limitation – a variation of what Katy Börner (2011) has termed a 'macroscopic' view of digital network communication. Fourth, I analyse the vernacular discourse surrounding vaccines on this very large Internet forum to demonstrate the potential of a macroscopic approach to this kind of research. With this combination of computational macroscopic viewing and the close analysis of documents and individual communication behaviours, it becomes clear that the extreme claims which drew my initial attention to this forum do not actually dominate the vaccine discourse. Instead, vernacular authority trumps the expertise of doctors through a pervasive distrust that lingers in the background, shaping the perception of vaccines more quietly.

CONFRONTING THE LIMITS OF DIGITAL ETHNOGRAPHY

I first discovered the *Mothering.com* Internet forum when I was working on my previous research project: *Digital Jesus* (2011). In that work, I used my long-term digital and face-to-face ethnographic work in online Christian fundamentalist communities to analyse communication enclaves where individuals share the belief that we are living in the 'End Times' based on a powerful sense that Jesus's Second Coming is imminent. While doing that work, a friend described a network location where radically progressive people were interacting with fundamentalist-leaning Christian conservatives and agreeing on things. Looking into it, I quickly discovered they were agreeing on notions such as the government and other institutions conspiring against them.

During my research for *Digital Jesus*, I developed the concept of 'vernacular authority' to account for how these individuals held such a powerful belief so totally rejected by the more mainstream discourse outside of their online communication enclave (Howard 2008a, 2008b). An alternative to institutional authority, vernacular authority emerges when an individual makes appeals that specifically are *not* institutional in the sense that they do not rely on any authority arising from formally instituted social formations like a church, newspaper company or academic journal. 'Vernacular' can best be defined as that which is opposed to its alternate term, 'institutional' (Howard 2011: 7–10). While this kind of authority can sometimes emerge in charismatic individuals claiming access to individual power, it is also often perceived as emerging from the aggregation of volition (Howard 2013a: 76). This aggregation occurs through the repeated expression of shared beliefs by different members in a community (Howard 2011: 20–1). These expressions can take many forms such as specific sayings like proverbs or riddles, generic conventions like knock-knock jokes or competencies such as table manners, or the ability to engage in debates about who might turn out to be the Antichrist.

While mass media locate the decision-making involved in the creation of global communication in the hands of institutionally empowered actors such as writers, producers and editors, participatory media offer everyday individuals more choice both in the media they consume and in the communication they enact. This increased freedom of choice combined with more opportunities to consume vernacular expression more quickly, increases vernacular authority because individuals can choose to consume ideas based on their already expected values. When they do this, perceived continuities and consistencies in the communication of others give rise to aggregate volition.

Aggregate volition occurs when individuals perceive themselves to be acting together. By finding a particular Internet location and sharing beliefs with others who seem to share those beliefs, individuals aggregate their volition by enacting continuities and consistencies in their expression. As a result, perceived vernacular authority is increased because the individuals are consuming media premised on their already-held values and thus aggregating more action into the same volitional expression of beliefs. When individuals frequent specific online locations that are linked by a shared value or interest, they enact what I have previously termed 'vernacular webs' (Howard 2008a, 2008b). Though webs of informal communication have always existed, the ability for individuals to access and enact very specific webs with more people than they could hope to find face to face is the mechanism through which network communication technologies are increasing the aggregating effect of communication and thus increasing the perception of vernacular authority (Howard 2015).

As optimistic media researchers like Yochai Benkler (2008) and Henry Jenkins (2006) have demonstrated, this increased choice in volitional aggregation can be very empowering because individuals can seek out, compare and assess large amounts of information before they make decisions. Similarly, it can create new opportunities for transformation as individuals access and are influenced by ideas with which they might not have otherwise come into contact (Howard 1997). On the other hand, there are less optimistic researchers, such as the Administrator of the White House Office of Information and Regulatory Affairs, Cass Sunstein (2007), who has demonstrated how this aggregation can be disempowering if individuals allow it to reify into communication enclaves that 'filter' out ideas which might give them access to useful information or challenge them to think in new ways (Sunstein 2007: 138; Howard 2011).

In order to better understand how these aggregative filtering effects might be working, researchers need maps of how authority emerges from the repetition of ideas in groups. I did this kind of work while researching *Digital Jesus* during the late 1990s and early 2000s 'by hand' in the sense that I used common search engines such as Google and Yahoo to find websites using the term 'End Times'. I archived those sites yearly. I searched them for links to other sites, and I surveyed and interviewed the builders and users of the sites – often driving across the country to meet people face to face when possible. I asked them what other sites they read and who they talked to and I was able to get a sense of who was talking to whom when they were talking about the 'End Times'. Using this variation of a multi-sited ethnographic approach, I confronted some significant limitations.

After fifteen years, I really had only closely followed about twenty of the 106 sites I was able to archive and the thousands of sites I catalogued – most of which I was never able to look at at all. These limitations are and have always been inherent to ethnographic and other highly qualitative work. Ethnography gives a small picture, a microscopic view of human behaviour. This is normal, of course, because the 'close analysis' that characterises so much qualitative ethnographic, literary and communication research requires the researcher to make judgements based on expertise they have developed observing real people communicating for a long time in a particular community. Having personal experience in a community is in many ways the hallmark of ethnographic authority and that authority emerges from revealing the complexity of the specific by being able to see particular situations in great detail. The small-scale nature of ethnography makes it excellent for deeply understanding and 'thickly describing' communities (Geertz 1973). However, this close-up view can block out the larger picture, especially when confronted with the reality that online we can easily find hundreds of thousands of documents to look at. Even a team of researchers can only interview so many people or read so many posts. Without a broader view, I could catalogue thousands of websites using a particular phrase, but I would barely be able to actually analyse a hundred.

How does the researcher make an appropriate judgement about which documents or individuals to talk to if they can never see the large relationships between them? After completing *Digital Jesus*, I wanted to find a way to get a better view of what the ten or a hundred documents I could look at were doing in the myriad sea of other documents in which I knew they were swimming. To understand how repetition of ideas aggregates volition into vernacular authority, I needed a larger view of a communication enclave: a macroscopic view.

A MACROSCOPIC VIEW OF VERNACULAR DISCOURSE

Much as my previous work was limited by its specificity, a purely quantitative approach cannot offer the powerful details that the microscope of participant-observation has mastered. Because online vernacular discourse can easily be accessed in huge numbers, the microscopic view of close analysis needed to be augmented by a macroscopic view that allowed me to see the few specific cases I was looking at in detail in relation to the overall online discourse. Even better, the macroscopic view of vernacular discourse could help me choose individual cases to zoom in on for close analysis in more productive ways.

Getting both the macro- and microscopic views is particularly important in ethnographies that take online communities as their focus because, on the one hand, online communities are like offline ones: to understand them deeply you have to get there and be in them. On the other hand, they can be huge and diffuse – having real large-scale processes that, in the case of vernacular authority at least, are a major source of their power to influence people. Today, people live in media worlds dominated by online communication. Much of that communication is not institutional. Much of it is not the product of media corporations. Instead, it occurs in the repetition of everyday communication events that matter most when they aggregate. As was the case with the End Times discourse and as would prove to be the case at *Mothering.com*, online communities can be important locations where individuals enact that aggregation. When individuals form opinions that will inform later actions based on that aggregated sense of vernacular authority about questions like 'Should I give the measles vaccine to my child?', researchers need to be able to account for how filtering processes might be amplifying that authority.

In a communication enclave, things like 'vaccines' are constantly being imagined and reimagined through a multitude of tiny media communications. There are so many, no one nor any group of researchers could get a clear view of how 'vaccines' are imagined on even just *Mothering.com*. While comments like those quoted at the outset from the forum offer really interesting opportunities for study, what role do they actually play in the overall discourse about vaccines occurring in this online forum? That question matters even more when more than 180,000 other people were using the forum when those exchanges occurred. What were the other 180,000 people saying while the few people I had already had a chance to look at imagined they should not give their children vaccines because those vaccines were part of a government conspiracy? Children's health is important, as is getting a view of the processes that result in healthcare choices people make for their kids. Online vernacular discourse is playing a role in this, at least for these 180,000 people. Getting a look at the big as well as the small picture of this discourse (and an untold number of ones like it) is important.

To do that, I turned to the ideas of information scientist Katy Börner at Indiana University. In 2011, Börner coined the term 'macroscope'. For her, 'Macroscopes let us observe what is at once too great, slow, or complex for the human eye and mind to notice and comprehend' (Börner 2011: 60). A few years later, UCLA ethnographer Timothy Tangherlini (2013) described 'the folklore macroscope' that 'would keep the researcher aware of the fundamental premise that folklore is created by people who live their lives in complex societies, embedded in both time and place' (11). Tangherlini's (2015) macroscopic tools, focused on the Evald Tang Kristensen historical archived texts, are far more complex and powerful than what I developed. However, I have adapted the 'macroscope' idea to online forums so that I can better trace the emergence of aggregate vernacular authority.

GRAPHING *MOTHERING.COM*

Mothering.com (MDC) is home to self-described 'venting' sessions where 'crunchy' hippies and fundamentalist Christians share techniques for avoiding taking vaccines or enrolling their children in public school. These individuals seemed united in a radical distrust of the medical establishment, including that which seems to career into paranoia. The MDC forums are part of *Mothering.com* website. Since the 1970s, *Mothering* has been focused on the topic of 'natural family living'. When the data sample was first taken on 11 June 2013, MDC had over 187,000 registered users who had posted in over 1.2 million threads for over 16 million individual messages. Today it has even more. Just focusing on this forum, you could spend 60 seconds on each post. Then in some 8,300 days or nearly 27 years (taking no breaks at all) you would read all the posts. And after all that reading, you would still have no easy way to create a map of how those posts fit together.

To create just such a map of the forum posts talking about vaccines on MDC, I worked with computer programmers to write PERL scripts. Hiring a graduate student from the electrical engineering department, I met with the first programmer to discuss the structure of the forum as well as other forums I was interested in downloading. We discussed the feasibility of downloading scripts and creating files from as many forums as possible. After the programmer wrote and tested the scripts, he initiated the downloads starting with MDC. For the second download, a second programmer reviewed the existing scripts and documentation. He updated them to accommodate changes in the forum and then reran the download in June 2013. In the end, we had downloaded all the 5.4 million MDC posts available on the site at that time (from 2004 to the spring of 2013 – see Figure 10.1).

Because forum software uses specific HTML code to create the webpages of the forum, those 'tags' can be used by the script to extract information and place it in into the database fields. For example, the text of each post is preceded and ended by specific HTML tags. The scripts recognise those tags and place the text that comes between them into the associated fields in the SQL database. This results in a database (see Figure 10.2) with different searchable fields for all the regular parts of the posts: the text of the post, if it was a reply,

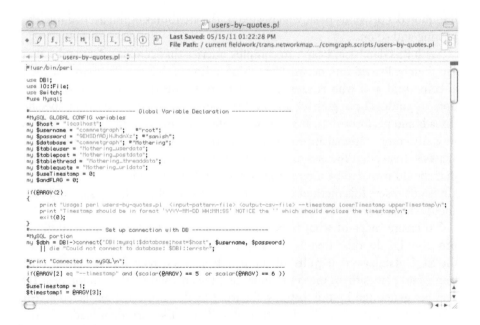

Figure 10.1 PERL scripts

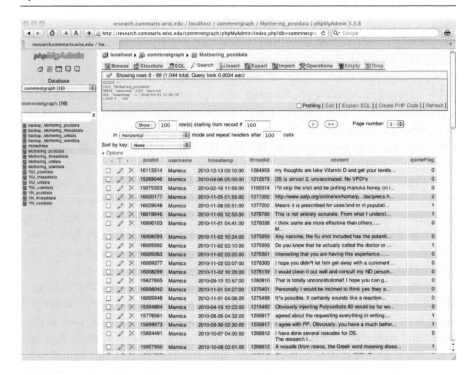

Figure 10.2 SQL database

if it quoted a previous post, who posted it, the attributes of the users doing the posting and so on.

With this database, I can run complex queries that generate data tables that can then be loaded into network graphing software that creates 'maps' of what is being said and who is saying it to whom. Using these network visualisations as guides, I can go back and pull the posts from specific users or specific threads and perform close analysis of specific documents or individuals. In this way, my computational approach does not replace any aspect of the qualitative analysis. Instead, it focuses my qualitative analysis on subsets of a mass of data that should prove to be interesting and useful for my study. The two primary kinds of subsets this method creates are data about what is being said and data about who is talking to whom.

To create maps of what is being talked about is by far the more difficult process. To do this, first I run a query from the phpMyAdmin pane for the SQL database that pulls all the text from each post for any given time frame and places them into individual text files named by the unique post ID number generated by the forum software. For this project, I extracted a year of posts into 492,870 individual text files. These files are then loaded into a language mapping software application called Automap that comes as part of the CASOS ORA Network Graphing Software package. The texts were then cleaned using the software. This cleaning includes: removing extra spaces, converting British to American spellings, fixing common typos, expanding all contractions, expanding common abbreviations, resolving pronouns and removing 'noise words'. Noise words include characters that are artefacts of the HTML coding and very common prepositions, articles and other words. These words are replaced with 'XXX' so that the number of words between words is kept the same. Further text refinement removes punctuation and converts all the text to lower case. So care has to be taken not to destroy things you might want to see later. For example, I was interested in the 'H1H1' virus so I changed all instances of it to 'HPNP' so that it would not be perceived as noise and removed by the software. After that, I created a delete list of the most common words. There are built-in delete lists. For this project, however, I sorted all the words used in the texts by frequency, exported all words with more than 100 occurrences in the data set and hand-culled the list of prepositions, HTML tagging or other noise words still present in the data. I then applied this delete list of noisy words. Finally, I saved the cleaned texts that now appear as unbroken strings of words punctuated only by frequent 'XXX' to mark the locations of the removed words.

Next, the Automap software can create a semantic network based on the cleaned text. It does this by using a 'word window'. In this network, each word will be a node and the strength of the connection between the nodes will be the number of times the linked words appear in this word window. You can set your word window to various numbers, but after experimenting with various lengths of windows I settled on seven words. So, each time two specific words appear within seven words of each other they get counted as a pair. The more times they are paired, the stronger the link between them in the network. Though it can be done in many ways, for this project I ran the window on all the texts from the earliest to the latest based on the date they were posted. The software generates the semantic network by running its seven-word window across all the texts in chronological order as if they were one long continuous stream of unpunctuated words.

Trying to visualise this network by itself is not useful, however, because all told it would be a picture of over 500 million links based on a 2.4 gigabyte text file. Instead, the network can be loaded into Automap's paired software ORA (Carley and DeReno 2006). ORA can visualise sphere of influence graphs that include only those nodes linked to a specific node through a specified number of intermediary nodes; this method produced useful topical maps. First, I used Automap to view lists of words that started with the letters 'v' and 'va'. Doing this, I found sixteen different terms and alternate spellings to refer to vaccination in the data set: 'vax | vaccination | vaccine | vaccinate | vaxed | unvaxed | nonvax | unvaccinated | nonvaxed | vaccinating | nonvaxer |

vaxs | provax | vac | vaxxing | vaccinates'. I combined these terms into a single term and then visualised a sphere of influence from that mega node. This process visualised networks showing only words that appeared within one link of a vaccination word. So the graph shows only words that appeared at least once within seven words of one of the sixteen vaccination words. When visualised, the sheer number of words still creates a useless 'hairball' (see Figure 10.3).

To reduce the ball, I dropped all nodes with links of less than four and ran a circle graph layout that put the most commonly connected words at the centre but pushed the pendants of words that tend to appear in clusters onto the outer edges of the graph. Locating the vaccination aggregate node, I could use the software to pull those nodes out and see which were connecting to which and how strongly (see Figure 10.4). Moving the nodes around in groups of those that were most linked, those groups of words suggested specific topics that were discussed in the text.

Though there are methods for producing purely computational topics such as creating an eigenvector[1] and looking for the words that cluster, this method allows the research to use the mathematics and software to visually explore what is being discussed. By clustering words by hand, element overlap and the larger shape of the topics can be seen. By looking at these clusters, I quickly discovered sixteen clearly important topics ranging from the obvious like the co-occurrence of 'vax' and 'baby' or 'child' to the revealing like the prevalence of 'vax' and 'exemption' showing how much of this discussion was about getting exemptions from institutional requirements for vaccines or the

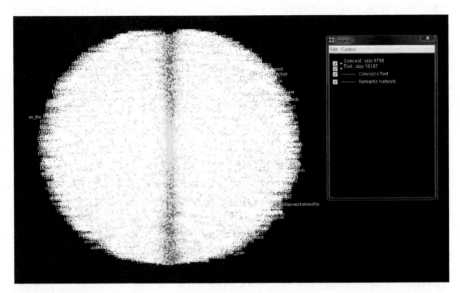

Figure 10.3 MDC hairball (Source: The author)

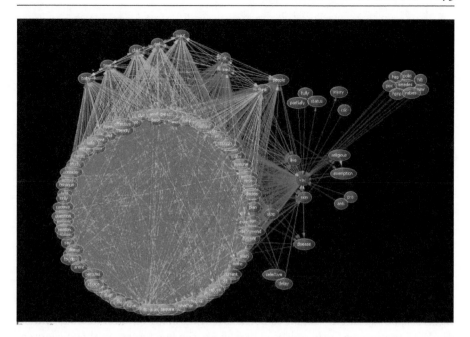

Figure 10.4 MDC topics graph (Source: The author)

really common discussions about what to expect from medical practitioners in the 'drs' (an aggregation of different ways to write 'doctor') and 'said' or 'say' topic.

This method reveals what is being talked about. It can also become the means by which we approach the second kind of subset of data: data about who is talking to whom when they are talking about vaccines. Returning to the SQL database, I queried each set of terms to create users-by-cothread graphs for each topic of interest. User-by-cothread graphs are graphs where the nodes are users and the links are the number of times the users appear in the same message threads on the forum. So by creating a query that returns all users who participate in threads that use all the words of interest, I can generate the second kind of data table. The scripts also create attributes files that include information about each user as it has been posted on their profile pages for the forum, but the reliability of most of this data made it unusable.

I can, however, very reliably create a table that lists each user as a pair of nodes and assigns each pair a value representing the number of times those two individuals posted to the same thread in the forum. In these graphs, each node is a user and the links are the number of times they appeared in the same thread that included the words that defined the topic. I created sixteen of these graphs and comparing them was interesting, but they did not differ that significantly from the largest graph: a user-by-cothread graph based on threads that used any one of the sixteen terms for 'vaccine' (see Figure 10.5).

In this graph, the researcher can locate interesting groups of people based on the amount of connections they have to others participating in the topically specific discussions on the forum. The strength of the connections are represented by the colour and thickness of the lines between the nodes: the thicker and redder, the more times those two users participated in the same thread about vaccines. The size of the users' nodes also represents the centrality of the user in the network based on a 'betweeness centrality' calculation. This kind of centrality is defined as: 'The centrality of node v is defined as: across all node pairs that have a shortest path containing v, the percentage that pass through v' (Carley and DeReno 2006: 89). The more between, the bigger the node.

Looking at those two elements, some very large patterns are immediately evident. First, Marnica and emmeline II talk a lot. They talk a lot to each other, and they also talk a lot with a fairly limited group of certain other key figures: claddaghmom, caned & able, Deborah, stacy05, ema-adama, and so on. We can now see fairly objectively who are the key figures in this discourse, but to really get at what each of those individuals is doing on the forum, we have to look at what they are saying – I have to engage in close analysis, get the microscopic view.

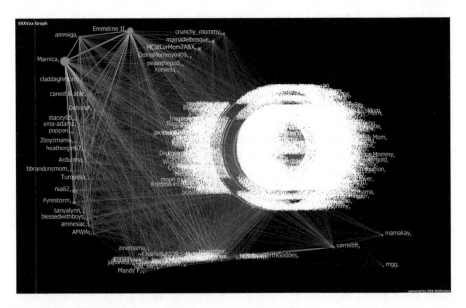

Figure 10.5 VAX graph (Source: The author)

CLOSE ANALYSIS OF *MOTHERING.COM*

The graph in Figure 10.6 reveals that the three primary participants are Marnica, emelinne II and ammiga in the sense that Marnica and Emmeiline II talk more than anybody else and ammiga talks to the two of them more than anybody else talks to anybody on the forum. We can see this on the graph because the lines connecting these three users are thicker and redder than any others. Ammiga speaks primarily to Marnica and emmeline II, but Marnica and emmeline II also speak to many other people. We can see this because those two are by far the most between on the graph while ammiga is not very between at all for how much talking she does. The three of them create a little triad-shaped enclave of red and orange communication about vaccines. While I had seen these users around when I was doing my participant observation reading of the forum, I had not realised how dominant these actors were.

Realising the huge role they played in the discourse, I could now go to back to the database to pull the actual texts this graph is based on. So doing I returned to the qualitative analysis that was typical of my humanist ethnographic methods – as in my work in *Digital Jesus*. I did not use the computational methods to replace my qualitative close analysis, but instead it has narrowed my attention from 5.4 million posts to 300–100 from each of these three users. Reading those posts closely, it turns out that they are all about vaccines – just as they should be.

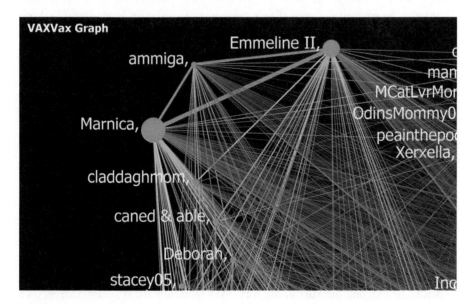

Figure 10.6 VAX graph detail 1 (Source: The author)

Marnica

One reason Marnica dominated this discourse was because there was also a lot of advice being given to other users who had questions and Marnica had a lot of advice to give. This advice ranged from tips on avoiding cervical cancer instead of taking the vaccine to folk remedies to use instead of getting a tetanus shot. Unlike the clearly conspiratorial discourse I quoted at the beginning of this chapter, however, this discourse was largely more tempered. For example, Marnica typically said things against doctors and vaccines such as: 'Any scientist/doctor that does not want to ruin their reputation, possibly change the course of their career forever, or have their funding dry up will NOT ask [. . .] questions publicly about vaccines' (Marnica 2010).

She does not explicitly say there is a conspiracy like the user above, but she does create an insider/outsider group dynamic with statements such as: 'The pharmaceutical companies also have a great deal to lose profit wise and the regulatory government agencies are largely funded by big pharma. [. . .] People like us here on MDC know their logic is flawed' (Marnica 2010).

emmiline II

Emmiline II was the second most dominant user in the discourse, but she contributed to the discourse with comments seldom more extreme than: 'I have read MANY anecdotal reports of children and adults having painful hard lumps, and/or pain in limbs or overall body ache post vaccination' (emmiline II 2010). The majority of emmiline's posts were focused on how to avoid taking vaccines and especially how to get a religious exemption for children so they could go to a public school without taking the required vaccines. This was an important topic in this discourse, and it even showed up as a topic in the topic analysis as I noted above. Because she was a big player in a top topic in the discourse, emmiline II became a big figure in the graph. Most often, emmiline II gave practical advice on this topic in her posts. She actually created a staggering amount of discourse doing just that on this forum. Because she did it a lot and because many different forum users had questions on this topic, she became 'highly between' on the graph.

ammiga

Ammiga was a third major contributor to the discourse and tended to post the more extreme conspiratorial and rumour-oriented statements. Of the three, she was the most focused on the 'unnatural' nature of vaccines. She linked this idea to a strong distrust of doctors: 'My trouble with trusting doctors as a reputable source is that [. . .] I find most pediatricians to be grossly uneducated about vaccines [. . .] Look at the perks they receive for vaxing their clients.' In this thread, Marnica responds to ammiga's rumour about the corruption of doctors with an overt statement about her own source of authority. She implores her fellow forum users: 'Listen to your Mommy instinct . . . it is more powerful than anything' (ammiga 2010a). In another similar exchange in another thread, ammiga breaks through into true conspiracy discourse in a response to Marnica: 'If you believe that the pharmaceutical/vaccine companies have their hands a little too deep in the government [. . .], you can start to connect the dots' (ammiga 2010b). This exchange is a good example of what turns out to be a somewhat rare expression of extreme distrust for vaccines in the closely analysed posts – but this statement is still highly visible and potentially influential because these individuals are the most read posters on the forum when it comes to talking about vaccines.

mgg

In addition to looking at the most central users in the discourse, it is useful to also consider the least central. Opposite from Marnica, ammiga and emmeline II down in the lower right of the graph, there is the very different triad of carriebft, mamaky and mgg (see Figure 10.7). Mgg is the least connected user on this graph.

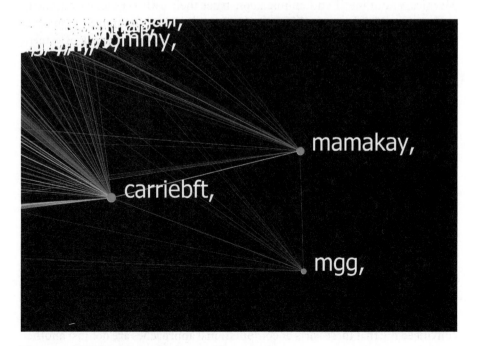

Figure 10.7 VAX graph detail 2 (Source: The author)

In fact, these three people were not highly connected to anyone. Mgg talked most to mamakay and cariebft who both talked to other people more than mgg did. What were these three significantly unconnected participants talking about? Looking at their posts revealed that they were actually not anti-vaccine. That is to say: they disagreed with Marnica, emmiline II and ammiga on the most fundamental issue in the discourse: whether people should take vaccines. While mamakay and carriebft sometimes did appear in the same thread as the main triad of Marnica, emmiline II, and ammiga, they both tended toward the 'selective vax' position: sometimes arguing that scientists are not in a conspiracy, but still maintaining you should research and think about the dangers that specific vaccines might have before you choose to take or give your child one. Mamakay and carriebft seemed reasonably able to engage even the strongly anti-vaccine forum users. Mgg, however almost never did. Why not?

Looking at her posts, it quickly became clear that mgg openly and consistently disagreed with the fundamental idea that pharmaceutical companies can manipulate doctors into giving more vaccines. She writes: 'It doesn't matter who does the study, or who funds the study. If another person or persons can replicate the study and get the same results, that is a much bigger factor in validation than who did the original study' (mgg 2010a). So who is mmg? Looking at her profile, she lists her occupation as 'pediatrician' (mgg 2010b).

Mgg is a representative of the very institutional authority against whom Marnica, emmiline II and ammiga construct their own vernacular authority as alternate. The dramatic difference between Marnica's or amiga's giant dots and thick links and mgg's tiny ones dramatically visualise the lack of esteem for medical institutions on this forum. In this discourse, at this network location, the graph demonstrates that at least in the discourse emergent from this set of words, vernacular authority dominates that of institutions. Acting against the vernacular authority of this forum, mgg was almost never replied to or quoted by anyone in the discourse. Because she is a doctor with significant expertise in issues of health, she does not exhibit signs of significant influence.

CONCLUSION: THE VALUE OF A MACROSCOPIC VIEW OF VERNACULAR AUTHORITY

Even just this basic deployment of network theory demonstrates the potential for methods that combine close analysis with a macroscopic computational approach in the research of everyday discourse online. Integrating these new software-based tools into my qualitative and critical ethnography increasingly convinced me that these sorts of computational approaches are not just another powerful tool researchers can use. Instead, these tools and the macroscopic view they can offer are maybe necessary if we want to make empirical claims that fairly generalise about large online discourses.

When I started working on MDC, I expanded the techniques I had used in my previous research. I found myself spending hours searching through this forum to find examples of really attention-grabbing discussions. Often, I found that individuals talking about governmental and other conspiracies provided some of the most interesting content. I even ran searches of the forum for the word 'conspiracy.' That produced some interesting results. However, those results were more about specific individuals than they were about the entire discourse on this forum.

Under the macroscope, I began to let the computers solve the problem of sheer quantity of data without undercutting my own qualitative judgement by directing my attention to the more influential agents in the network – or (in the case of mgg) the least influential. And what did my efforts to embrace these computational methods yield? Most importantly, they demonstrated that while extreme claims to conspiracy do not dominate this discourse, they linger in the background specifically because a few individuals whose authority is powerfully anti-institutional, powerfully vernacular, dominate the discourse about vaccines here.

This is important at least because many people use the discussions on this forum as a basis for medical choices about their children. And this is just one example. As individuals have increasingly sought out information online instead from media institutions or institutional experts, it is important that we develop research methods and theoretical frameworks to keep apace with the rapidly changing media world in which we all now live, not least because they become the basis on which significant numbers of people may make important life decisions.

ACKNOWLEDGEMENTS

I would like to thank Sanish Mahadik, Ashish Maurya, the Hamel family, the Vilas Associate Award Committee and the University of Wisconsin Office of the Vice Chancellor for Research and Graduate Education for the expertise and funding that have made this ongoing project possible. I would also like to thank Timothy Tangherlini, the Institute for Pure and Applied Math at UCLA and the National Endowment for the Humanities, for including me in the 2010 'Networks and Network Analysis for the Humanities: Advanced Topics in Digital Humanities' workshop that spawned my interested in pursuing computational humanities.

NOTE

1. Eigenvectors are a special set of vectors associated with a linear system of equations. ORA calculates 'the eigenvector of the largest positive eigenvalue of the adjacency matrix representation of a square network' (Carley and DeReno 2006: 90).

REFERENCES

AllyRae (2009) 'Fine and jail time for not taking swine flu in MA????!!!', *Mothering.com*, at <http://www.mothering.com/discussions/showthread. php?p=14283818> (accessed 15 July 2010).

ammiga (2010a) 'Doctors and vaccines', *Mothering.com*, at <http://www. mothering.com/forum/47-vaccinations/1223917-doctors-vaccines.html> (accessed 5 June 2013).

ammiga (2010b) 'I was appalled this A.M.!', *Mothering.com*, at <http://www. mothering.com/forum/47-vaccinations/1232869-i-appalled-m.html> (accessed 5 June 2013).

Benkler, Y. (2008) *The Wealth of Networks: How Social Production Transforms Markets and Freedom*. New Haven, CT: Yale University Press; also <http:// yupnet.org/benkler/archives/8> (accessed 1 September 2008).

Börner, K. (2011) 'Plug-and-play macroscopes', *Communications of the ACM*, 54: 3, pp. 60–9.

Carley, K. and DeReno, M. (2006) *ORA 2006: User's Guide* (Carnegie Mellon University), at <http://www.casos.cs.cmu.edu/publications/papers/ CMU-ISRI-06-113.pdf> (accessed 5 June 2011).

emmiline II (2010) 'So, what do I do about a rusty nail', *Mothering.com*, at <http://www.mothering.com/forum/443-i-m-not-vaccinating/1212272- so-what-do-i-do-about-rusty-nail.html> (accessed 5 June 2015).

Geertz, C. (1973) *The Interpretation of Cultures: Selected Essays*. New York: Basic Books.

Gitti (2009) 'Anyone else totally creeped out?', *Mothering.com*, at <http:// www.mothering.com/discussions/showthread.php?p=13999035> (accessed 15 July 2010).

Grahamsmom98 (2005) 'Avian flu', *Mothering.com*, at <http://www.moth ering.com/discussions/showthread.php?t=351849> (accessed 15 July 2010).

Howard, R. G. (1997) 'Apocalypse in your inbox: End Times communication on the internet', *Western Folklore*, 56, pp. 295–315.

Howard, R. G. (2008a) 'Electronic hybridity: the persistent processes of the vernacular web', *Journal of American Folklore*, 121, pp. 192–218.

Howard, R. G. (2008b) 'The vernacular web of participatory media', *Critical Studies in Media Communication*, 25, pp. 490–512.

Howard, R. G. (2011) *Digital Jesus: The Making of a New Christian Fundamentalist Community on the Internet*. New York: New York University Press.

Howard, R. G. (2013) 'Vernacular authority: critically engaging "tradition",' in T. J. Blank and R. G. Howard (eds), *Tradition in the 21st Century: Locating the Role of the Past in the Present*. Logan: Utah State University Press, pp. 72–99.

Howard, R. G. (2015) 'Why digital network hybridity is the new normal (Hey! Check this stuff out!)', *Journal of American Folklore*, 128: 509, pp. 27–59.

Jenkins, H. (2006) *Convergence Culture: Where Old and New Media Collide*. New York: New York University Press.

laohaire (2009) 'Do I have to worry about the school administering vaccines?' *Mothering.com*, at <http://www.mothering.com/discussions/showthread.php?t=1125154> (accessed 15 July 2010).

Marnica (2010) 'Another SIDS death "not" attributed to vaccines', *Mothering.com*, at <http://www.mothering.com/forum/47-vaccinations/1188808-another-sids-death-not-attributed-vaccines-2.html> (accessed 5 June 2013).

mgg (2010a) 'Curious case of non-vax children and autism', *Mothering.com*, at <http://www.mothering.com/forum/47-vaccinations/1249337-curious-case-non-vax-children-autism.html> (accessed 5 June 2013).

mgg (2010b) 'Profile', *Mothering.com*, at <http://www.mothering.com/forum/members/155924-mgg.html> (accessed 5 June 2013).

MyLilPwny (2009) 'Vaccination for worse living conditions?', *Mothering.com*, at <http://www.mothering.com/discussions/showthread.php?t=1141695&highlight=> (accessed 15 July 2010).

MyLittleWonders (2006) 'Former neighbor (picu nurse) told me to vax . . .', *Mothering.com*, at <http://www.mothering.com/discussions/archive/index.php/t-428052.html> (accessed 15 July 2010).

NaomiLoreli (2006) 'If you were stocking up on NT foods due to Bird Flu what would you stock up on??', *Mothering.com*, at <https://www.mothering.com/discussions/showthread.php?p=4779332> (accessed 26 July 2009).

Sunstein, C. (2007) *Republic.com 2.0*. Princeton: Princeton University Press.

Tangherlini, T. (2008) 'Sites of (re)collection: a digital approach to the folklore collection of Evald Tang Kristensen', at <http://dev.cdh.ucla.edu/~newmedia/DFL2/> (accessed 5 June 2013).

Tangherlini, T. (2013) 'The folklore macroscope: challenges for a computational folkloristics', *Western Folklore*, 72: 1, pp. 7–27.

CHAPTER 11

Dealing with Big Data

Tobias Blanke and Andrew Prescott

BIG DATA AND ITS ANXIETIES

As the United States grew rapidly in the late nineteenth century, its government sought to collect more information about the state of the country. The vast amount of data collected in the 1880 census was still being transcribed by clerical staff nine years later. A new method was required for the 1890 census and Herman Hollerith, a census employee, proposed that census returns should be analysed by the use of punched cards sorted by an electro-mechanical machine. Operators made holes in the cards which corresponded to (for example) the number of people in a family, and the cards were automatically sorted to provide statistics on family size. Using Hollerith's machines, between 12.5 and 15 million individual records were processed in less than two years in the 'first truly mass-scale state information processing project to be mechanised' (Driscoll 2012: 8). Hollerith's 'Tabulating Machine Company' went on to form part of IBM, and by the 1920s automated information processing was used for US government processes ranging from income tax to fingerprinting of criminals, with other governments following the US lead (Driscoll 2012; Agar 2003).

The potential and perils of automated data processing have fascinated governments and the governed ever since. During the First World War, the British government discussed linking all government registers into a vast national register but was deterred by concerns about civil liberty (Agar 2003). Other public bodies, such as libraries, adopted punched cards and made them familiar to a wider public. Given the long history of automated data processing, it is surprising in 2015 to find government ministers such as Francis Maude, the British Cabinet Office Minister, describing data as 'the new raw material of the 21st century'.[1] Big data has caused similar excitement among academic researchers, with Marshall declaring that 'Big Data is surely the Gold Rush of the Information Age' (Marshall 2012: 1). This excitement reflects two recent developments: the growing quantities of data in machine-readable form which can be processed without extensive preparation; and the availability of advanced methods to analyse this data.

Two examples quoted by Marshall illustrate why big data generates such enthusiasm. The first is Twitter (see also Chapter 5 in this volume), where each tweet is short but has a great deal of metadata associated with it describing the time, place, language, author, etc., of the message.[2] Twitter archives are highly suitable for data mining and can be readily used to create maps showing linguistic groups in a city[3] or visualisations of Russian political groupings (Kelly et al. 2012). While such Twitter mining offers exciting research possibilities, the Twitter archive only extends back to its launch in 2006, limiting its relevance for many humanities scholars, while its evidential value is increasingly compromised by the purchase by political and other figures of non-existent followers and by the automated generation of tweets.[4] Marshall's second illustration of the research potential of big data techniques is the Google Ngram Viewer,[5] which shows word trends from millions of books digitised by Google. The Ngram Viewer enables the public for the first time to run their own linguistic analysis of the millions of words in printed books. The inventors of Google NGram Viewer declared that: 'The Ngram Viewer's consequences will transform how we look at ourselves . . . Big data is going to change the humanities, transform the social sciences, and renegotiate the relationship between the world of commerce and the ivory tower' (Aiden and Michel 2013).

Despite the enthusiasm of its creators, there is little evidence at present that the Google Ngram Viewer is generating major new research findings. Gibbs and Cohen (2011) used Google Ngram to analyse references to religion to investigate the crisis of faith and growth of secularisation in the Victorian period. They found that from 1851 there was a decline in the use of the words 'God' and 'Christian' in the titles of books, suggesting that perhaps the Victorian crisis of faith began earlier than previously thought. But Gibbs and Cohen admit that their experiments were very preliminary and Underwood has pointed out that a different selection of words can give a completely opposite result.[6] The hazards of Google Ngram Viewer are further illustrated by a study of the use of the words 'courtesy' and 'politeness' in the eighteenth and nineteenth centuries. A Google Ngram search seemed to show that there was a huge growth in the use of these two words in about 1800. However, until 1800 the letter 's' was frequently printed in a long form so that it looked like an 'f', meaning that these words looked like 'courtefy' and 'politeneff', so the Ngram Viewer missed them. This practice ceased around 1800, so the apparent rise in use of these words reflects typographical changes, not cultural shifts

(Jucker 2012: addendum). Other humanities researchers have complained that Ngram results are trivial (Kirsch 2014), and it is certainly true that Ngram often simply provides a visual representation of what we already know. It is not yet clear how we can interrogate Ngram in such a way as to generate new intellectual insights and ideas. It is probable that, in using the big data created by Google Books, researchers will come to prefer more sophisticated search tools, such as that developed by Mark Davies at Brigham Young University.[7]

Big data has many definitions (Jacobs 2009) which often only agree that big data cannot be defined. Some link big data to data sets of a certain size in the petabyte and exabyte range.[8] However, there is no objective reason for categorising these byte ranges as 'big'. Handling a terabyte was problematic ten years ago but is now routine. Big data cannot be seen simply as data that is bigger than the scales we currently experience (Jacobs 2009). For big data, size matters, but the experience of size can only ever be relative. The format of the data is also an issue; large quantities of alphanumeric data may be easier to process than multimedia data. In 'Pathologies of Big Data' (Jacobs 2009) a thought experiment is used to explore the storage of simple demographics about every person on the planet. In the end, there will be 'a table of 6.75 billion rows and maybe 10 columns'. While for humans, this might be an impressive number of data items, such quantities are not a problem for standard computers to process. On the other hand, 8.5 million images of medieval manuscripts[9] can be more difficult for computers to process than eight billion genome sets (for reasons we will explore) and it may be that humans can deal more readily with such big image data. It is impossible to define big data in terms of a particular number of bytes, because 'as technology advances over time, the size of data sets that qualify as big data will also increase' (Chui et al. 2011: 1). We need to think about big data in terms of what computers can store and process and what humans can analyse using current techniques. Big data 'should be defined at any point in time as data whose size forces us to look beyond the tried-and-true methods that are prevalent at that time' (Jacobs 2009). Data is big not just in terms of its quantity, but also in terms of what we would like to do with it, how we seek to extract research value from it and the type of infrastructures available to support this extraction of value. As Lynch (2008) emphasises, data can also be big in different ways, making demands in such areas as long-term preservation or description which challenge current computational methods.

Doug Laney's celebrated 2001 'three Vs' description of big data provides a good framework for further analysis: 'Big data is high volume, high velocity, and/or high variety information assets that require new forms of processing to enable enhanced decision making, insight discovery and process optimization' (Laney 2001: 1). High Volume, or the first V, means that big data needs a certain size to be big. Such high volume mainly stems from data that is produced not just once, but again and again, perhaps as a result of an experiment, such as the Large Hadron Collider, or through repeated re-transmission, as for example in an e-mail conversation. It is this re-transmission which helps determine the second V, or Velocity. The third V describes how data assets of differing format or origin can nevertheless be exploited as big data when combined together in information repositories. For example, the family history service Ancestry had over fourteen billion records in August 2014 and was adding two million daily.[10] However, these records are taken from many different sources and thus show great Variety. While the three Vs of Volume, Velocity and Variety provide a clear conceptual framework, they do not cover every aspect of big data and it has been proposed that a number of other Vs should be added to the mix such as Veracity and Value. Many business and government executives are uncertain how accurate their data is and the level of Veracity can have a big effect on predictions made from data.[11] Where large quantities of accurate data can be used to predict sales movements or other business cycles the data has a monetary Value.[12]

Big data developments frequently attract controversy, often as much for social and cultural reasons as for any practical computing issues. Some extreme claims by proponents of big data have prompted extensive debate. In particular, Chris Anderson in 2008 *Wired* magazine declared the 'end of theory', as he argued: 'This is a world where massive amounts of data and applied mathematics replace every other tool that might be brought to bear. Out with every theory of human behavior, from linguistics to sociology . . . With enough data, the numbers speak for themselves' (Anderson 2008: 1).

The claim of the 'end of theory' was meant as a provocation and may superficially be read as a plea to use the availability of large quantities of data to return to positivistic methodologies. Anderson apparently suggests that research questions should derive not from the broader intellectual concerns of a particular discipline but rather from numerical patterns and anomalies in large data sets. Many commentators see such data-driven research, which looks for patterns without explaining them, as the chief characteristic of big data methods (Mayer-Schönberger and Cukier 2013). A more cautious reading of Anderson's piece might suggest that he was only proposing the abandonment of some theories of human behaviour, particularly sociological ones, and their replacement with mathematically based models. Nevertheless, the idea that focusing on data means that critical and theoretical frameworks can be abandoned has been influential. An article on the digital humanities in the *New York Times* in 2010 echoes Anderson's impatience with critical theory:

A history of the humanities in the 20th century could be chronicled in 'isms' – formalism, Freudianism, structuralism, postcolonialism –

grand intellectual cathedrals from which assorted interpretations of literature, politics and culture spread. The next big idea in language, history and the arts? Data.

Members of a new generation of digitally savvy humanists argue it is time to stop looking for inspiration in the next political or philosophical 'ism' aand start exploring how technology is changing our understanding of the liberal arts. This latest frontier is about method, they say, using powerful technologies and vast stores of digitised materials that previous humanities scholars did not have.[13]

Callebaut (2012) has dismissed as fundamentally flawed the idea that scientific and other research can be data-driven, pointing out that Anderson misrepresents the role of modelling in biological research and emphasising that research questions, methods and interpretation remain fundamentally driven by the current theoretical understanding of the relevant discipline. Callebaut quotes Charles Darwin who declared that 'all observation must be for or against some view if it is to be of any service' (Callebut 2012: 74). The analytical and predictive techniques used in big data are themselves founded on statistical and mathematical theories (Mayer–Schönberger and Cukier 2013: 70–2). The idea that 'raw data' represents an objective factual quarry is an illusion (Gitelman 2013). Much of the disruptive power of big data for traditional fields of inquiry stems not from giving up theory but rather from the way in which very large quantities of data challenge existing methodologies and require researchers to explore the use of new theoretical models, perhaps drawn from other subject areas that had previously seemed alien (Boyd and Crawford 2012). West (2013: 1) declares that 'Big data needs a big theory'.

The second major area of concern about big data is the use of data in surveillance or 'dataveillance', which describes 'the systematic monitoring of people or groups, by means of personal data systems in order to regulate or govern their behavior' (Degli Espositi 2014: 1). Following the revelations by Edward Snowden of the enormous scale to which the intelligence agencies of America and its closest allies harvest e-mail, mobile phone and other communications, big data has become linked in the popular imagination to the perfection of state surveillance, although such forms of big data as meteorological data have little to do with surveillance. Before big data 'all surveillance was inherently partial and analogue in nature and produced varying levels of recorded data, ranging from observations that were unrecorded to detailed logs or continuous recordings, sometimes applied to samples' (Kitchin 2014: 88). The East German secret police, the Stasi, famously collected all information it could get on almost everybody in the German Democratic Republic until the end of that state in 1989. Nowadays, smartphones collect more information about their owners than the Stasi could have dreamt of, and Snowden has revealed how modern security agencies make use of that. Compared to the Stasi records, this data is real-time and delivers valuable information such as location and movement in a format computers can easily use. The Stasi was limited in how deeply it could analyse the data or represent it in graphs. With big data, it has become much easier to analyse relationships and networks in great depth. Moreover, big data can be used for pre-emptive actions by police and security agencies, as Lyon (2014) explains:

> Big Data reverses prior policing or intelligence activities that would conventionally have targeted suspects or persons of interest and then sought data about them. Now bulk data are obtained and data are aggregated from different sources *before* determining the full range of their actual and potential uses and mobilising algorithms and analytics not only to understand a past sequence of events but also to predict and intervene *before* behaviors, events, and processes are set in train. (Lyon 2014: 4)

Another area of controversy around big data is the use of quantification. The role of statistics is regarded with particular suspicion in the humanities, where the use of mathematical modelling and computing in the 1950s and 1960s in such controversial disciplinary developments as 'cliometrics' in history or the 'new archaeology' had caused bitter debates (Fogel and Davis 1966; Clarke 1973). Consequently, big data causes long-standing tensions about the relationship of quantification to more hermeneutical work in the humanities to resurface. Moreover, the use of statistical techniques to predict human behaviour and cultural trends seems antagonistic to many of the values traditionally associated with research in the humanities. Mayer-Schönberger and Cukier declare that 'Predictions based on correlations lie at the heart of big data' (2013: 55). They describe a widely reported case in which the American retailer Target identified two dozen products that enabled the company to calculate a 'pregnancy predictor' score for each customer, which even calculated the due date of the pregnancy. Mailings sent by the store using this predictor revealed the pregnancy of a high-school girl before her parents were aware of it (ibid.: 57–8). Predictive data analytics are now being used for applications ranging from dementia research[14] to improving the content of film scripts.[15]

For many humanities scholars, such techniques are at best irrelevant and at worst dangerous. Adam Kirsch declares that: 'In humanistic study, quantification hits its limits (even if quantifiers refuse to recognise them). It is much easier to measure the means – books published, citations accumulated – than the ends' (Kirsch 2014: 1). For the sociologist Emma Uprichard, big data reuse of methods from physical, engineering, computational and mathematical sciences leads to 'reductionist approaches', is 'deeply positivist' and will finally end up in a 'methodological genocide'.[16] For Uprichard, the enthusiasm for statistical analysis of data offers few intellectual insights or frameworks for addressing grand challenges:

> Let's face it, big data is not going to solve our big social problems, such as global warming, violence, genocide, war, social divisions, sexism, racism, disability, homophobia, water and food security, homelessness, global poverty, health and educational inequality, infant mortality, care for the elderly, and so on.[17]

This chapter will attempt to counter such anxieties about the role of big data in the humanities by focusing on approaches which, by being firmly grounded in the traditional values of humanities disciplines, enhance existing methods to produce fruitful humanities research. Big data poses many methodological challenges, but these pressures should prompt humanities scholars to pay much closer attention to methodological issues than they have in the past.

DATAFICATION OF THE HUMANITIES

Many very large new data sets have been created in the past decade for humanities scholars. For example, as of the end of 2013, the European Union Cultural Heritage aggregator Europeana had made available over thirty million digital objects through its portal.[18] If big data is simply the extension of data from the giga- and terabyte domains into the peta- and exabyte (and beyond), then the humanities already deals with such big data. While nothing matches the 200 petabytes generated by the Large Hadron Collider in the search for the Higgs Boson, 'big humanities' can nevertheless rival scientific data in size (Hand 2011). The Sloan Digital Sky Survey, for instance, had brought together about 100 terabytes of astronomical observations by the end of 2010. This is big data, but not as big as some humanities data sets. The Holocaust Survivor Testimonials Collections by the Shoa Foundation contained at the same time 200 terabytes of data. The American English data set from Google Books contain 200 billion words,[19] while another typical digitisation project, the Taiwanese TELDAP archive of Chinese and Taiwanese prints, images and other heritage objects, had over 250 terabytes of digitised content in 2011.[20] This is not surprising considering that most of these collections have multimedia files which tend to be bigger than other types of data. Where videos and images dominate, tera- and petabyte sets are readily produced.

This kind of multimedia data can be entertaining for humans, but computers have problems processing it because it is unstructured. Without going into too much detail, in computing, unstructured data refers to text, images, etc., while a good example of structured information is a spreadsheet. A good analogy for understanding the difference between structured and unstructured data is comparing the way in which an address book organises information (structured) with a box full of unlabelled photographs (unstructured). Structured data is often organised in relational databases which follow a standard that has not significantly changed over the last twenty years. It is called Structured Query Language (SQL) and is based on analysing and processing sets of data; its return produces sets of records that comply with certain conditions. So, for instance, a typical query would return all records of people born on 28 August 1975. Organising data so it can be interrogated by SQL can be very laborious, and the conventions used to label the information in SQL are often difficult for humans to work with. However, for computers this kind of data is easier to understand because there are unambiguous identifiers describing the information in the record or how records can be joined up.

If the data is unstructured or unstructured queries are allowed, more computational intelligence needs to be added to the application so that the unstructured information can be transformed into something a computer can process. A commonly used method to transform unstructured into structured information is information extraction (Cowie and Lehnert 1996). Google mail, for instance, identifies what it believes to be dates and times for appointments in e-mails and lets the user add those directly to his or her calendar. Extracting information such as appointment details in e-mails is never a perfect process, but it helps with the organisation of e-mail content. Information extraction (IE) does not target the whole document (like the content of an e-mail) but individual facts found there.[21] IE's aim is therefore to find and process smaller parts of documents and extract facts from them, such as who did what and when. Relationships can also be extracted, for instance that Rome is the capital of Italy. In this way structured data is derived from unstructured information – texts in this case.

There are many openly accessible IE tools now on the web, of which OpenCalais from Reuters is one of the better known. You can use this tool yourself. Simply go to <http://viewer.opencalais.com/> and submit any English text. Figure 11.1 shows the results using the first paragraphs of the Wikipedia entry on Indonesia.

You can see how the OpenCalais tool annotates words in the text such as places or organisations. While this tool is easy to use and potentially has a lot of applications in humanities research, it is immediately obvious from Figure 11.1 that this is not a perfect process and contains mistakes. Current IE systems are very good at identifying documents of a specific type and then extracting information according to pre-defined templates, such as a list of all places. But IE can easily fail if the spelling is slightly different or other

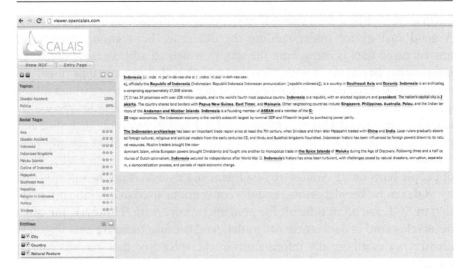

Figure 11.1 OpenCalais extraction of information from Wikipedia entry on Indonesia
(Source: The author)

factors hide the original name, as in Figure 11.1, where the adjective form of
Indonesia is not recognised. While IE is helpful in retrieving information from
a particular group of sources, such as news wires, its more extensive deployment in historical texts requires further linguistic research in order to establish
how words relate to one another so that computers can be programmed to
recognise the different functions of words. Despite IE's limitations, it gives
a good idea of how it is necessary to identify information such as names and
places if we are to transform the unstructured information in (say) the text of
a Victorian novel into data.

We tend to use the term 'digitisation' very generically. There is a difference between a book which has been scanned to produce a digital image
which has been made available as unstructured data, and a text which has been
keyboarded and marked up for automated processing so that it is structured
data. The process of creating structured data has been described as 'datafication' (Mayer-Schönberger and Cukier 2013). Mayer-Schönberger and Cukier
(2013) define data as everything that can be digitally repurposed and analysed
by machines. For Mayer-Schönberger and Cukier, 'to datafy a phenomenon
is to put it in a quantified format so that it can be tabulated and analysed'
(Mayer-Schönberger and Cukier 2013: 78). This is different from the process
of producing a digital surrogate based on digitising originally analogue content
by (for example) transferring a microfilm of a book to digital form or making
an MP3 version of a taped interview. Mayer-Schönberger and Cukier (2013)
rightly point out that big data is not related to the kind of digitisation work
which libraries and museums undertake to provide access to their collections,

but rather to the desire to produce quantifiable pieces of data a computer can ask relevant questions against.

The concept of 'datafication' has particular significance in the humanities, since it suggests that for big data work unstructured data is not enough. This would mean that the digitised files of sound recordings of interviews of Holocaust survivors in the Shoa Foundation described above are not big data as such. If the large collections of images, sound or video commonly used by humanities researchers are not big data, then what is? For Mayer-Schönberger and Cukier (2013), the Google Ngram Viewer is a perfect example of how humanities content can be 'datafied' by splitting it up into n-grams or smaller chunks of data. Ngrams are here simply 'n' letters in a word joined together. The word 'data', for instance, contains two 3-grams: 'dat' and 'ata'. N-grams are often used in linguistic analyses to counteract the challenges of heterogeneous data, if, for instance, texts generated by automated optical character recognition packages contain recognition errors. N-grams help with processing those words with inaccuracies. N-grams might not help humans understand texts better but they definitely provide computers with a way to parse large amounts of inconsistent and incoherent texts. Other examples of large sets of structured data used in the humanities are library catalogue records or linguistic corpora. Like n-grams, these data sets are sufficiently large that they cannot be effectively deployed without sophisticated computational methods.

METHODS

The computational methods associated with big data, far from undermining the humanities, can revitalise long-standing methods used by humanities scholars and give them renewed relevance. Prior to the computer, scholars laboured with difficulty to compile Domesday statistics and geographies from the vast inventory of information about eleventh-century England preserved in the Domesday Book. Domesday Book has now been 'datafied', with all the information placed in a database so that it can be searched, analysed and mapped, allowing landholding patterns, values, estate structures and much else to be analysed.[22] This work on Domesday Book reflects the long-standing interest of humanities scholars in analysing the membership of historical populations and groups. Prosopography is the writing of a collective biography of groups that share certain attributes and is 'a means of profiling any group of recorded persons linked by any common factor' (Magdalino 2003: 43). Prosopography investigates 'what the analysis of the sum of data about many individuals can tell us about the different types of connection between them, and hence about how they operated within and upon the institutions – social, political, legal, economic, intellectual – of their time' (Keats-Rohan

2000: 2). According to the Byzantine scholar Paul Magdalino prosopography is 'a powerful analytical tool which literally reduces history to atoms, for a *prosōpon* is an *atomon*, the indivisible unit of human existence' (Magdalino 2003: 46).

The compilation of prosopographies has a venerable history in the humanities, but their publication in big printed volumes makes them both cumbersome to use and expensive. The *Prosopography of the Later Roman Empire* (Jones et al. 1980), which contains biographies of much of the recorded population of the late Roman world from CE 260 to 641, was published in three volumes containing altogether 4,157 pages and costing over $1,000. A reviewer commented: 'The book is very fat, and the sheer quantity of matter it contains is an impediment to judicious assessment' (Bowersock 1976: 85). The 'datafication' of a volume like this not only makes it easier to use but also allows the information it contains about individuals to be explored in new configurations so that networks, patronage and patterns of movement can be reconstructed. A project has recently been started to digitise the *Prosopography of the Later Roman Empire*.[23]

Prosopographical studies are used for many different cultures and societies. A project at the University of California Berkeley is developing a prosopography from a set of Hellenistic Babylonian legal texts in ancient cuneiform script, and is using this to test an open-source prosopographical toolkit that generates interactive visualisations of the biological and social connections that individuals documented in legal and administrative archives.[24] The Department of Digital Humanities at King's College London has developed a series of prosopographical projects which cover the populations of the Byzantine Empire, Anglo-Saxon England and medieval Scotland as well as more modern groups such as the Clergy of the Church of England (Bradley and Short 2005; Bradley and Pasin 2013). The databases developed by those projects have been used to examine such major research questions as the development of the sense of national identity of the lowland Scottish population and the operation of social networks in medieval society (Hammond 2013: 3–4). The potential for prosopography to contribute to the humanities work in Big Data was recognised by the Arts and Humanities Research Council in the UK when it funded as part of its portfolio of Big Data projects two prosopographical projects in such different domains as Greco-Roman histories and archival research.[25]

Because prosopographies catalogue all recorded persons from a particular country or time period, they provide insights into the ordinary people often overlooked in historical research. Magdalino describes prosopographies as being 'like a police file' (2003: 47) and the same analytic techniques that cause concern when used by security agencies or by retailers like Target can be used to identify trends, networks and social structures in historic populations. One of the best-known digital humanities projects is the Proceedings of the Old

Bailey, which created a searchable edition of over 197,000 trials at the central criminal court in London between 1674 and 1772, containing over 127 million words of text.[26] The Old Bailey Proceedings contain biographical details of approximately 2,500 men and women executed at Tyburn and is the largest body of texts concerning the lives of non-elite people ever published. The Old Bailey data has been used to analyse the life and behaviour of beggars in eighteenth-century London (Hitchcock 2005). A data-warehousing tool is provided which enables graphing and visualisation of data from the trials.[27] In a project called 'Data Mining with Criminal Intent', sophisticated text mining and statistical software were used to investigate the word count for each individual trial. Changes in the length of reports suggests that major changes in the conduct and function of the trial occurred in the nineteenth century, with the increasing use of counsels and the rise of adversarial proceedings (Cohen et al. 2011). An example of the potential synergies between prosopographical studies and big data analytics is a study which uses the Jensen–Shannon divergence, a popular method of measuring the similarity between two probability distributions, to show how a distinction emerged between violent and non-violent crimes in trials at the Old Bailey in the early nineteenth century (Klingenstein et al. 2014).

The European Holocaust Research Infrastructure (EHRI)[28] investigates, collects and integrates Holocaust material from archives across Europe. Again, the aim is to link the material in archives into virtual collections so that, for example, prisoners of Auschwitz can be traced with regard to their countries of origin, other camps where they were prisoners, etc. This once more illustrates how the linking, identification and cross-referencing of records which characterises big data is also at the heart of much traditional historical research. The EHRI illustrates the potential difficulties of building such links. For the Holocaust, a great deal of work on identifying and also preserving documentation on the Holocaust has already taken place, mostly by Yad Vashem in Israel[29] and the United States Holocaust Memorial Museum (USHMM).[30] Both have collected huge numbers of Holocaust documents. Initially this was done by photocopying, more recently by digitisation. Yad Vashem and USHMM hold massive copy collections in both analogue and digital form, and the EHRI's work in integrating material from these archives has to discriminate carefully not only between copies and originals, but also between older copies and more recent copies. Consequently, the EHRI has to reconstruct how the copy collections were built up. The EHRI shows how, in building up large resources that survey and link material from different collections, it is essential to consider the provenance and status of individual records, disentangling copies and originals.

The EHRI is undertaking experiments with social network analysis, which is used in the social sciences to analyse the interaction between individuals or groups. This generally involves the application of quantitative methods to represent communities as networks, in which the nodes correspond to individuals and the links between nodes to the relationships between individuals (Easley and Kleinberg 2010). (The exciting field of social network analysis is discussed in more detail in Robert Glenn Howard's chapter in this volume.) One of the key features of social network analysis as described by Easley and Kleinberg (2010) is the idea of strong and weak ties between actors in social networks. In the EHRI, weak ties could be indicated by fewer historical relationships (by, for instance, living in different communities or belonging to different temples) between two actors, while strong ties require more exchanges. One might assume that those with the strongest ties are also those who help each other make decisions, but this is not necessarily the case. If one runs out of ideas to solve a certain problem, one needs new perspectives. Under such circumstances, it might be necessary to activate the weak ties to connect to new contexts. Weak ties are often more important than strong ties to keep clusters of actors together (Easley and Kleinberg 2010), so that weak ties might be more important in (say) finding a new job, because they will know about a different set of job opportunities than will strong ties. For the EHRI, we are investigating whether weak ties helped people to survive during the Holocaust. In which network did Jews take part that supported their survival? How did they participate in these networks? How were these networks structured nationally and internationally?

EHRI reminds us that not everything is digital yet. The coordinator of the project is the Dutch War and Genocide research institution NIOD in Amsterdam. Their archives are 2.5 kilometres long but only 2 per cent of them are available in digital format and then not always accessible online. The objective for 2016 is for 7 per cent of the collections to be available in digital format. NIOD is a well-funded archive and is not alone in that the vast majority of its collections remain undigitised. Recent figures for the British Library, for instance, reveal that only 5 per cent of their collections are digitised. Any kind of big data project in the humanities that aims to link across archives therefore needs to find ways of uniting analogue and digital information. To this end, the EHRI has a twofold strategy of providing virtual access to Holocaust archives through its portal[31] as well as physical transnational access to archival material through fellowships.

If we want to undertake humanities research using only digital material then we need to restrict our research to so-called 'born-digital' material, that is data such as websites or tweets that were created digitally and have never had an analogue form. As already mentioned, such born-digital material is attractive for data analytics work because it is not necessary to undertake the expensive and time-consuming process of turning the information into digital form first. Tweets offer many opportunities for historians or literary scholars to explore social and cultural trends (Kirschenbaum 2012) while web archives will form a major primary source for future research in the humanities (Brügger and Finnemann 2013). One born-digital medium whose potential is sometimes underestimated but which will offer great opportunities for historical and literary research in the future are e-mail archives. The George W. Bush Presidential Center, for example, holds in its collections 200 million White House e-mails of the second Bush administration from the Executive Office of the President.[32] The Bush e-mails are subject to the provisions of the US Presidential Records Act and are only just becoming available for access under the US Freedom of Information Act so we do not know what kind of insights they will produce. In analysing such a vast amount of material, we will probably want to look at patterns of communications and networks of activity, in just the same way that Edward Snowden has shown that the National Security Agency analyses metadata from the e-mails of the general population: '[H]istorians can look for clusters of emails around various events and see, perhaps, the discussions that went on and the thinking and the mindset of individuals in the White House during the various stages of those big events.'[33] We could use the number of emails an individual sends out to estimate his or her influence. It is probably then also a good idea to investigate the patterns of replies to those e-mails. The from–to relationship is part of all e-mail communication metadata, as is the time an e-mail was sent. We can thus easily identify at which time of day most e-mail communications are happening, which might, for instance, indicate how work on particular policies or legislation proceeded. We could even perform 'sentiment analysis' on words used in e-mails and produce statistical analyses of the mood in the White House at different times.

This kind of research has been done with the publicly available Enron data set, which contains e-mails made public during the legal investigation into the collapse of the Enron corporation (Klimt and Yang 2004). Russell (2013) gives detailed instructions on how this e-mail data can be interrogated. Simply counting numbers of e-mails and correspondents and tabulating the frequency of contact can 'tell you so much with so little effort' (Russell 2013). Such simple tabulation, making use of the rich metadata and structured information associated with e-mails, is a good first step in analysing such data sets. It is not difficult, for instance, to track the number of documents sent out at a certain period of time of day during a week. From these groupings it is easy to cluster groups of e-mailers who are involved in frequent, direct communication with each other. Most users would probably not be adventurous enough to download the Enron e-mail archive, but a sense of what is possible can be easily achieved by analysing your own e-mail. MIT have produced a tool called 'Immersion' which analyses the metadata of messages in any g-mail box (precisely the method used by the security agencies) and produces visualisations showing the relationship between correspondents, enabling any user to explore the potential of the data produced by e-mail activity.[34] You can easily and safely try Immersion for yourself.

There are many other aspects to the exploration of e-mail archives which could be discussed here, such as the way in which natural language processing techniques can be used to investigate word occurrences. Russell (2013: 261–4) shows how simple text mining techniques involving the identification of terms such as 'raptor' can be used on the Enron corpus to identify which executives were aware of the use of fraudulent financial instruments. However, in conclusion, we would like to draw attention to one aspect of the study of e-mails which has given renewed relevance to a venerable humanistic method. Diplomatic is the study of the layout and formulae of ancient charters and is essential to establishing their authenticity. Its origins lie in the techniques used in the fifteenth century by the humanist scholar Lorenzo Valla to establish that the Donation of Constantine, a document supporting claims of papal supremacy, was a forgery. The critical tools of diplomatic were further developed by the French monk Jean Mabillon in writing saints' lives in the seventeenth century, and Mabillon wrote a treatise on diplomatic method, *De Re Diplomatica* (1681). The archival theorist Luciana Duranti has pointed out that e-mail presents many similarities to medieval documents because it can be difficult to establish the authenticity of an individual message. In her book *Diplomatics: New Uses for an Old Science*, Duranti argues that the methods of diplomatic provide tools for assessing the authenticity of such born-digital material (Duranti 1998). The techniques developed by the monk Mabillon thus have renewed value in the world of big data.

CONCLUSION

Some aspects of big data seem at first sight antagonistic to fundamental values of humanities research: the assumption that, if the data set is large enough, inaccuracies and individual peculiarities will not affect the result; the idea that answers will emerge from just looking at the data; an impatience with contextual discussion; and, above all, the claim that behaviour can be mathematically predicted if you have enough data. But, on closer examination, big data methodologies have more in common with traditional research preoccupations of the humanities than might at first be thought. The police file of the prosopographer is not dissimilar to the mobile phone data gathered by the security agencies. Historians wishing to link references to individuals in different archives have concerns similar to security officers trying to trace a suspect across various social media. The seventeenth-century monk Jean Mabillon can help in exploring e-mail archives.

In a blog post called 'Big Data, Small Data and Meaning', Tim Hitchcock, a leading light in the Old Bailey Proceedings project, has expressed concerns about the way in which some historians, in response to big data, advocate a 'macroscope' view of history emphasising the big picture.[35] For Hitchcock, such approaches share with big data the assumption 'that the "signal" will come through, despite the noise created by outliers and weirdness. In other words, "Big Data" supposedly lets you get away with dirty data. In contrast, humanists do read the data; and do so with a sharp eye for its individual rhythms and peculiarities – its weirdness.' Hitchcock is not unsympathetic to big data approaches. Indeed, he collaborated in the use of Old Bailey data to develop a statistical 'bootstrap model' of the sort used in predictive analytics (DeDeo, Hawkins, Klingenstein and Hitchcock 2013). Hitchcock found that 'working with "Big Data" at scale and sharing methodologies with other disciplines is both hugely productive, and hugely fun'. But what Hitchcock missed in these collaborations with mathematicians and scientists was the close reading of a single datum. For Hitchcock, the humanities are as much about the microscope as the macroscope.

In April 2012, the *Guardian* published a map purporting to show British trade routes between 1750 and 1800, under the headline '18th century shipping mapped using 21st century technology'.[36] The map, surprisingly, shows no trade routes connecting with a number of major ports such as Liverpool or Hull. This was because the ships' logs used in the visualisation were from the Royal Navy; no movements of merchant ships are included. The map shows royal naval ship movements, not trade routes – its creator had failed to think about the provenance of his data. The ease with which data can be visualised and transformed can create a suspension of disbelief in which fundamental critical awareness is forgotten. In using large data sets it is essential to be conscious of the origins of each record, as the need to disentangle copies and originals in the EHRI project shows. This point has been eloquently made by Huggett (2014: 3): data are not 'out there', waiting to be discovered; if anything, data are waiting to be created. As Bowker has commented, 'Raw data is both an oxymoron and a bad idea; to the contrary, data should be cooked with care.' Information about the past is situated, contingent and incomplete; data are theory-laden and relationships are constantly changing depending on context.

In reminding us of the importance of the single datum, Hitchcock is warning us not to forget our fundamental critical tools. Hitchcock urges greater awareness and the 'radical contextualisation' of the language of large data sets: 'We need to be able to contextualise every single word in a representation of every word, ever. Every gesture contextualised in the collective record of all gestures; and every brushstroke, in the collective knowledge of all painting.'[37] This is not a quixotic demand since the data sets exist which would allow such links to be made and recent developments in computing are moving in the direction Hitchcock describes. Among the biggest data used in the humanities are corpora used for research into language, such as the *Historical Thesaurus of English* at the University of Glasgow.[38] If big data techniques were used to link thesauri to such resources as the Old Bailey Proceedings, Hitchcock's vision would have been realised and a virtuous circle made between big data and close reading.[39]

NOTES

1. <http://www.theguardian.com/public-leaders-network/2012/apr/18/francis-maude-data-raw-material> (accessed 27 February 2015).
2. <http://blogs.wsj.com/digits/2014/06/06/in-a-single-tweet-as-many-pieces-of-metadata-as-there-are-characters/> (accessed 2 March 2015).
3. <http://twitter.mappinglondon.co.uk> (accessed 1 March 2015).
4. <http://quantifyingmemory.blogspot.co.uk/2013/06/putins-bots-part-one-bit-about-bots.html> (accessed 1 March 2015); <http://ro.ecu.edu.au/isw/54/ (accessed 1 March 2015).
5. <http:// books.google.com/ngrams> (accessed 1 March 2015).
6. <https://digitalcriticaltheory.wordpress.com/2012/03/11/two-different-ways-of-thinking-about-religious-vocabulary/>(accessed 26 February 2015).
7. <http://googlebooks.byu.edu/x.asp> (accessed 6 March 2015).
8. A bit is a binary digit; a byte comprises eight bits; a gigabyte (GB) comprises a million bytes. A terabyte (TB) is 1,000 GB; a petabyte (PB) is 1,000 terabytes; an exabyte (EB) is 1,000 petabytes. A petabyte is enough to store the DNA of the entire population of the United States three times over; an exabyte of storage would contain 50,000 years worth of DVD-quality video. Further up the scale, 1000 exabytes = 1 zettabyte; 1,000 zettabytes = 1 yottabyte; 1,000 yottabytes = 1 brontobyte; 1,000 brontobytes = 1 geopbyte.
9. <http://aalt.law.uh.edu> (accessed 2 March 2015).
10. <http://www.fiercebigdata.com/story/how-ancestrycom-uses-big-data/2014-08-04> (accessed 3 March 2015).
11. <http://www.ibmbigdatahub.com/infographic/four-vs-big-data> (accessed 3 March 2015).
12. <http://www.wired.com/2013/05/the-missing-vs-in-big-data-viability-and-value/> (accessed 3 March 2015).
13. <http://www.nytimes.com/2010/11/17/arts/17digital.html> (accessed 2 March 2015).
14. <http://www.slideshare.net/davidderoure/big-data-for-dementia-research> (accessed 6 March 2015).

15. <http://www.slideshare.net/davidderoure/big-data-for-dementia-res earch> (accessed 6 March 2015).

16. <http://www.discoversociety.org/2013/10/01/focus-big-data-little-questions/> (accessed 6 March 2015).

17. <http://www.discoversociety.org/2013/10/01/focus-big-data-little-questions/> (accessed 6 March 2015).

18. <http://epthinktank.eu/2014/04/09/europes-cultural-heritage-on line/>

19. <http://googlebooks.byu.edu/x.asp> (accessed 6 March 2015).

20. <http://culture.teldap.tw/culture/index.php?option=com_contentandt ask=blogcategoryandid=1andItemid=181andlimit=5andlimitstart=364> (accessed 6 March 2015).

21. <http://gate.ac.uk/ie/> (accessed 2 March 2015).

22. <http://domesday.pase.ac.uk/> (accessed 4 March 2015).

23. <https://kclpure.kcl.ac.uk/portal/en/projects/digitising-the-prosopo graphy-of-the-man-republic(5d0713a1-14a5-406b-b208-1c3a9521037f). html> (accessed 4 March 2015). For further background on this prosopog raphy, see Mathisen (2003).

24. <http://berkeleyprosopography.org> (accessed 4 March 2015).

25. <http://www.ahrc.ac.uk/News-and-Events/News/Pages/Digital-Transformations-in-the-Arts-and-Humanities---Big-Data-Projects-Call. aspx> (accessed 4 March 2015).

26. <http://www.oldbaileyonline.org/> (accessed 6 March 2015).

27. <http://www.oldbaileyonline.org/static/API.jsp> (accessed 6 March 2015).

28. <http://www.ehri-project.eu> (accessed 28 February 2015).

29. <http://www.yadvashem.org/yv/en/about/archive/> (accessed 28 February 2015).

30. <http://www.ushmm.org> (accessed 28 February 2015).

31. <http://portal.ehri-project.eu> (accessed 28 February 2015).

32. <http://www.georgewbushlibrary.smu.edu/Research/Electronic-Records.aspx> (accessed 7 March 2015); <http://www.zdnet.com/special-report-g-w-bush-presidential-center-to-release-200-million-white-house-emails-to-archivists-7000013632/> (accessed 7 March 2015).

33. <http://www.zdnet.com/special-report-innovative-application-of-modern-analytics-techniques-to-presidential-email-7000014308/> (accessed 7 March 2015).

34. <https://immersion.media.mit.edu> (accessed 6 March 2015). Immersion only accesses metadata of your inbox and there is an option to delete the data at the end of the session. Similar analytic tools are available for born-digital information in other social media such as Facebook: <http://www.wolframalpha.com/facebook/> (accessed 6 March 2015).

35. <http://historyonics.blogspot.co.uk/2014/11/big-data-small-data-and-meaning_9.html> (accessed 7 March 2015).
36. <http://www.theguardian.com/news/datablog/2012/apr/13/shipping-routes-history-map> (accessed 7 March 2015).
37. <http://historyonics.blogspot.co.uk/2014/11/big-data-small-data-and-meaning_9.html> (accessed 7 March 2015).
38. <http://historicalthesaurus.arts.gla.ac.uk> (accessed 7 March 2015).
39. And see now <http://www.gla.ac.uk/schools/critical/research/fund edresearchprojects/samuels/> (accessed 7 March 2015).

REFERENCES

Agar, J. (2003) *The Government Machine: A Revolutionary History of the Computer*. Cambridge, MA: MIT Press.

Aiden, E. and Michel, J.-B. (2013) *Uncharted: Big Data as a Lens on Human Culture*. New York: Riverhead Books.

Anderson, C. (2008) 'The end of theory', *Wired Magazine*, 16: 7, at <http://archive.wired.com/science/discoveries/magazine/16-07/pb_theory> (accessed 3 March 2015).

Bowersock, G. (1976) 'Review of Jones, Martindale and Morris, 1971–1992', *American Journal of Philology*, 97, pp. 84–6.

Boyd, D. and Crawford, K. (2012) 'Critical questions for big data: provocations for a cultural, technological, and scholarly phenomenon', *Information, Communication and Society*, 15, pp. 662–79.

Bradley, J. and Pasin, M. (2013) 'Structuring that which cannot be structured: a role for formal models in representing aspects of medieval Scotland', in M. Hammond (ed.), *New Perspectives on Medieval Scotland 1093–1286*. Woodbridge: Boydell & Brewer, pp. 203–14.

Bradley, J. and Short, H. (2005) 'Texts into databases: the evolving field of new-style prosopography', *Literary and Linguistic Computing*, 20, pp. 3–24.

Brügger, N. and Finnemann, N. O. (2013) 'The web and digital humanities: theoretical and methodological concerns', *Journal of Broadcasting and Electronic Media*, 57, pp. 66–80.

Callebaut, W. (2012) 'Scientific perspectivism: a philosopher of science's response to the challenge of big data biology', *Studies in History and Philosophy of Science Part C: Studies in History and Philosophy of Biological and Biomedical Sciences*, 43, pp. 69–80.

Cameron, A. (ed.) (2003) *Fifty Years of Prosopography: The Later Roman Empire, Byzantium and Beyond*, Proceedings of the British Academy 118. Oxford: Oxford University Press.

Chui, M., Brown, B., Bughin, J., Dobbs, R., Roxburgh, C. and Manyika, A. H. B. J. (2011) *Big Data: The Next Frontier for Innovation, Competition, and Productivity*. Washington, DC: McKinsey Global Institute.

Clarke, D. (1973) 'Archaeology: the loss of innocence', *Antiquity*, 47, pp. 6-18.

Cohen, D., Gibbs, F., Hitchcock, T., Rockwell, G., Sander, J., Shoemaker, R., Sinclair, S., Takats, S., Turkel, W. J. and Briquet, C. (2011) *Data Mining with Criminal Intent*, Final White Paper, at <http://criminalintent. org/wp-content/uploads/2011/09/Data-Mining-with-Criminal-Intent-Final1.pdf> (accessed 4 March 2015).

Cowie, J. and Lehnert, W. (1996) 'Information extraction', *Communications of the ACM*, 39, pp. 80–91.

DeDeo, S., Hawkins, R., Klingenstein, S. and Hitchcock, T. (2013) 'Bootstrap methods for the empirical study of decision-making and information flows in social systems', *Entropy*, 15, pp. 2246–76.

Degli Esposti, S. (2014) 'When big data meets dataveillance: the hidden side of analytics', *Surveillance and Society*, 12, pp. 209–25.

Driscoll, K. (2012) 'From punched cards to "big data": a social history of database populism', *Communication +1*, 1, article 4.

Duranti, L. (1998) *Diplomatics: New Uses for an Old Science*. Lanham, MD; London: Scarecrow Press.

Easley, D. and Kleinberg, J. (2010) *Networks, Crowds, and Markets*. Cambridge: Cambridge University Press.

Fogel, R. and Davis, L. (1966) 'The new economic history', *Economic History Review*, 19, pp. 642–63.

Gibbs, F. and Cohen, D. (2011) 'A conversation with data: prospecting Victorian words and ideas', *Victorian Studies*, 54, pp. 69–77.

Gitelman, L. (2013) *Raw Data Is an Oxymoron*. Cambridge, MA: MIT Press.

Gold, M. (ed.) (2012) *Debate in the Digital Humanities*. Minneapolis: University of Minnesota Press.

Hammond, M. (2013) *New Perspectives on Medieval Scotland 1093–1286*. Woodbridge: Boydell & Brewer.

Hand, E. (2011) 'Culturomics: word play', *Nature*, 474, pp. 436–40.

Hitchcock, T. (2005) 'Begging on the streets of eighteenth-century London', *Journal of British Studies*, 44, pp. 478–98.

Huggett, J. (2014) 'Promise and paradox: accessing open data in archaeology', in C. Mills, M. Pidd and E. Ward (eds), *Proceedings of the Digital Humanities Congress 2012*, at <http://www.hrionline.ac.uk/openbook/chapter/dhc2012-huggett> (accessed 13 March 2015).

Jacobs, A. (2009) 'The pathologies of big data', *Communications of the ACM*, 52, pp. 36–44.

Jones, A. H. M., Martindale, J. R. and Morris, J. (1980) *The Prosopography of the Later Roman Empire*. Cambridge University Press

Jucker, A., Taavitsainen, I. and Schneider G. (2012) 'Semantic corpus trawling: expressions of "courtesy" and "politeness" in the Helsinki Corpus', *Studies in Variation, Contacts and Change in English*, 11 [online].

Keats-Rohan, K. (2000) 'Prosopography and computing: a marriage made in heaven?', *History and Computing*, 12, pp. 1–11.

Kelly, J., Barash, V., Alexanyan, K., Etling, B., Farls, R., Gasser, U. and Palfrey, J. (2012) *Mapping Russian Twitter*. Cambridge, MA: Berkman Center Research Publication: 3, at <ssrn.com/abstract=2028158> (accessed 1 March 2015).

Kirsch, A. (2014) 'Technology is taking over English departments: the false promise of the digital humanities', *New Republic*, 3 May, at <http://www.newrepublic.com/article/117428/limits-digital-humanities-adam-kirsch> (accessed 1 March 2015).

Kirschenbaum, M. (2012) 'What is digital humanities and what's it doing in English departments?', in M. Gold (ed.), *Debate in the Digital Humanities*. Minneapolis: University of Minnesota Press, pp. 3–11.

Kitchin, R. (2014) *The Data Revolution: Big Data, Open Data, Data Infrastructures and Their Consequences*. London: Sage.

Klimt, B. and Yang, Y. (2004) 'The Enron corpus: a new dataset for email classification research', in *Machine Learning: European Conference on Machine Learning 2004*. Berlin: Springer, pp. 217–26.

Klingenstein, S., Hitchcock, T. and DeDeo, S. (2014) 'The civilizing process in London's Old Bailey', *Proceedings of the National Academy of Sciences*, 111, pp. 9419–24.

Laney, D. (2001) *3-D Data Management: Controlling Data Volume, Velocity and Variety*, META Group Research Note, 6 February, at <goo.gl/Bo3GS> (accessed 1 March 2015).

Lynch, C. (2008) 'Big data: how do your data grow?', *Nature*, 455, pp. 28–9.

Lyon, D. (2014) 'Surveillance, Snowden, and big data: capacities, consequences, critique', *Big Data and Society*, 1: 2, at <http://bds.sagepub.com/content/1/2/2053951714541861> (accessed 13 March 2015).

Magdalino, P. (2003) 'Prosopography and Byzantine identity', in A. Cameron (ed.), *Fifty Years of Prosopography: The Later Roman Empire, Byzantium and Beyond*, Proceedings of the British Academy 118. Oxford: Oxford University Press, pp. 41–58.

Marshall, C. (2012) 'Big data, the crowd and me', *Information Services and Use*, 32, pp. 215–26.

Mathisen, R. (2003) 'The prosopography of the later Roman empire: yesterday, today and tomorrow', in A. Cameron (ed.) *Fifty Years of Prosopography: The Later Roman Empire, Byzantium and Beyond*, Proceedings of the British Academy 118. Oxford: Oxford University Press, pp. 23–40.

Mayer-Schönberger, V. and Cukier, K. (2013) *Big Data: A Revolution that Will Transform How We Live, Work, and Think*. Boston: Houghton Mifflin Harcourt.

Mills, C., Pidd, M. and Ward, E. (2014) *Proceedings of the Digital Humanities Congress 2012*, Studies in the Digital Humanities. Sheffield: HRI Online Publications, at <http://www.hrionline.ac.uk/openbook/chapter/dhc 2012-huggett> (accessed 4 March 2015).

Russell, M. A. (2013) *Mining the Social Web: Data Mining Facebook, Twitter, LinkedIn, Google+, GitHub, and More*, 2nd edn. Sebastobol, CA: O'Reilly Media.

Weingart, S. (2011) 'Demystifying networks, parts I and II', *Journal of Digital Humanities*, 1: 1, p. 1.

West, G. (2013) 'Big data needs a big theory to go with it', *Scientific American*, 308, p. 5.

Notes on Contributors

Dawn Archer is a Professor at Manchester Metropolitan University. She has experience of (co-)developing (1) corpora, (2) pragmatic annotation schemes (with J. Culpeper, Lancaster) and (3) corpus linguistic tools (with P. Rayson and A. Baron, Lancaster).

Tobias Blanke is a Senior Lecturer in the Centre for e-Research, Department of Digital Humanities, at King's College London. His main research interests lie in infrastructures for research, (big) data and advanced computational methods for humanities.

Coppélie Cocq is a Research Fellow at HUMlab, Umeå University, Sweden. Her research interests centre on storytelling, place-making, revitalisation and folklore in digital environments. Recent publications include 'Indigenous Voices on the Web: Folksonomies and Endangered Languages', *Journal of American Folklore*, 2015, 128: 509, pp. 273–85; 'From the Árran to the Internet: Sami Storytelling in Digital Environments', *Oral Tradition*, 2013, 18: 1; and 'Anthropological Places, Digital Spaces and Imaginary Scapes: Packaging a Digital Samiland', *Folklore*, 2013, 124.

Stefan Gelfgren is Associate Professor at HUMlab and the Department of Historical, Philosophical and Religious Studies at Umeå University, Sweden. His research interests centre on transformations within the Christian sphere in relation to societal and technological changes, with special focus on the nineteenth and twenty-first centuries.

Gabriele Griffin is Professor of Gender Studies at the University of Uppsala, Sweden. She has a long-standing research interest in research methods for the humanities and in women's cultural production. Recent publications include

The Emotional Politics of Research Collaboration (co-ed.; Routledge 2013) and *The Social Politics of Research Collaboration* (co-ed.; Routledge 2013).

Matt Hayler is a Lecturer in English at the University of Birmingham specialising in Digital and Cyberculture Studies, specifically phenomenology and cognitive science-influenced approaches to e-reading and to technology more broadly. He acts as network coordinator for the AHRC-funded Cognitive Futures in the Humanities research network and is a steering committee member for the AHRC Digital Reading network.

Natalie M. Houston is Professor of English at the University of Massachusetts Lowell. Her current research project, *Digital Reading: Poetry and the New Nineteenth-Century Archive*, uses large-scale computational analysis to explore the cultural function of poetry within Victorian print culture. She was the Project Director for an NEH-funded project to develop *VisualPage*, a software application to identify and analyse visual features in digitised printed books.

Robert Glenn Howard is Director of Digital Studies, Chair of Comparative Literature and Folklore Studies, and Professor in the Department of Communication Arts at the University of Wisconsin – Madison. Most broadly, his research seeks to uncover the possibilities and limits of empowerment through everyday expression on the Internet by focusing on the intersection of individual human agency and participatory performance.

Anna Johansson is an Associate Senior Lecturer in ethnology at HUMlab, Umeå University. Following on from her PhD in 2010, her research has focused on social media and health, gender and the body in digital culture. She is currently working on a project that explores the ways in which digital technologies enable particular performances of mental suffering and mental health identities. Her major theoretical and methodological interests are discourse theory and digital ethnography.

Maria Lindgren Leavenworth is Associate Professor in English Literature at the Department of Language Studies, Umeå University. She has published extensively on fan fiction within the project *FAN(G)S: Fan Fiction and the Vampire Trope*, funded by the Swedish Research Council.

Anna Sofia Lundgren is Professor of Ethnology at the Department of Culture and Media Studies, Umeå University. She is associated with the Ageing and Living Conditions Programme. Her research interests include discourse studies and she is currently involved in a study on reproduction narratives of the parents of the baby-boomer generation.

Andrew Prescott is Professor of Digital Humanities at King's College London. He was formerly a Curator of Manuscripts at the British Library and has written extensively on British social history as well as the history of libraries and archives.

Gabriel K. Wolfenstein is a Project Manager and Researcher for the Center for Spatial and Textual Analysis (CESTA) Mellon Project at Stanford. CESTA is a Humanities and Social Science Digital Humanities Lab at Stanford University.

Index